CAPTAIN S   J. CRAIG
U.S. COAST GUARD RESERVE (RETIRED)

ALL PRESENT AND ACCOUNTED FOR

The 1972 Alaska Grounding of the Coast Guard Cutter *Jarvis* and the Heroic Efforts that Saved the Ship

Hellgate Press   Ashland, Oregon

ALL PRESENT AND ACCOUNTED FOR

Published by Hellgate Press
(An imprint of L&R Publishing, LLC)
Hellgate Press
PO Box 3531
Ashland, OR 97520
email: sales@hellgatepress.com

Cover Design: JD Smith Design (*front*) and L. Redding
Interior Design: L. Redding
Ship photo provided by Jack Hunter
Page vi and vii: *Jarvis* ship drawing by George Bieda. Windjammer Arts, Silverdale, Washington

Cataloging In Publication Data is available from the publisher upon request.
ISBN: 978-1-55571-964-7

Printed and bound in the United States of America
First edition 10 9 8 7 6 5 4 3 2 1

To the thousands of men and women, past and present, who have served in the U.S. Coast Guard—active, reserve, civilian and auxiliary— and to the families who gave them unconditional support.

"When you go to sea you are mostly on your own. If you run into serious trouble, there are no first responders to get you out of it. You either remedy the trouble or die. The Coast Guard Cutter *Jarvis* and its crew was assailed by a sailor's worst enemy—hellish foul weather. The author makes you part of the crew pulling, you into peril with them. Your ship is sinking and being shoved toward a rocky Alaskan shore where it will break up, sending you into freezing seas where your chance of survival is nil. Although human nature rises to heroic action in the worst situations, after reading this book you may never want to get on a ship again!"

—*CWO4 Paul C. Scotti, USCG (Ret.)*
Author: Coast Guard Action in Vietnam

"Captain Steve Craig has captured the core values of the Coast Guard: Honor in the explanation of our service, Respect for those who came before us and the challenge of each Coastguardsman to equal or exceed their accomplishments, and Devotion to Duty in the daily routine of being underway and the can-do-and-persevere attitude when faced with the challenge of saving their shipmates and the *Jarvis*. BRAVO ZULU CAPT Craig."

—*Admiral Steve Day, USCGR (Ret.)*

"Throughout history, the dedicated men and women of the United States Coast Guard have unselfishly risked their lives to save those in peril on the high seas around the world. Captain Craig has accurately captured the riveting, untold story of CGC *Jarvis* and its crew, unexpectedly finding themselves on the brink of disaster in the treacherous, unforgiving waters of Alaska. His writing encompasses the raw emotion and desperation of the crew, as we fought to prevent the ship from sinking and the most certain death of all onboard. His book embodies the unwavering, heroic efforts of the crew to save *Jarvis* and themselves."

—*Commander Richard G. Brunke, USCG (Ret.)*

"It is a fine piece of research and writing that should be required reading for anyone in a leadership position who is entrusted with ensuring the safe operations of a ship that operates in harm's way."

—*Rear Admiral Bobby Hollingsworth, USCG (Ret.)*
Second Commanding Officer of the CGC Jarvis

Contents

Built by Avondale Shipyards, New Orleans, LA

USCGC JARVIS WHEC-725

Displacement: 3050 tons

Dimensions: 378 ft. length, 43 ft. beam, 20 ft. draft

Main Machinery: Two gas turbines, two diesel engines, two shafts, 7,200 bhp., 28.4 kts.

Armament: One 5-inch, 38 cal. Mk30 gun; two 81mm Mk 2 mortars; two 50 cal. mg; and two triple-tube ASW torpedo launchers

Helicopter: One HH-52A Sea Guard

Complement: 20 officers and 158 enlisted

"*Jarvis* Log"

Anchored in the harbor
Unalaska by the sea
We spent Nov 13th
by the mountains for our lee

The quiet night woke us
as the ship began to roll;
the winds were blowing fiercely
pushing us to the shoal

Though we fought to hold her safely;
the winds our fearless foe,
We stood out the harbor
with a hole way down below

The crucial hours that followed
finally brought the cheerful sound
that the *Jarvis* was again seaworthy
and ready for homeward bound

Southward bound we set her
with every number of the crew
turned thoughts to homes and loved ones
on our island of Oahu

Two months ago, we left her
for the patrol in our 50th state;
now the time had arrived for leaving;
No-one foresaw our fate

Two hours out they caught us
these seas and winds we fear;
Our mighty ship was laboring
bad weather drawing near

Our damage control parties
gave their all high and low
but the water kept coming in
14 inches now below
Then a terrifying feeling befell us
the words came like a shout

An SOS sent thru the night
how long before we'd know
if help was coming to us;
40 inches now below

Not knowing what was happening
we feared the worst by chance
but our doubts soon were answered
as we heard our Captain's voice

"Our *Jarvis* may be crippled
but she's gonna make it through;
a Japanese vessel has heard us
by the name of *Koyo Maru*"

Certain precautions must be made
but do not be alarmed
We'll keep the *Jarvis* floating
safely and unharmed

Singing filled the ship that night
all ratings side by side
the spirit on the *Jarvis*
some simply call it PRIDE

An hour away from danger
our rescue vessel came,
a Japanese fishing vessel
Koyo Maru was her name

The rest is only history;
many tales will be told of that night;
did the spirit on the *Jarvis*
saved a Coast Guard ship that night

—QMC Jim Herman

PREFACE

The U.S. Coast Guard and America in the 1970s

I N 1972 RICHARD M. NIXON was President and Spiro Agnew was the Vice President. The average cost of a new house was just over $27,000 and the average price of a used home was $7,300. Gasoline prices were thirty-four cents per gallon, stamps cost eight cents, and milk was thirty-six cents a gallon.

The nation itself was in turmoil during the '70s; the Vietnam War was still three years away from ending, and race riots were hitting the streets of major cities such as Los Angeles and Chicago. Airline companies began the first inspections of passengers and baggage, but we all know how effective that was. China was known, universally as "Red China" and had maintained an isolationist posture until President Nixon visited the country that year. That visit was the beginning of the opening of China to the world. Communism had run rampant throughout the world, only to crumble a couple of decades later. The term, "Better dead than red," was often stated when referring to communism. I still remember the nuclear bomb drills in the first grade in Ontario, Oregon, where all the students had to drop beneath their desks upon hearing the sirens.

On the entertainment front, outdoor rock concerts, fueled by the success of Woodstock, abounded throughout the United States, quite often just as an excuse for thousands to get "high and loaded" in a group session. Future legislation and insurance requirements reduced these types of concerts to the history books of America. Released in 1972, *The Godfather* opened in movie theaters to huge audiences. The Home Box Office network, referred to as HBO, was launched to millions of television viewers. *The Waltons*, *The Streets of San Francisco*, *The Bob Newhart Show* and *M*A*S*H* premiered on television networks. Dwayne ("the Rock") Johnson, Shaquille O'Neal the basketball star, and Cameron Diaz were born that year. The Summer Olympics in Munich observed the tragic massacre of eleven Israeli athletes, resulting in additional security measures enforced for other significant events or ceremonies.

Coast Guard

In those days the Coast Guard active duty personnel were all men, with the primary recruiting emphasis on bringing in minorities, and, a couple of years later, women. In an agreement with the Philippine government, hundreds of Filipinos served, proudly, in the Coast Guard as well as the U.S. Navy. When asked how the Coast Guard selected my fellow Filipino yeoman for enlistment, he said he just stood in a straight line with dozens of other applicants in Manila, and the recruiter went down the line picking every tenth person as Coast Guard, and the rest as Navy.

The draft was still in place, with many enlisting in the Coast Guard to avoid going to Vietnam. Most were good workers, while a few whined about the injustice of being in the service. The Coast Guard had two recruit training centers (boot camps): one was in Alameda on the west coast; the other located at Cape May, New Jersey. Later, Alameda was closed, leaving Cape May as the lone boot camp for the Coast Guard.

There were three primary advanced training facilities: one at Governors Island in New York City, another in Yorktown, Virginia, and the third in Petaluma, California. Later Governors Island was closed permanently due to budget and personnel issues. While students tended to get into various types of trouble in downtown New York City, those personnel problems disappeared when surrounded by dairy cows in the countryside of Petaluma or the fields of historic Yorktown.

During the early 1970s, personal computers didn't exist. "Whiteout" was an exciting discovery. If you were lucky, you had an IBM Selectric electric typewriter and plenty of carbon paper. Storekeepers maintained your pay records. Months could go by before a Coast Guard member was paid, should that record get lost. Contractors didn't mow the grass or paint buildings; Coast Guard personnel did. Television didn't exist on ships. Saturday night was a special night with pizza and beer to go along with the showing of 16 millimeter (mm) movies that had been checked out to the unit the previous week. Many

Coast Guard bases did not have manned security, let alone fences, to protect the personnel and the facilities. Coast Guard barracks often featured a common sitting room with one television and a beer vending machine. Bingo was quite popular at the larger bases, with the halls often filled with many of the nearby residents from outside the station. Petty officers in many Coast Guard rates (job classifications) could be transferred within the district by the District Commander. Due to some abuses and the need for better management by Headquarters, this personnel transfer policy ended in December of 1973.

The Pacific Ocean waters could be most treacherous, even in waters off the Hawaiian Islands. In 1973, while temporarily assigned on board the Coast Guard buoy tender *Planetree* out of Honolulu, I learned an invaluable lesson regarding the dangers of the sea. On my first sea voyage to the Big Island of Hawaii, we came upon a severe storm that night that rocked the 180-foot ship like a cork in a bathtub. As a young man from a landlocked community in eastern Oregon, I had never seen an ocean storm, nor realized the potential size of the waves. Curiosity got the better of me. I went topside to check it out, stepped outside, closed the hatch, and turned to see the front of the ship disappear into a huge wave, that sent me spiraling between the rails of the ship. I quickly grabbed the rails, then crawled back onto the deck and re-entered the ship, soaking wet. There I met a chief who very distinctly exclaimed, "What the f… are you doing outside?" Mortified, I explained I was curious, at which he spouted off a couple more lessons to learn by. Quite frankly, that was a lesson well learned without the commentary.

Farther north, just six months earlier, the CGC *Jarvis* had run aground during a violent storm near the Aleutian Islands, Alaska, resulting in a breach in the ship's hull. After temporarily patching the hole, the ship then proceeded toward Honolulu, only to be struck by a more violent storm— one that was described by the XO (Executive Officer), Commander White as "…the most tremendous seas I had ever seen with snow, wind, and rain."

Ensign James Richardson described the situation: "We were in seas thirty-five to forty feet high. A seventy-knot wind was off our starboard quarter. We were rocking with a tilt of about thirty-five degrees. Our bridge is forty-four feet high, but the tops of the oncoming waves appeared to be up to our feet."

The temporary patch failed, the engine room filled with water, the ship lost all power, and for one of the few times in Coast Guard history, the emergency message SOS broadcast was sent by a Coast Guard vessel.

In 1973, I was a young nineteen-year-old, working at my first Coast Guard unit at Base Honolulu. While there, I ran across another young man who was a crewmember aboard the *Jarvis*. He relayed the story of the near sinking to me and how the crew positively responded to the accident. As he said to me, "If anyone tells you they were not afraid, he is lying. There was no panic, but there was fear." Over the years, I have always felt a need to tell the story of the Coast Guard Cutter *Jarvis*, the Coast Guard's newest ship at that time, and the heroic efforts of the crew to save it from the treacherous and frigid waters of Alaska. From commissioning in 1972 to decommissioning in 2012, over 2,000 men and women would proudly serve on the Coast Guard Cutter *Jarvis*, the "Queen of the Fleet."

PART ONE

Chapter 1

"TRAPPED"

Point Barrow, Alaska
September 1897

"A philosophical common sense is a great help in living in the Arctic regions, as elsewhere. If you are subjected to miserable discomforts, or even if you suffer, it must be regarded as all right and simply a part of the life, and like sailors, you must never dwell too much on the dangers or suffering, lest others question your courage."

—David Jarvis, March 16, 1898 log entry

THE HUNT WAS on for bowhead whales, deep in the icy waters north of Point Barrow, Alaska. Buggy whips, clothespins, pie cutters, and carriage wheels, along with the extremely popular women corsets, were all profitable products made from whale bones. Nine whaling ships, including the *Alexander, Jesse H. Freeman, Belvedere, Orcas* and the *Rosario*, were convinced they had several weeks of good weather in which to complete their missions. On the morning of September 1, 1897, the temperature plunged, and a thick ice layer swept in from the distant sea.

The crew was not overly concerned, and many believed the nor'easter winds would arrive and drive the ice out. Benjamin Tilton, captain of the whaleship *Alexander*, had grave misgivings and became greatly concerned about the lack of discipline of the other captains, many of whom chose to party the hours away while waiting for the much-needed winds. Unfortunately, when the winds did arrive, it was too late. The sea surface was frozen solid. Those captains who previously were unconcerned now realized the precarious position of their vessels and crew members.

Weather in Alaska could be unforgiving, particularly in the winter months, and Tilton knew it. He realized their position near Point Barrow would mean twenty-four-hour days without sunshine, for months on end. Temperatures would drop to sixty degrees below zero; aided by severe winds, the ice could move with such force as to demolish a ship completely and with very little notice. The fact they only carried food enough to last a couple of more months further complicated the situation. If the *Alexander* were to survive the winter, the ability to escape the ice would not occur until later in the spring.

> "The difference between care and carelessness is slight, in Arctic travel, and the first let-up is sure to bring its reminder in the shape of a frosted toe or finger or a frozen nose. One must be on guard, and the slightest tinge in the nose or cheek must be heeded, and circulation started again by vigorous rubbing. Though somewhat disagreeable and painful, freezing these parts is not necessarily harmful unless too long neglected. It is the easiest thing in the world for a man to suffer severely in such a climate, but it is possible, by good care and attention, to avoid what one might call extreme suffering, and live there with only the unavoidable discomforts of the country, to which a man in good health sooner or later grows accustomed."
>
> —*David Jarvis's journal*

Fortunately, Captain Tilton was piloting one of the newer ships that was powered by steam as well as sail. For eighteen hours, Captain Tilton ordered the *Alexander* to ram the ice repeatedly. Slowly making progress, the *Alexander* finally broke free of the ice and arrived on open seas. However, none of the other eight whaleships had the same steam capability of the *Alexander*, and they were now trapped or destroyed in the Arctic ice. The ships *Orca* and *Freeman* were both crushed as both crews abandoned ship and boarded *Belvedere*. The *Rosario* was close to Point Barrow on the west side, while the other vessels *Newport, Fearless,* and *Jeannie* were at various distances close to Point Barrow. The whaleship Wanderer was known to be in the area; however, her whereabouts were still unknown. When realizing that no overland rescue expedition had ever been sent to Alaska in the dead of winter to rescue such a large number of individuals, the 300 stranded men grew more frustrated and hopeless. Captain Tilton, understanding the seriousness of the situation, immediately set sail for San Francisco to relay news of the looming disaster.

Those men who had evacuated their ships managed to make it to other vessels that were still intact. However, 100 men could not be accommodated adequately on the other whaleships due to the lack of space. One solution included a nearby whaling station owned by Charlie Brower, Point Barrow's lead resident. An abandoned building, though in disrepair, was immediately overhauled to accommodate some of the men. However, there still existed a shortage of space, and a nearby resident, Ned McIlhenny agreed to use his building to meet the needs at this time.[1] Despite his family's business background, Ned had two primary interests: collecting biological specimens and seeking adventure. He pursued both by obtaining a commission from the University of Pennsylvania's Natural History Museum to retrieve samples from Alaska.

With the housing situation under control, Brower sent one of his assistants, along with Ned McIlhenny, by dogsled, to the ship Belvedere where he relayed the offer of lodging to those on board. Forty crewmembers volunteered and embarked on a treacherous sixty-five-mile journey through two feet of snow, in temperatures well below zero. Most of the men beginning this journey were well past middle age. A week later, the second group of sixty-five men arrived via dogsleds, with many frozen about the face and hands and several unable to walk.

Brower now turned his attention to providing food and heat for the stranded men. He soon began sending men out to collect driftwood along the beach, while also employing the local population to hunt for geese, ducks, caribou, and whatever else they could find. This food was stored below in his ice cellar, but there was a concern the food supply would run out for the stranded men remaining at this station. With the severe winter months approaching, hunting would soon come to an abrupt halt.

Conditions aboard the ships and at the whaling stations were deteriorating. With so many men crammed into the small cabin, the house would sweat, and in turn, would freeze, resulting in a foot of ice on the floor, thus cooling the environment even more. Morale was declining, with the whaling captains unwilling or unable to assist in maintaining discipline. Men were

---

[1] Ned's family was the infamous McIlhennys, founders of the popular food-seasoning sauce Tabasco.

selected to help with hunting for food but often refused, complaining of the bitter cold or claiming sickness. Further exasperating the situation, some of the crewmembers had taken to robbing the graves and cellars of the local community, searching for clothing or food. McIlhenny grew frustrated at the lack of order and honesty, warning anyone caught stealing would be shot.

On November 19th, the sun disappeared and would not reappear again until February. The onset of winter weather brought extreme temperatures, with many bitterly cold nights, some which were fifty degrees below zero. If help did not soon arrive, many of the whalers would perish.

October 1897

In late October, the whaleship *Alexander* steamed into San Francisco Harbor with Captain Tilton spreading the news of the trapped ships in the Arctic. Reports quickly spread throughout the west coast, notably in Seattle, a bustling maritime community. Almost immediately calls were made for a rescue to the remote region, despite the incredible odds of performing the mission. Company owners of the whaling ships, along with other organizations, and family members of the trapped crew, made passionate pleas to President William McKinley asking for immediate assistance in forming a rescue mission.

Three weeks later, the United States Revenue Cutter *Bear* arrived in Seattle. The *Bear* had just returned from a six-month trip in the Alaska region providing aid to local tribes and other ships in need. The *Bear*'s captain, Francis Tuttle, was on the deck, reading his latest set of orders, relayed on behalf of the President of the United States. The official papers outlined a mission to rescue of the 265 crewmembers in the Point Barrow area, who were at last report, in dire distress.

"Report of the Cruise of the U.S. Revenue Cutter *Bear*: LETTER OF INSTRUCTIONS. Treasury Department, Office of the Secretary, Washington, D.C. November 15, 1897. "Sir: The best information obtainable gives the assurance of trust to the reports that a fleet of eight whaling vessels are ice-bound in the Arctic Ocean, somewhere in the vicinity of Point Barrow, and that the 265 persons who were, at last accounts, on board these vessels are in all probability in dire distress. These conditions call for prompt and energetic action, looking to the relief of the imprisoned whale-men. It, therefore, has been determined to send an expedition to the rescue."

In further detail, the instructions outlined how the *Bear* would transit as far north as the icy conditions dictated, then put ashore three of its officers who would then proceed to Point Barrow, a journey of over 1,500 miles through the Alaskan territory.

Captain Tuttle was quite aware of the weather conditions in the Arctic region, where temperatures could plunge from fourteen degrees above zero to thirty-five degrees below, in just a few hours. Sunny weather could change just as fast to fierce storms as well. Those men selected would have to be physically fit and have knowledge of the Alaskan landscape. Despite it being 1897, much of Alaska was unmapped. Those few maps that did exist were inaccurate, at best. The three officers selected must be volunteers and realize it could take up to seven or eight months to complete the journey. Every member of the ship volunteered, including those who were inexperienced and unaware of the life-threatening challenges and severe weather conditions. After reviewing the crew for those best qualified, it was an easy decision for Tuttle to select his first choice: First Lieutenant (LT) David Jarvis.

David Jarvis was born in Maryland and appointed to the Revenue Cutter Service in 1881. Two years later, he graduated from its officer's training school and finished at the top of his class. After graduation, his primary duty was developing maritime activities in Alaska and the Bering Sea. It was during this period that he assisted in the rescue of several ships and a large number of individuals. An eight-year veteran of the Alaska Arctic, he had learned Alaskan Eskimo and the native dialects of every village along the Alaskan coastline. He was described as a "small, mild-mannered, seemingly placid but a man with an iron will and indomitable courage." Throughout his career, no matter how dangerous the task, he never assigned his men a job, without facing the same dangers.

The second man chosen was the *Bear's* surgeon, Dr. Samuel Call. His first experience in Alaska was serving as a doctor at an Alaskan trading post, a position which required traveling to various villages in extreme weather conditions. Despite the medical proficiency that could have rewarded him with a more lucrative job in the "lower 48," Dr. Call preferred the Alaskan wilderness, where his skills were much needed and were more rewarding than monetary gain. His selection to the team was crucial, as there surely would be medical needs along the way and on the scene in Point Barrow. Unknown to the other officers, Call also had another passion: photography. His skills would be invaluable in compiling a visual record of the trek to Alaska.

The third person chosen for the assignment was a newcomer to the *Bear*, Second Lieutenant Ellsworth Bertholf. Bertholf's background was colorful; he loved the sea, and at the young age of sixteen he was admitted to the U.S. Naval Academy. While seemingly quite intelligent, he had a side of him that disliked authority and loved to play pranks, which ultimately lead to his dismissal from the Academy. Learning his lesson, he soon applied and was accepted to the officer's training school with the Revenue Cutter Service, and shortly after he was assigned to the legendary ship *Bear*. Being chosen as part of the rescue effort was the dream of a lifetime, and he wasn't about to screw it up.

Once on the ground in Alaska, David Jarvis and his two accomplices were to proceed to two reindeer stations located on the Seward Peninsula. Once there, the plan was for the two stations to agree to give up their herds, and escort the reindeer to Point Barrow, where food provisions were running low. The owners, Tom Lopp, and local native, Charlie Artisarlook, were familiar with David Jarvis, and they would need to be convinced to donate their herds for the sake of saving the whalers. David was no stranger to reindeer; he had participated before in expeditions that brought reindeer over to Alaska from Siberia. Additionally, he was familiar with Point Barrow, where he had previously supervised the building of the whalemen's refuge station.

Winter 1897

On November 27th, the *Bear* departed Seattle en route to Dutch Harbor in the Aleutian Islands. Loaded with provisions and barrels of salted meat, the *Bear* also carried a large contingent of noisy, sled dogs. Upon reaching Dutch Harbor ten days later, the ship took on more coal and purchased additional sled dogs for the upcoming trek.

On December 13th, the *Bear* made landing at the small village of Tunu-nak where a small group of residents greeted the men and assisted with off-loading of the supplies. There, Jarvis, Bertholf, Call, and a Russian dog handler known only as Koltchoff began their mission, with the provisions

David Jarvis, Dr. Call, and others. Photo courtesy of the Alaska State Library.

lashed to nine-foot wooden sleds. The first day proved to be quite arduous with the men having to cross a range of mountains 1,500 to 2,000 feet in height while herding a considerable amount of supplies, sleds, and dogs. Thus, they began their 1,600-mile journey, a trek that included many challenges along the way—harsh winds, freezing low temperatures, and rugged trails. Several dogs suffered fatigue, and finding replacements was difficult. When passing through the small villages, Jarvis attempted to hire local guides familiar with the region, to avoid getting lost or incurring a mishap.

Traveling through Alaska proved to be difficult, particularly when attempting to acquire sled dogs along the way. As David Jarvis wrote in his journal:

"We would buy or hire dogs, only to have them run away and return to their owners after going but a short distance with us. Native dogs are very unlikely to remain with anyone but their owners."

Little more than two weeks later, they arrived at their first destination of St. Michael. After discussions with the local population, Jarvis and his crew were able to procure the necessary clothing required for the extreme temperatures they would encounter on their journey. However, the commander of the army post was alarmed at the exhausted status of Jarvis's dogs. Many of the dogs displayed cut and swollen feet, a condition that the commander felt would make it near-impossible for the dogs to complete the journey. But he offered a solution. As the military authority for the area, he would order Dr. Albert Kettleson, superintendent of the herd at Port Clarence, to provide enough of the strong reindeer to pull his sleds to their destinations.

Kettleson (Kittilsen) himself, had been educated at the University of Wisconsin and the Rush Medical College in Chicago and was living in Wisconsin at the time of his appointment in 1896 where he also served as assistant superintendent. As part of his contract, his permit allowed a limited private practice. As a pioneer doctor in northwestern Alaska, traveling was quite harsh in the cold environment, as he later wrote:

"I am now, more than 200 miles from Port Clarence to call on a sick white child. A Lapp and I made the trip in five days with reindeer. We travel without tent or stove, hoping to arrive each evening at an Eskimo village and to sleep in a house; but one night we had to spend in the snow. This, however, did us no harm, as we are prepared for anything. We have sleeping bags made of reindeer skins; with them one can be warm anywhere. It is pleasant to travel with deer; on level surfaces they are much faster than horses, and they go through where it is so uneven that a horse wouldn't think of making it. Last year they did this, three times. So far, they have not got out of my control, although they have been able to smash two sleds for me."

Soon after, Kettleson would move to Cape Nome and lay claim to some of the richest gold claims in the area and later operate a saloon in Anvil Creek. While initially penniless when he first arrived in Alaska, Kettleson was now recognized as one of the richest men at Cape Nome.

Two days later, Jarvis departed for the next major destination, Cape Rodney, where they would acquire their first reindeer herd. Meanwhile back at Point Barrow, Charlie Brower and Ned McIlhenny were dealing with a situation that had gotten much worse. The snows had increased, temperatures had dropped, and thick ice now formed inside the building. To top it off, a number of the whalemen had come down with scurvy, a flesh-eating disease often resulting in death. Sanitary conditions were dismal, and a general lack of discipline amongst the crew added to the dire situation at hand.

January – March 1898

En route to Cape Rodney, on January 10th, Jarvis made his first contact with Dr. Kettleson, who would be asked to supply the first herd of reindeer needed for the expedition. Kettleson read Jarvis's orders to provide the reindeer, and immediately he agreed to the supply order and also to volunteer with driving the reindeer to the next destination. Jarvis and Call were now required to learn how to operate reindeer-pulled sleds versus dog sleds. The significant difference was in their handling and the speed of the reindeer; if any man were to fall off, they would never catch up to the sled.

Two days later, Jarvis, and his small contingent, departed for Cape Rodney with the reindeer, only to run into a fierce blizzard. They pressed on in the blinding storm, and if not for the natural instincts of the reindeer to seek the safety of a village, they all would have perished on the trail. Temperatures were now thirty below zero with snow blowing so hard, the men could hardly stand. They finally reached the village of Opiktillik where they were compelled to remain for three days because of the blizzard. But on the fourth day, Jarvis's patience had worn out and he ordered the party back on the trail. By now, the blizzard had actually grown in intensity with Jarvis and his men now having to don snowshoes to tramp down the snow in front of the dogs, and in some cases, dig a path for the animals. By late evening, the now cold and exhausted Jarvis and his party were forced to pitch their tents and wait until the next day to finish this leg of the trip.

The next day, they entered the village of Cape Rodney and obtained the second herd of reindeer from Charlie Artisarlook. The next phase of the rescue included a treacherous journey of at least a thousand miles. To assist further in this effort, Charlie agreed to lend himself and a couple of his herders who would lead the herd to Point Barrow. The next stop of the journey was Cape Prince of Wales to acquire the last herd of reindeer, owned by Tom Lopp.

After days of traveling through some of the worst weather yet encountered, including blizzards and temperatures of thirty degrees below zero, Jarvis and his group arrived at Cape Prince of Wales and then proceeded to Tom Lopp's house. Together with Charlie's and Kettleson's herds, the reindeer now numbered over 400 and would be required to traverse 700 miles over snow-covered mountains and across frozen bodies of water, with Tom Lopp and his herders leading the way.

The last 700 miles tested human endurance to the limit. The harsh, challenging weather conditions including blowing snow, blizzards, rough terrain, and short days, added to the misery. Jarvis and his fellow companions also had to manage the dogs and the reindeer as well. In his log entry, Jarvis describes the conditions:

> "We had ideal weather for traveling, clear and cold, the thermometer ranging from minus thirty degrees to minus forty degrees the whole way, and we had to keep moving. With plenty of food and plenty of driftwood along the beach, we were able to fortify ourselves against the cold, and by exercising care and paying attention to our noses and cheeks, we were not touched even in these sensitive places."

By mid-March, the supply of dog feed had shrunk, and during times of idleness, the dogs went unfed. The Alaska natives, as a rule, do not feed their dogs except when working, and now Jarvis and his crew had to do the same. The only feed the dogs received was a type of "flour" soup, which they received for two days. As a consequence, the dogs would eat everything not nailed down, including parts of the sled, or even more importantly, clothing. Anything edible, especially boots, had to be raised off the ground, out of reach of the dogs.

> "Upon telling one of the natives what we wanted, he simply told us to go into his ice house and help ourselves. No price was asked; no stipulation made. He saw what our needs were, and, so far as he was able, or as much as he had, he would help us gladly. It is refreshing to meet such simple, true-hearted people in time of need and to have dealings with them."
>
> —David Jarvis, March 8 log entry

March 26, 1898
Point Barrow

After 100 days and 1,500 miles, the relief expedition sighted the first of the marooned vessels, the Belvedere, and days later, the refugee camp. Of the 448 reindeer acquired during the trip, 382 survived. Lieutenant Jarvis writes in his journal:

> "We drew up alongside at 4 p.m. and going aboard announced ourselves and our mission, but it was some time before the first astonishment, and incredulousness could wear off and welcome extended to us."

Here Jarvis found outbreaks of scurvy, food shortages, and deplorable living conditions. Morale was non-existent, with many just waiting for death. The provisions of reindeer meat immediately provided the much-needed vitamins to offset scurvy. Jarvis took charge and organized baseball games and duck-shooting contests to counter the boredom and depression. He also imposed mandatory physical exercise by the crews through daily walking to and from the fields. The duck-hunting competition proved so successful that in one day, over 1,100 ducks were killed, helping add to the meat supply. Living conditions and morale greatly improved.

Jarvis immediately set upon improving the sanitation of the men and their clothing. Soap was increased to one pound a month, depending on availability. But challenges remained, as the water had to be melted from the ice, and the ability to accomplish this was limited. Jarvis continued his log:

> "It was difficult at first to get some of the men to make any effort to clean themselves; but later, after the majority saw they had the means to do it, and could, they united to complete the others and were quick to report any great neglect. It was not long before the general appearance of all was greatly improved. I instituted a system of daily inspection of the quarters and clothing by Surgeon Call and myself, and kept it up until the men were finally put aboard the *Bear*; and they were never allowed to lapse from the condition or order, discipline, good health, and cleanliness we instituted."

Alaska State Library - Historical Collections

David Jarvis at Point Barrow. Photo courtesy of the Alaska State Library.

These activities and rules continued for months until help could arrive. There was not much else to do but wait for the ice break-up, and that would generally occur in late July. As Jarvis was in charge, he maintained discipline and arbitrated disputes where required. As he stated in his journal: "In the matter of exercising discipline and control, it was better that the men be divided into small groups, separated at good distances, as they now were, for so many idle men in one crowd would breed all manner of disturbances and troubles."

The weather continued to plague the region; in early July, a violent gale struck the coast, shoving ice against the beach and the *Rosario* whaleship. The crushing ice tore her keel away, took the rudder and sternpost, and put a hole in her bow. While it all happened in minutes, the crew managed to escape, and it was now necessary to lodge them at Point Barrow, with the other survivors. Nearby, the men of the Jeannie watched as ice floes were shoved repeatedly onto the beach, atop each other, to an incredible height of forty feet in some sections.

July 1898
Point Barrow

Jarvis knew the *Bear* would return and sent Bertholf to Port Lay, a 220-mile trek down south where he hoped he would be able to contact the ship. Upon finding the ship, Bertholf relayed Jarvis's message, that should the *Bear* not arrive by August 1st, the situation would be dire, and he would be forced to start sending the whalemen south along the coast and hopefully to safety.

Faced with the immediate deadline on hand, Captain Tuttle made repeated attempts, over a five-day time period to leave Port Lay, but the ship was turned back by the thick ice. Finally, on July 27th, enough open passages appeared, and the *Bear* departed in the late evening under the Arctic midnight sun.

The next day, the men at Point Barrow sighted the Revenue Cutter *Bear* approaching. James Allen, an engineer aboard the *Freeman*, would write:

> "How well I remember July 28, 1898! Smoke was reported to the south. Everyone was guessing what ship. Finally, the masts were sighted and then the yards. It turned out to be that grand old Revenue Cutter U.S.S. *Bear*, to me, one of the most beautiful ships that was ever built." As the *Bear* pulled next to the crushed hulk of a whaling ship at Point Barrow, one lone figure walked across the ice to meet the cutter. Lieutenant David Jarvis marched up the gangway, saluted the colors, and requested permission to come aboard.

Departing from Point Barrow proved to be a difficult task for the *Bear*. The ship was quickly surrounded by ice, trapping the vessel. Farther out to sea, those whaleships not severely damaged, were able to transit and set sail south, leaving the *Bear* behind until the ice broke up. With conditions improving, on August 16th, the Revenue Cutter *Bear*, packed with the whalemen from bow to stern, finally forced her way through the ice and into open seas.

September 1898
Seattle, Washington

On September 13, 1898, ten months after the men had been stranded in Alaska, the Revenue Cutter *Bear* arrived in Seattle. Astonishingly, of the 268 whalers and crewmembers aboard, 265 survived.

Captain Tuttle, Commanding Officer of the *Bear*, would write to the Secretary of the Treasury:

> "The officers and crew bore the monotonous isolation with the greatest patience, complaints being almost unheard of. The courage, fortitude, and perseverance shown by the members of the overland expedition is deserving of the highest commendation. Starting over a route seldom traveled before by dog sleds, with a herd of over 400 reindeer to drive and care for, they pushed their way through what times seemed impassable obstacles, across frozen seas, and over snow-clad mountains, with tireless energy until Point Barrow was reached and the object of the expedition successfully accomplished. I respectfully recommend that the heroic services of First Lieutenant D. H. Jarvis, Second Lieutenant E. P. Bertholf, and Surgeon S.J. Call should meet with such recognition as the Department sees fit to bestow."

Nearly four years later, Congress awarded LT Jarvis, LT Bertholf, and Dr. Call, Congressional Gold Medals for what President McKinley termed "a victory of peace." Additionally, one of the Coast Guard's most prestigious awards given annually is the David H. Jarvis Award for Inspirational Leadership.

Lieutenant Jarvis would later become captain of the *Bear*, succeeding Captain Tuttle. Returning to Alaska, Jarvis was instrumental in the rescue of dozens of miners trapped in freezing conditions near Kotzebue Sound, further enhancing his reputation throughout the country. In 1902, President Theodore Roosevelt appointed him customs collector of Alaska. Three years later, he retired from government employment and retreated to the private sector. Ellsworth Bertholf would continue his impressive career in the Revenue Cutter Service. In 1915, the Revenue Cutter Service combined with the United States Life-Saving Service to form today's U.S. Coast Guard, a name suggested by Bertholf to President Wilson. President Wilson not only took his suggestion, but appointed Bertholf as the first commandant of the new service.

A little over seventy years later, construction would begin at Avondale Shipyard, New Orleans, on the Coast Guard's cutter, the *Jarvis* (WHEC 725), named in honor of David Jarvis. Called the "Pride of the Fleet" by many, the *Jarvis* would participate in numerous search-and-rescue missions and fisheries patrols in the northern Pacific for many years after commissioning. But all of these missions would take a backseat to the events of November 1972 when, much like David Jarvis many years before, the crew would be tested beyond normal human endurance to save the ship.

PART TWO

Chapter 2

FREDERICK WOOLEY

The Bering Sea
For ne'er can sailor salty be
Until he sails the Bering Sea,
And views Alaska's dreary shore
And fills himself with Arctic lore.

Columbus and Balboa too,
With Nelson form a salty crew,
But they are fresh to you and me –
They never sailed the Bering Sea.

So when you boast of fiercest gale,
That ever ocean you did sail,
You can not salty sailor be
Until you cruise the Bering Sea.

Trident Society – *The Book of Navy Songs*

The Atlantic, 1944

CROSSING THE ATLANTIC on the merchant mariner vessel William B. Rogers (often referred to as simply the Will Rogers) always made Chief Mate Frederick Wooley nervous. Despite the heavy losses sustained by the German U-boats in 1944, many still plagued the waters, looking for any merchant vessels of the Allies carrying supplies for the war effort. Wooley's job as chief officer bore the responsibility of being in charge of the ship's cargo and deck crew. His concern was well founded; he had had several run-ins with the U-boats, including one involving a small convoy, where a

German U-boat may have sunk one of his ships. The cause may have been exacerbated by weather or by a mechanical failure, but the exact cause was never determined. The ship had disappeared with all hands lost, and it was a memory that would follow Wooley the rest of his life.

The fear of those sailing on merchant mariner ships was justified; merchant seamen suffered a higher rate of fatalities than those serving the military services. One person out of each twenty-five never made it home. With over a 4% casualty rate, this was far higher than the near 3% of the Marines or 2% of the Army. Even worse, while the military services' pay would continue regardless if their ship were destroyed, it was not so in the merchant marines. If your ship was sunk, your wages stopped once you hit the water. To add further insult, if you were declared dead, but showed up later alive, you were now required to pay back any death benefit pay awarded to your family.

Built in 1942 as part of the war effort, the *William B. Rogers* was part of the Liberty-ship class that had its beginnings at the end of 1941. Over 2,700 Liberty ships were built within five years to transport men and supplies to the front. The first Liberty ship took 244 days to construct; that figure dropped to under forty days by the end of 1945. But the German U-boats found the Liberty ships easy targets due to their limited speed; in 1943 a new class of merchant ship was created. The new Victory line proved to be faster than the older Liberty ships, making it safer and quicker to move cargo and personnel.

"Wooley," as he was known to his friends and workers, first entered the merchant marines as a cadet in 1940, with his first assignment in 1942. Standing 5' 9'' with a slight build of 150 pounds, Wooley's only known vice was cigarettes, with which he struggled with all his life. In any spare time he found, he would delve into painting or sculpturing.

His heart's desire was to attend forestry school, but he did not have the finances to do so. Early in his life, he attended art school while boxing on the side for extra cash. After a short while, Wooley realized a new direction was necessary for long-term success. His paternal grandfather had been a merchant mariner. This occupation appeared to be an attractive career, and thus he joined the Merchant Marines.

While his training as a cadet was mostly uneventful, he received a rescue citation for trying to save a shipmate who had fallen into the frigid Galway Bay in Ireland. As reported in *The New York Times*:

"Marine Cadet Wins a Rescue Citation. Fourth Class Cadet Frederick O. Wooley of the United States Liner *Washington*, risked his life in an attempt to rescue another member of the ship's crew from the Bay of Galway, Eire, June 13, has received a commendation 'for heroic action' in line of duty' from the United States Maritime Commission, it was announced yesterday."

The article described how Wooley was detailed as a handler in a motorboat when, upon returning to his ship, he encountered rough water that threw his fellow crew member into the water. The article continued:

"Cadet Wooley dived from the bow of the motorboat and swam about 100 feet to Phillips, who was foundering in the rough waters. He turned Phillips on his back and carried him to within twenty feet of the boat, where John Gorman, a seaman, dived in and aided in bringing Phillips aboard. Phillips died later."

Because of this life-saving incident, Frederick Wooley tended to be more prone to pneumonia for the rest of his life.

The article further noted that Cadet Wooley had been one of 166 successful applicants in the national competitive examination of the Merchant Marine Cadets, held April 17, 1939. Upon completion of the preliminary training at the Cadet Training Station, Wooley served as a Deck Department Cadet, Fourth Class, on board the liner ship *Washington*.

The liner *Washington* had an exciting history during June of 1940. It was designed as an ocean liner and launched in 1932. The 705-foot long *Washington* carried a crew of 478, along with transporting 580 passengers in Cabin class, 400 in Tourist, and 150 in Third Class. The ship quickly earned a reputation for its high standard of service and luxury, not to mention being the fastest passenger liner of its time. Initially slated for the New York to Hamburg, Germany, route, it was soon changed to New York-Naples-Genoa due to the outbreak of WWII.

In June of 1940, its last voyage was to repatriate U.S. citizens from Italy and France with a scheduled stop in Galway, Ireland. On June 11th, two days before Frederick Wooley would attempt to save the crew member's life, the ship encountered a German U-boat off the coast of Portugal. The German submarine first signaled to "stop, heave to" with immediate compliance. The second signal stated that the ship had "Ten minutes to abandon ship." With over 1,000 passengers and 570 crew on board, the demand was next to impossible to fulfill.

Captain Harry Manning, the skipper of the liner, signaled the German submarine that *Washington* was an "American Ship," and therefore protected, as the United States had not yet entered the war. As the captain would write, "Watertight doors were closed, the general alarm was sounded, and the operation of stowing the passengers in the boats consummated with commendable calm and lack of confusion. Not a passenger showed signs of hysteria or confusion. The crew behaved well, obeying orders without question or criticism. Women and children went first. We maintained radio silence."

Ten tense minutes went by, and nothing occurred. Finally, the submarine signaled, "Thought you were another ship; please go on, go on!"

Not too long after, another U-boat appeared off the port beam. Rather than face another encounter, the captain swung the ship into the sun, hoping to obscure the vision of the sub. This maneuver possibly blinded the sub, and it soon disappeared.

For their work in bringing the ship safely through combat waters, the United States Lines later awarded a medal to each member of the crew, plus a ten percent bonus in their monthly paychecks. John Gorman and Frederick Wooley, as previously noted above, both received the company's Distinguished Service Medal for their role in the rescue of the crewman from the rough waters of Galway. The ship was sold for scrap in 1965.

Rising quickly in the ranks, Wooley's assignment as chief officer aboard the *Will Rogers* was his first significant position with the company. At the age of twenty-eight, he was second in command of a vital shipping vessel; his next assignment would be chief officer of the merchant vessel *Sea Serpent* in February 1945.

The *Will Rogers*, however, would suffer damage two months later in the Irish Sea when it was struck by a torpedo on the starboard side, causing flooding of both compartments. While the ship was towed to safety, the nine officers, thirty-four crewmen, and twenty-seven armed guards stayed onboard. She returned to service the following December. In the meantime, Wooley would continue to serve on various merchant vessels until January 1951, when he was released to join the U.S. Coast Guard.

Despite having a successful career in the merchant marines, his time away from the family on these extended trips took a toll. After one return, his daughter cried because she didn't know who the strange man was. Wooley decided the time was right to join the Coast Guard where he could spend more time with the family.

His assignments in the next twenty-plus years included serving as operations officer aboard two ships, and as executive officer aboard the Coast Guard Cutter *Boutwell*. Additionally, he spent eleven years in the marine inspection field of work and three years in charge of the merchant marine detail in Bremen, Germany, located in the northwestern part of the country.

Upon his transfer to the CGC *Boutwell* from the assignment in Germany, the Consulate General of the United States sent a letter to the Commandant of the Coast Guard, Admiral Bender, speaking highly of Wooley's performance. The letter, dated July 28, 1970, read in part:

> "The uniformly favorable and often glowing reports on Commander Wooley have come in the main from Germans in important positions who have had the opportunity to know Commander Wooley and estimate his worth as a professional. These German spokesmen represent shipping and shipbuilding companies, a variety of official German organizations concerned with the broad field of shipping (including the German Navy, police officials, and the German Society for the Rescue of Shipwrecked). The few American businessmen concerned with shipping in this district share the sentiments of their German colleagues."

In his nearly ten years of merchant marine experience, Frederick Wooley served on as many as twenty vessels of various gross tonnages, in positions of either chief officer or master in charge of the ship. In the Coast Guard, he completed over twenty years of commissioned service, all related to the maritime industry. His vast and extensive career on the sea made him a natural choice to be the first commanding officer of the Coast Guard's latest ship, the Coast Guard Cutter *Jarvis*.

Chapter 3

THE BEGINNING

"A better seaman I've never seen, next to Harry Parker (a retired rear admiral) who I was with on Pontchartrain. I do remember one thing I'll never forget. Captain Wooley saw the *Jarvis* from original plans, keel laying to detail. He loved that ship."

—*Roy Montgomery*

ON AUGUST 4, 1790, the U.S. Congress authorized the construction of ten vessels to combat smuggling and to enforce new federal tariff and trade laws. This new agency would be known as the Revenue Marine or, alternatively, as the Revenue-Marine and, later as the Revenue Cutter Service in 1863. For the first eight years of its service, the Revenue Service was the only armed maritime service of the United States. The Revenue cutters were known for their versatility and speed, having the ability to travel into shallow water, making them better able to protect the coastline. To this day, the Coast Guard refers to any of their vessels sixty-five-feet and longer as a cutter.

As the nation grew, so did the service's duties and responsibilities. In 1915, the U.S. Congress merged the Revenue Cutter Service with the U.S. Life-Saving Service to form the current day U.S. Coast Guard, with the primary duties to save lives and enforce maritime laws. In 1936, Congress enacted legislation that assigned the service to administer the International Ice Observation and Ice Patrol Service; previously the Coast Guard had already been conducting ice patrols near Alaska and the northern Atlantic. In 1939, the Coast Guard assumed responsibility for this country's aids to navigation and lighthouses when President Franklin Roosevelt transferred the Lighthouse Service. In 1946, merchant marine licensing and merchant vessel safety responsibilities were assigned to the Coast Guard as well.

The Coast Guard remained under the Department of the Treasury until 1967 when the agency transferred to the new Department of Transportation. With the Coast Guard recognized as the premier armed service protecting this country's shorelines, and as a result of the 9/11 attacks, the service was once again transferred, this time under the newly created Department of Homeland Security in 2003.

The U.S. Coast Guard has a proud history of serving in every one of this nation's armed conflicts. From the transfer of military personnel to the shores of Normandy for D-Day of WWII to patrolling the river waters of Vietnam or inspecting suspect vessels during the Persian Gulf War in 1990, the Coast Guard has performed with distinction. Of the latter, three port security units (PSU's) consisting of 550 Coast Guard reservists reported in support of Operation Desert Shield, the first involuntary overseas mobilization of reservists in the history of the reserve program. Overall, 950 Coast Guard reservists would answer the call. The largest call-up of reservists for a military response would occur as a result of the 9/11 attacks, with over 1,100 reservists on the job by September 14th with another 900 reporting soon after.

The Coast Guard is also responsible for search and rescue, and nowhere can a better example be made than its response to the devastation caused by Hurricane Katrina in 2005. In late August of that year, the third major storm of the season struck the United States, hitting the Gulf Coast region especially hard. The storm caused the deaths of 1,200 people and more than 200 billion dollars in damages. Over a million people were displaced, causing the most significant humanitarian crisis to this country since the Great Depression. Along with over 5,600 active duty and reserve Coast Guard men and women, the Coast Guard deployed twenty-six cutters, thirty-eight helicopters, fourteen fixed-wing aircraft, 119 boats and eight Marine Safety and Security Teams and Disaster Assist Teams. In a special 2005 edition of the Coast Guard magazine dedicated to the Katrina response, the Commandant of the Coast Guard, Admiral Collins, reflected on the staggering numbers:

"Team Coast Guard members descended on the devastated city of New Orleans and the Mississippi coastal communities, with winds still howling and in uncertain waters, only to find the utter horror of great spans of country under water, neighborhoods completely flattened by hurricane force winds, and thousands of survivors clinging to rooftops. Every available Coast Guard boat and helicopter immediately launched into action. Our people teamed with first responders from our local and state partners and integrated seamlessly with our DOD counterparts.

"And a full 10 days later we had executed one of the largest search and rescue operations in United States history by saving and evacuating more than 33,544 lives. To put this in perspective, in a typical, but nonetheless busy year, we might rescue a little over 5,000 people, so in less than a two-week period, the Coast Guard conducted over six years of rescues.

"During the same post-Katrina timeframe, the Coast Guard executed our other missions of ensuring safe and secure passage within impacted waterways and responded to pollution cases totaling over 8 million gallons of oil and huge amounts of sewage and toxic chemicals.

"What makes these events particularly compelling is the fact that Team Coast Guard members who accomplished all of these amazing feats were also victims of Katrina. Over 28% of the workforce either lost their homes or sustained intense property damage.

"I've never been prouder of the Coast Guard. Our team of multimission men and women: active duty, reserve, civilian, and auxiliary, are performing brilliantly. Their ability to adapt to a quickly changing operational environment, squeeze excellence out of our over-extended systems, and provide the face of calm, reassuring professionalism to those in dire need embodies who we are: guardians, warriors, patriots, and life savers."

The Coast Guard continues its missions every year: search and rescue, ice-breaking, maintenance of aids to navigation, maritime law enforcement including drug interdiction, port security, licensing, fishery patrols, and monitoring oil and hazardous material spill—to name just a few of the primary duties. It does so with approximately 40,000 active duty personnel, 7,000 reservists, 7,000 civilians, and 26,000 auxiliarists. Considering that the U.S. Army has over 470,000 active duty members, it is by far the smallest service but has a huge responsibility.

New Orleans, 1970

The birth of the Coast Guard Cutter *Jarvis* began in the shipyards at Avon-dale Shipyard in New Orleans, Louisiana, on September 9, 1970. Con-structed of top-quality materials, the *Jarvis* was built in sections that were later welded together. At 378-feet, the ship would be one of the largest cutters in the Coast Guard fleet. The high-endurance cutters of the *Jarvis* class were able to carry enough food, water, fuel, and men for extended periods at sea. With the missions assigned, the capabilities were particularly important when carrying out lengthy fishery patrols in the north Pacific waters.

The *Jarvis* was one of twelve of the High Endurance class eventually built with the first commissioned in 1967. The High Endurance class of cutters missions would include long-range search and rescue, law enforcement, de-fense support and operations, and oceanographic research. Before the wide-spread commercial use of satellites, the *Jarvis* would also assist aircraft and ships with navigational and weather information. Late in the 1980s, the "378s" were significantly updated and remodeled to enhance their mission performance capabilities. One of the more notable physical changes was the strengthening of the flight deck to accommodate the newer, more massive Coast Guard helicopter. While the previous version of the ship would show six rectangular portholes on the side, the new would show five. This material change is one of the more apparent distinctions when viewing pictures of this class of ship to determine the original era of the vessel.

With two large Fairbanks-Morse diesel, 7,000 HP engines, the *Jarvis* could operate at a cruising speed of twenty knots. Operating at this cruising speed, the ship would have the capability of traveling 10,000 nautical miles. Additionally, two Pratt and Whitney gas turbine 36,000 HP engines, similar to those used on Boeing 707 airplanes, could also power the *Jarvis*. Opera-tion of the gas turbine engines would be for special rescue missions where a faster response time would be required. The diesel and gas turbine engines could not be used together.

On April 24, 1971, the Coast Guard's newest ship, the Coast Guard Cutter *Jarvis*, was officially launched from the shipyard in New Orleans. Not yet complete, the ship was then towed within the shipyard where she was to be dressed and outfitted before her first sailing later in December.

Meanwhile, the Pre-commissioning Detail was formed up and established

Jarvis commisioning at the Avondale Shipyard. Photo provided by Jack Hunter.

on Ford Island, Hawaii, on September 19, 1971, with Ensign James Nagle as the first man to report via the ferry service, commonly called the "liberty launches." Later, 140 personnel would report as future crewmembers of the *Jarvis*. Housed in an old and decrepit WWII building, the place would serve as their temporary home and office for the next eight months. Located next to Hickam Air Force Base, the bathrooms were truly pre-war style without toilet partitions. Upon arrival and described many of the crewmembers as "termite infested," with a few minor repairs and fresh paint, the building looked brand-new again. On resupplying the building with new furniture and supplies, Petty Officer Strutton commented: "We just told the chief, 'Don't ask where it came from or how we acquired them.'"

It was here that a dozen or so training schools including fire-fighting training would commence at the Navy Fleet Training Group school. As several of the crewmembers stated later, the shipboard training they received would prove to be invaluable and probably saved their lives. To effectively manage

First picture of the CGC *Jarvis* after leaving New Orleans. Photo provided by Jack Hunter.

the administrative side for the *Jarvis*, a massive number of manuals and publications were assembled and stored. Other crewmembers, notably the enginemen, stayed on the mainland to attend more advanced schools before reporting to the *Jarvis*.

Ford Island, located in the waters of Pearl Harbor, was named after Dr. Seth Ford, a Honolulu physician. The U.S. Army purchased the island during WWI and transferred it over to the U.S. Navy in 1932, where the ownership remains today. During the attack on Pearl Harbor in 1941, Ford Island was at the epicenter, with Japanese planes destroying all of the patrol planes and disabling the Pacific Fleet's battleship force. Today, it is an active military base and home to several museums, including the USS *Missouri* Battleship, the USS *Utah* Memorial, the USS *Oklahoma* Memorial, the Pacific Aviation Museum, and the most famous, the USS *Arizona*. [On a trivia note, the movie *In Harm's Way* with John Wayne, was filmed on this island.]

Petty Officer Third Class Robert Loftin also reported aboard with this same pre-commissioning group, he and several others flown there on an Air Force C5 Galaxy transport plane. Since the men arrived after the workday had ended, they were allowed to sleep late the next day. When they awoke, they cleaned up the barracks, stowed their gear, and proceeded out to the yard where they received further orientation. At the end of the workday, Boatswain's Mate Chief (BMC) Walt Stanczyk, instrumental to the future of the *Jarvis*, told the men "I want you guys to suck up that liberty, drink that beer, and be a man."

Chief Walt Stanczyk, known to his friends as "Stan," was born in Connecticut where he attended grade school, then a technical school learning the machine trade. Enlisting in the Marine Corps at an early age, he stayed for three years, then enlisted into the Coast Guard. Here he rose to the rank of warrant officer until his retirement after twenty-seven years of active Coast Guard service. The chief was highly respected and revered by all for his strong belief in hard work, common-sense leadership, and a "no-bullshit" attitude. The chief would often work alongside his men to get the job done. Petty Officer Strutton commented, "If the crew stayed late, he stayed late. He wouldn't have them do anything that he wouldn't do himself."

Seaman Lawler, one of the deck force enlisted working for Stanczyk, stated that the "Chief was always chewing on someone but always had a smile on his face when he did so." The common theme from his workers was that "When the Chief told you to jump, you asked how high."

Ensign Carl Schramm was a "newly minted Ensign," reporting to his first ship after graduation from the Academy. Arriving at Ford Island to begin his new career on a Sunday, he inquired at the Bachelor Officer Quarters (BOQ) on where to officially report. He was further directed to the officer's club, where, as he tells it:

> "When I got to the O-club I went inside. Someone was sleeping on the pool table, and most of the other JOs (junior officers) were sitting at the bar nursing drinks and a hangover. I think I announced to someone—probably the Ops boss—that I was 'Ensign Schramm reporting for duty.' The reply was 'Welcome aboard. Have a drink.' And that pretty much set the tone. The camaraderie that developed among those of us on Ford Island is something that I'll never forget."

At his office in building 86, on Ford Island, the new executive officer, Commander Kenneth White, otherwise known as the "XO," oversaw the new crew arrivals and training required for a new ship. Commander White's reputation was almost as big as the man itself. Reportedly the most decorated man in the Coast Guard at the time, White had served previously in the Navy, completing tours in Vietnam and participating in the Bay of Pigs in-

Commander Ken E. White. Photo from *Wake Behind Us,* used with permission.

vasion. Forty-six years old, standing near 6'4" and weighing over 250 pounds, the Commander was often described by his men as always "firm but fair."

(Chief Warrant Officer) Keoni Shaw: "Let me add that Ken White...the X/O, was, in my opinion, a *great* leader...and, of course, wardroom 'God.' Some of the guys were wary, even fearful of Ken, but that guy was such an inspiration in many ways."

As a youth, and much like the rest of the country, he wanted to sign up for the service right after the Pearl Harbor attack in 1941. White initially signed up for the Navy in 1941 at the age of fifteen, using his brother's birth certificate; however a postcard from Australia to his mother while stationed aboard a submarine revealed his location to the family. With information received from the family, the Navy dismissed White from the service due to his age. Two years later, this time with his father's written approval, White again entered the Navy as an enlisted man, working as a fire controlman. In 1950, he was discharged from the Navy so he could join the Coast Guard, working as the first fire-control technician for the service. Five years later, he was accepted into the Officer Candidate School (OCS) despite lacking the full college educational background, a testament to his achievements and supervisory endorsements. Notably, later in his career, he was the first Coast Guard officer accepted into postgraduate training at the Armed Forces Staff College.

White believed that the chiefs ran the Coast Guard and that people who deserve it, should be promoted (sometimes with a kick in the pants), with firm, but fair leadership. He loved the military life, and he was a strong proponent of the captain. While having a strong belief in the military formalities, he would sometimes bend the rules to accommodate the men. Petty Officer Third Class Denny Strutton relates the following:

"Once I went to request mast with a request chit disapproved by all my chain of command.[2] I asked for the day off because it was such a beautiful day outside in Hawaii. Commander White looked at me like I was nuts and stepped outside his office, opened the hatch and looked around. He said, 'You're right, and I will approve this chit.' I think he did it because he could. I tried to pattern my chiefdom after him and made my decisions based on what I thought he would do."

While under construction in New Orleans, the *Jarvis* was continually being inspected by Coast Guard personnel, several who ended up serving on her when the inspections were complete. Knowing that shortly you will be working on a ship will almost guarantee the vessel construction evaluations will be thorough. Chief Warrant Officer Third Class (CWO3) Bill Strickland, EM1 Neil Metzbower, and FT2 Lee Cearley were three of the personnel assigned to the Resident Inspection Office (RIO). Petty Officer Metzbower recalled the *Jarvis* being constructed in five pieces, upside down, then flipped over and welded together. His job was to x-ray every weld to ensure they were acceptable before the ship was to be launched. He became intimately knowledgeable of the ship, having inspected every pipe and electrical component.

Additionally, the ship had another set of eyes—those of the future commanding officer: Commander Frederick Wooley.

On December 14, 1971, the *Jarvis* was declared ready for builders' trials out on the water. Leaving Avondale Shipyard down the Mississippi River, she entered into the Gulf of Mexico to undergo extensive sea trials. All tests completed successfully; the vessel returned to the shipyards two days later. The next few days were devoted to correcting minor problems and to make ready the Coast Guard's most modern and finest 378 ship.

In late December, the crew of ninety-one officers and enlisted men were flown from Honolulu to New Orleans via a C-141 airplane, where for the next few weeks the entire ship would have the final outfitting, including bedding and food. At the end of December, the ship was turned over by the Resident Inspection Office (RIO) to Commander Frederick Wooley, later promoted to captain in just a few short weeks. On January 17, 1972, the

---

[2] Those times that the commanding officer or the executive officer make themselves available to crewmembers to hear concerns, complaints, or requests.

Captain Frederick Wooley. Photo from *Wake Behind Us*, used with permission.

ship went through a pre-commissioning ceremony with attendees including Congressman F. Edward Hebert, Rear Admiral John D. McCubbin, Master Chief Petty Officer of the Coast Guard *Charles Calhoun*, and others. The next day, the *Jarvis* set sail for the Coast Guard Yard near Baltimore. Once out of the Gulf of Mexico waters, Captain Wooley lit off the turbines to test the ship; as George Fewell relayed: "We had a big rooster tail behind us. With the Gulf Stream pushing us, we were almost flying."

Arriving in Baltimore four days later, *Jarvis* spent the next four-plus months adding or modifying equipment according to the latest specifications. Among the changes, adding a new sonar, new electronic equipment, and other changes were added that would improve the capabilities of *Jarvis*.

Winter weather in Baltimore was not as inviting as Honolulu or New Orleans, but crewmembers still found the time to visit nearby Washington, D.C., and other tourist sites.

Homeward Bound
March 1972

Finally, March 29th saw the departure of the Coast Guard Cutter *Jarvis* from Baltimore, en route to her new permanent home at Coast Guard Base Honolulu. Months of mundane ship preparation was now complete, and the crew was excited to start participating in actual Coast Guard missions. Along the way there would be stops at the Panama Canal and a final stop in San Diego before the last leg of the trip across the Pacific, but not without a couple of minor incidents.

Before departing from Baltimore, the command asked the crew that, due to some extra time, there was a possibility of a layover in one of the Caribbean islands that lay on the course to the canal. The resulting vote from the men revealed Aruba as the island most would like to visit. The command staff contacted the U.S. State Department with approval granted.

After departure from Baltimore, there was to be a brief stop at the Naval Station in Norfolk to run the ship through the degaussing range. Unfortunately for the crew, degaussing of the *Jarvis* had to commence due to the amount of magnetism detected, most likely caused during the construction phase of the ship. Life-time mariner David Martin would explain:

> "Magnetism is a problem if you are near magnetically triggered mines or torpedoes. It is also a problem for the accuracy of your magnetic compass. The degaussing system is used to reduce the ship's effect on the earth's magnetic field by preventing the generation of the magnetic disturbances. The application of the degaussing system started during World War II to prevent the naval ships from triggering magnetic mines and torpedoes."

This process unexpectedly took five days and involved stringing huge cables around the ship, then "zapping" the vessel to remove the magnetism. The delay resulted in the cancellation of the Aruba visitation.

One of the primary purposes of high-endurance cutters, such as the *Jarvis*, was is to conduct search and rescue (SAR) where needed. On April 9th, the *Jarvis* received her first SAR call while on her journey to the Panama Canal. The M/V *Compromise* had lost power and was adrift; after a short search, the *Jarvis* found the vessel floating several hundred miles north of Panama. Boatswain's Mate First Class (M1) Charlie Greene, along with two others, boarded the yacht to assist with towing to a port in Panama. Once there, the boat was released. This SAR case, along with the previous degaussing action, had effectively canceled the Aruba stopover.

The next day the *Jarvis* entered the canal without incident if you ignore the "mooning" from the crew of an identified cargo ship directed toward the men of the *Jarvis* for reasons unknown. Soon the ship was transiting into the Pacific to San Diego where she moored on April 19th. Taking on supplies and getting some R&R for the crewmembers, the week in San Diego was relatively uneventful. There were minor issues that normally occur with young men, such as a non-rate, probable age around nineteen, who was arrested and returned to the ship for intoxication and having a fake ID. Probably the most exciting event was the anti-war demonstration against the *Jarvis* later in the week. One needs to understand the country was involved heavily in the Vietnam conflict, and the war was unpopular back home. Local police notified the *Jarvis* of the impending demonstration and the crew responded by laying out high-pressure water hoses, should they be necessary, along with extra security. Despite rumors that an estimated 700 demonstrators were to attempt boarding of the *Jarvis*, a whopping twenty-one demonstrators showed up with no incidents occurring. Finally, on April 28th, the "Pride of the Fleet" departed San Diego for her new home in Honolulu.

The Hawaiian Islands consist of six major islands for visitors and residents including Oahu, Kauai, Molokai, Lanai, Maui, and the big island of Hawaii. Oahu is the business and tourist visitor centerpiece of the chain. The 1970 census figure lists a population of just over 630,000 for the city and county of Honolulu. Today that figure has grown to over 950,000.

Culturally, Hawaii is one of the most diverse demographic places in the country, with over fifty ethnic groups spread throughout the islands. But what sets the islands apart from the rest of the country is the consistently warm weather and beauty. Being assigned to the *Jarvis* and living on Oahu can hardly be considered rough duty for a Coastie.

On May 3, 1972, the CGC *Jarvis* arrived and moored at the Coast Guard Base on Sand Island, located across the harbor from the city of Honolulu. After several months away from home, many of the crew were anxious to be in Honolulu with their friends and families. Those without families would soon spend time with hobbies, swimming, weight-lifting, or working part-time jobs. Non-rates Cortez[3] and DeLeon worked part-time as bouncers in a Honolulu nightclub whenever the ship docked; DeLeon was described as a fairly big man who could handle himself in a tough situation, while Cortez was described by his mentor, Chief Stanczyk, as "someone I wouldn't mess with even if I had five guys behind me." Both Cortez and DeLeon, who both had discipline issues on previous assignments, shined while working their butts off for Chief Stanczyk, who would label them both as "proven sailors." Fellow crewmember Petty Officer Mike Large spent his off-time enjoying recreational scuba diving, a hobby that would turn into a full-time career later in life and

---

[3] A Non-Rate is an E-2 or E-3 who has not attended an "A" school or completed a Striker (Qualification) Program.

would prove pivotal in the future of the ship. Seaman Mike Campbell was even more adventuresome; he loved to skydive. More importantly, the entire crew was eager to show off the Coast Guard's latest ship, the *Jarvis*.

That same day, many Coast Guard personnel reported to duty, including one member who had "missed movement" (another way of saying that he failed to report to the ship on time when it departed from Baltimore.) This member, who was Captain Wooley's duty driver in Baltimore, had overslept past the ship's departure. He ended up hitch-hiking across the country and borrowing money from a girlfriend to fly to Hawaii so that he could report before the ship arrived. Because of his extra efforts to report, not to mention his relationship with the captain, the punishment at his Captain's Mast came down to "dismissed with a warning."

Another member reporting this day would be Seaman Richard Brunke, "ready to save the world," as he would later quip. Standing six-feet tall and weighing 155 pounds, Brunke came from a middle-class family near Chicago. The son of a Marine Corps veteran, Brunke was like so many young men of that generation; it was either college or the military. He chose the Coast Guard.

The base was also home to another high-endurance cutter, the CGC *Mellon*, and two buoy tenders, the CGC *Planetree* and the CGC *Buttonwood*. The missions of the high-endurance cutters are concentrated on search and rescue (SAR) and fisheries patrols, while the buoy tenders' primary mission was to maintain the hundreds of aids of navigation buoys surrounding Hawaii and other regions of the Fourteenth Coast Guard District. This area included over fourteen million square miles, stretching from Hawaii to Japan.

With a new crew, comes extensive training. In the next few months, the *Jarvis* crew would be involved in various forms of training and exercises, ranging from tests regarding engineering, gunnery, seamanship, search and rescue, and nuclear preparedness. Of vital importance were the preparedness tests regarding General Quarters (GQ)[4] and damage control drills. If the participants didn't appreciate the value of those drills then, they surely would in the future.

All of the men, whether enlisted or officer, had undergone water survival training. Training for the officers would have been most likely at the

---

[4] General Quarters—A member's designated assignment during a ship's emergency.

Academy, while enlisted completed their qualification and training at boot camp, either in Alameda, CA, or at Cape May, NJ, depending on which one was closer to their home of residence. In 1972, all recruits were required to complete several swimming tests, including swimming an Olympic size pool the entire length and return, jumping off the high diving board to simulate jumping off a ship, and a flotation test in which a person would inflate their trousers with air and be able to stay afloat without moving. This flotation test involved the crewmember floating in the water, taking their pants off and tying the ends of the pant legs into a knot. Flailing the pants above the water, the member would capture enough air to inflate the pant legs and use them as a floatation device. Failure to complete all phases of the swim tests would disqualify a person from the Coast Guard.

That is not to say there was no leeway in applying the rules. A former crewmember recalls one recruit from a small desert town in eastern Oregon who swam most of the way but for the last fifteen feet, crawled on the bottom of the pool to the finish line, with three lifeguards walking along topside, closely monitoring the situation. Another recalls a recruit refusing to jump from the diving board, choosing instead to cling upside down to it; a lifeguard proceeded to pry his arms off the board, and he fell flat on his back into the water. As far as the Coast Guard was concerned, he passed the test.

During the shipboard training, on June 18th, the *Jarvis* was ordered to assist with a search and rescue (SAR) case 500 miles southwest of Honolulu involving the Japanese fishing vessel, the *Kaigata Maru*. The ship had caught fire 500 miles southwest of Honolulu and had issued a MAYDAY distress signal. The *Jarvis* raced to the scene and attempted to locate any of the twenty-one crewmembers aboard. Ten days later, a C-130 airplane did find one crewmember, and he was picked up shortly by the *Jarvis* helicopter.

No other members of the ship were found despite the searches. The lone crewman told the story that, with the vessel ablaze, the captain decided to have each of the crew jump in the water one mile apart. By placing the shipmates in line with an equal distance apart, the captain felt it would be easier for the rescuers to find; unfortunately, the rescue of only the last crewman occurred. As it were, the fire burned itself out, and the ship did not sink; if the crew had stayed on board, they would have survived. With the *Kaigata Maru* now posing as a hazard to navigation, permission was granted by the owner for the *Jarvis* to sink the vessel, which was accomplished by gunfire.

Finally, on July 21st, the training was completed, with the ship earning four "E's" for excellence from the sea trials conducted; these included excellence for Ship Control and Navigation, Seamanship, Operations, and Engineering.

In the military, violations of the Uniform Code of Military Justice, commonly called UCMJ, will often result in Captain's Mast where the commanding officer will hear the evidence and dispense justice to the member. More often than not, the violations are minor; such as alcohol-related incidents, fights, failure to follow orders, or failure to report to work on time, to name a few. Violations of a more severe nature will often lead to a court-martial. While a civilian court action may follow a person throughout their life, a Captain's Mast is confidential with the records closed for public release.

The punishment handed out could involve forfeiture of pay, reduction in rank, or restriction to the command; all dependent on the seriousness of the offense and the Commanding Officer's judgment. Discipline issues are common with young men, and the *Jarvis* was no exception during this initial training period. While most were minor, one entry in the *Jarvis* ship logs curiously stated that the member was sent to the brig, a military jail, by the XO for "safe keeping."

Chapter 4

COMMISSIONING CEREMONY

"This memorable occasion ended with good cheer and celebration by all. Many months' work had been spent planning for this day. The *Jarvis* was now the 'Pride of the Fleet.'"

—*Coast Guard Cutter Jarvis Commissioning Ceremony*
From The Wake Behind Us

Honolulu, Hawaii
August 1972

ON AUGUST 4, 1972, the *Jarvis* crewmen spent the early afternoon shining their shoes, squaring away their white uniforms, and lastly, donning their flat hats (also referred to as "Donald Duck" hats) for the official ceremony. Petty Officers Loftin and Berry ascended to the flying bridge, where they proceeded to hoist the Coast Guard ensign (flag). The halyard line[5] bounded the ensign; Petty Officer Loftin pulled the line, and the Coast Guard ensign unfurled. As Loftin recalls, "There I was in a historic moment and thrilled to pull on that halyard."

At 4:30 p.m., Coast Guard Cutter *Jarvis* became the first Coast Guard vessel to be commissioned in Hawaii. The commissioning ceremony was conducted at the Coast Guard Base Sand Island with Mr. James Beggs, Under Secretary of Transportation, as the principal speaker. Mr. Beggs was

---

[5] A line used to hoist or lower a flag.

the vessel's sponsor and had christened the ship at her launching in New Orleans on April 24, 1972. Also, in attendance was the seventy-seven-year-old daughter of Captain David Jarvis, Miss Anna T. Jarvis,[6] and the future commanding officer of the *Jarvis*, then Commander Bob Hollingsworth. Noteworthy of the date was that it was the 182nd anniversary of the founding of the U.S. Coast Guard.

A week later, *Jarvis* departed for its first ocean mission, officially called "Ocean Station November," scheduled for twenty-one days. Stationed halfway between Honolulu and San Francisco, what many would refer to as "the middle of nowhere," the primary duty for the ship was to collect and provide the U.S. Weather Bureau with meteorological information. Additional responsibilities included gathering seawater samples and furnishing overseas flights with radar fix information. While on station, *Jarvis* serviced over 2,700 aircraft.

With the mild August weather and with time to kill after drills and work were completed, crewmembers could participate in fishing or "swim call." On one Saturday afternoon, the seas were warm and calm, so the call went out for swimming. Calm seas were a requirement in order to observe if there were any sharks in the area; a gunner's mate was posted on the bridge with an M-16 rifle to serve as a shark watch. Petty Officer Third Class Richard Brunke, so eloquently tells the story:

"The ship's accommodation ladder was lowered, and the crew would jump from the main deck (about thirty feet above the waterline) into the water. The propellers were secured, as well as the sewage discharge pipe that came out of the ship at the water's edge, right where the accommodation ladder platform would hit the water. As *Jarvis* gently rocked, the crew would gather and wait for the platform to come into the water when several members of the men would get on and climb the ladder up the ship.

"About thirty minutes into swim call there were about twenty-five people in the water, when everyone started screaming and swimming toward the small boat with ground up toilet paper and shit all over their heads and ears. Someone in the engine room energized the sewage discharge and was pumping raw sewage all over the crew in

---

[6] Anna Jarvis, born Nov 7, 1897, deceased December 5, 1991. (Source: Ancestry.com)

the water. The pipe was about ten inches in diameter and sewage came out in a solid stream.

"The OOD (Officer of the Deck) was yelling into the 1MC (loudspeaker system) to "SECURE THE SHITTERS, SECURE THE SHITTERS!" The 'shitters' were turned off, but there was a pool of human waste all around the accommodation ladder platform, and no one would swim through it. There were too many people in the water to put in the small boat, the CO could not start the engines to move the ship because there were people in the water, and no one would swim through the human waste. The decision was made to lower the bow thruster and move the vessel ahead until the water was clear. It was a sight to behold, seeing that many people swimming next to the ship as it slowly moved forward. Once in clean water, everyone came aboard and took showers.

"That was the last swim call I remember having onboard the *Jarvis*."

Now with swim calls relegated to the history books, the remainder of the free time was spent on more ship drills and exercises, playing bingo, watching movies, or playing poker to fill the void. Mercifully, for the crewmembers, *Jarvis* was relieved of duty on time by the CGC *Klamath* and returned to Honolulu. Regular work schedules and liberty prevailed upon the arrival back in Honolulu until the end of September, when the ship departed for Alaska.

Alaska

Toward the end of August, a new assignment was passed to the CGC *Jarvis*: Alaska Patrol. Here she would provide for law enforcement, fisheries treaty enforcement, and ocean study along the Aleutians and the Bering Sea. The Coast Guard Marine Science Technician (MST) would take oceanographic samples along the way; ordinarily, *Jarvis* would have two of these designated crewmembers on board to assist with the sampling.[7]

---

[7] In 1972, the patrols had been highly effective. Before the *Jarvis* arrived for the Alaska Patrol, six Japanese fishing vessels were detained in violation of an international fisheries agreement. In total, over $430,000 had been collected from court actions.

The Coast Guard Alaska Law Enforcement Patrol is a joint effort with the National Marine Fisheries Service (NMFS). The two agencies conduct patrols in the North Pacific Ocean and the Bering Sea to fulfill fishery enforcement obligations as directed by statute and several international treaties. These patrols require surveillance of foreign fishing vessels to ensure compliance. Another objective was to visit local fishing communities to assure the local population that the patrols are being conducted in their interest. The Seventeenth Coast Guard District designates large patrol areas to those Coast Guard vessels assigned to these duties. The commanding officer was given broad discretion as to how best to patrol these areas.

While many of the crew looked forward to the new adventure in "the land of the midnight sun," there was concern regarding the frigid conditions of the most northern state in the union. According to the National Weather Service, the Gulf of Alaska is one of the stormiest places on earth in the dead of winter, with gale force winds present fifteen percent of the time and ocean swells topping seventeen feet. In an average year, hurricane-force winds strike two or three times. Hurricane winds are defined as winds in excess of sixty-four knots (seventy-four mph).

Hypothermia is a considerable concern, should a person be submerged in the frigid Alaska waters. With water temperatures below thirty-two degrees, your body is immediately immobilized upon entry and exhaustion or unconsciousness can occur within fifteen minutes. At best, the expected survival time is between fifteen to forty-five minutes dependent on the physical condition of the person. Surprisingly, or perhaps not, heavier people are most apt to survive longer in the freezing waters as "fat is a very efficient insulator against heat loss" as commented by noted cold-water expert Dr. Alan Steinman. Regardless of this, your chances of survival in the freezing waters of Alaska, coupled with the potential for drowning from the sea waves, is not good. Those who have experienced Alaska, know the dangers.

Captain Webster Balding, commanding officer of the *Jarvis* in later years, was quite aware of Alaska's risks, having over thirteen years of sea service under his belt. At his Coast Guard *Jarvis* change of command ceremony in 2012, when being relieved, he commented, "I've been aboard a ship in Dutch Harbor in hurricane strength storms before. The weather in Alaska is very unforgiving; especially in November as low-pressure systems roll in, one after the other, across the Bering Sea from Siberia."

Many Coast Guard members stationed in Alaska have stories of tragedies that can never be forgotten. Crewmember Joe Borosh commented that often they would receive an SOS from a fishing vessel and upon arrival, find only debris and bodies. In one particularly unsettling case, they arrived at the location and saw a man floating: "He was waving at us, and we proceeded towards the man. On arrival, I grabbed the man's hand only to realize he was dead, frozen solid. He was bobbing in the water rather than waving at us."

As Captain Balding stated, "The weather in Alaska is very unforgiving," with proof given in the numerous ship disasters that have occurred in Alaskan waters. Coast Guard regulations regarding the fishing industry have gradually improved safety through the years, but have not prevented accidents from happening, a reminder that Mother Nature is still in charge. On April 1, 2001, the *Arctic Rose* sank in the Bering Sea, with the loss of fifteen men. It was deemed one of the worst commercial fishing accidents in the last century. Weather conditions at the time were reported as treacherous, with winds up to forty-five knots and seas to twenty-four feet. In March of 2008, the fishing trawler Alaska Ranger sank 120 miles west of Dutch Harbor. Forty- two of the forty-seven crewmembers survived the ordeal. Many were suffering from hypothermia.

Familiar to most television viewers, the Discovery Channel hosts the highly rated show *The Deadliest Catch*. This is a reality television show based out of the Aleutian Islands port of Dutch Harbor. The selection of Dutch Harbor for the television series was due in large part for it being the number one fishing port in the nation, particularly for crab fishing. While the show highlights the fishing industry in this part of Alaska, the real stars of the show are the dangerous weather conditions of Alaska. Freezing rain, snow, gale-force winds, and huge swells that roll the fishing vessels, all contribute to the show's popularity.

The Aleutian Islands themselves, are widely known as a graveyard of past shipwrecks. Since the first grounding of a Japanese whaling ship in 1780 near the western end of the 1,100-mile volcanic archipelago, there have been at least 190 shipwrecks in the islands. These shipwrecks are due in large part to the geography of international shipping; it is the shortest route between ports of Asia and North America. An estimated 3,100 vessels travel this route each year. In the past two decades, shipwrecks have become less frequent, but larger.

In 1997, the freighter *Kuroshima* ran aground on Unalaska Island spilling over 39,000 gallons of fuel. In December, 2004, the 738-foot Malaysia-flagged vessel *Selendang Ayu*, ran aground, spilling over 328,000 gallons of fuel, the second largest spill in Alaska since the *Exxon Valdez* spill in 1989. This incident inspired the book *On the Edge of Survival*, by acclaimed author Spike Walker.

Walker describes the rescue of the ship's crew in severe Alaskan winter conditions as "One of the most incredible Coast Guard rescue missions of all time."

Unalaska, home to the Port of Dutch Harbor,[8] is a quiet village that had a population of 400 people in the 1960s. As of this writing, it has now become a prosperous port town of over 4,000 residents, resulting from an increase of large crab fishing processing plants.[9]

Another weather concern amongst Coast Guard members were "williwaws." A williwaw, or katabatic wind, is described as a sudden violent gust of cold land air, common along mountainous coasts at high latitudes. They are quite common in Alaska in which cold, dense air is pulled down from the mountains toward the ocean where it will stir up winds and waves. Former *Jarvis* crewmember David Landis, who has over fifty years sea time, commented that, "The Aleutian chain is a series of islands that jut upwards from sea level in an almost vertical ascension. Also known is that winds in this area particularly, are susceptible to higher gusts thru bays and passes, giving rise to williwaws. Dutch Harbor is a bay, and you have passes on either side."

Captain Peter Garay, a former maritime pilot with over fifteen years of years of western Alaska sailing, very distinctly describes his experiences with williwaws:

"The williwaws, powerful winter winds that come avalanching down the steep slopes of the surrounding mountains, are the worst. Forget

---

[8] Some folks may be confused as to the proper name of Unalaska. The island and the town are both named Unalaska. There is a body of water called Dutch Harbor and many people refer to the town as Dutch Harbor or simply Dutch. Technically, there is no town named Dutch Harbor on Unalaska Island. (City of Unalaska website)

[9] Of historical note (and not well known to those outside of Alaska), a foreign military bombing of two American military installations occurred at Unalaska/Dutch Harbor on June 3, 1942, by twenty Japanese planes from the Imperial Japanese Navy. Noted as the only attack on U.S. soil outside of Pearl Harbor. A few days later, the islands of Attu and Kiska were seized and occupied by Japanese forces until liberated by U.S. forces on May 30 of the following year.

about the normal physics of ship handling; they don't work. Nothing goes right. Imagine being at work and the ship you are on no longer behaves in any conventional manner. Suddenly you are heeling over 10° as a wall of wind and snow crashes against the ship's sides. Visibility drops to zero, and your vessel starts to move sideways like a giant crab. Everyone is scared."

Jarvis crewmember Richard Brunke believed that a flaw of the 378-foot cutter was the design of the bow structure. In times of severe wind, especially with williwaws, it would catch "the wind like an umbrella, and at times could affect the maneuverability of the vessel."

Onward to Alaska
September

On September 28, CGC *Jarvis* departed from Honolulu for Alaska to begin a forty-four-day fisheries patrol, arriving in Kodiak on October 6th after collecting oceanographic samples along the route. Normal shipboard routine during the transit included standing an eight to twelve-hour work shift, then spending the rest of your time reading, playing bingo, watching movies, or playing poker, as previously stated. Sonar Technician Petty Officer 3rd Class (ST3) Joe Borosh was so bored that he read the *World Book Encyclopedia* three times! His crewmates agreed that he was tough to beat at trivia games.

Seaman Edwards, showing his job versatility, would operate the 16mm movie projector as one of his many shipboard duties. These movie times often included servings of soup and bread made by the cook, Warrant Officer Lape. Brunke explained the ship's routine for *Jarvis*:

"The underway routine consisted of the usual ship's work during the morning, and after lunch we did drills. The 0400 - 0800 / 1600 - 2000 (4:00 a.m. – 8:00 a.m. / 4:00 p.m. – 8:00 p.m.) watches were the worst for me. You were on watch early in the morning, did ship work after watch, and had lunch. The routine for that watch was to be able to hit the rack in the afternoon, but we always had drills, so that never happened. Thursday was steak day, so for dinner, we always had steak. Friday was fish day, so we had a good selection of seafood for lunch every Friday. Saturday was inspection day, so the ship's crew spent all morning cleaning the ship, and at 10:00 the inspection parties would go throughout the ship making lists of discrepancies to be fixed by the next inspection. That usually lasted until lunch, and after lunch, we had 'holiday routine.'

"Every Saturday underway was also pizza night. Each week a different department would make pizza for the crew for dinner. Pizza night was usually a good time! We were also given two beers each. The beer was a great treat because you were not supposed to have alcohol on board.[10] The Chiefs did not pay attention to this as they always had whiskey in the Chiefs Mess. I had several friends that did not drink so I would trade them soda for their beer; I usually ended up with a six pack each Saturday. Saturday was also when we had movies on the Mess Deck, poker games throughout the ship, and everyone just let their hair down. Sunday was holiday routine. There were religious services at 10:00, and brunch until noon. The cooks left the food out, and you cooked what you wanted yourself.

"As Boatswain's Mate of the Watch, I had to make rounds of the entire ship every hour, checking to ensure there was no flooding or fire. As the seas got rougher, the inspection of the forward part of the ship became harder because it was rocking, rolling and pitching so much. If I was down there too long, I would get seasick (so would the other BMOWs, but they would never admit it).

"The paint locker was all the way forward, so our inspections of the forward compartments were very important. If the paint locker caught on fire, it could blow the bow off the ship. Sometimes on the night watches, I would wake up the duty cook and tell him everything in the galley was flying around, and he had to get up and secure it. They never wanted to get up, so I would offer to do it for him if he gave me the keys. His keys also had the key to where the ice cream was kept, so I would get ice cream and eat it on my rounds. There was never anything banging around in the galley!"

---

[10] The times were different in the 1970s. Alcohol use was more tolerated, and violations often ignored. An alcohol incident today would possibly lead to dismissal from the Coast Guard.

It was during slow periods that the command felt it was essential to maintain a state of readiness. Captain Wooley, with coffee in hand, (lots of sugar he would joke) would often roam the passageways, reviewing the crew's performance, and stopping personnel during his walk to converse about their career goals or their families. The men of the *Jarvis* loved and respected the captain; there was no doubt about that. As former crewmember David Landis stated: "As I look back at the years from my many years as a mariner, I see Captain Wooley as a true professional mariner and yes, loved and respected! His leadership style was ahead of the times. There was a lot of talent on the *Jarvis*, and he made use of it."

The XO, Commander White, was highly respected by the crew as well, and he believed in transparency. He often utilized the ship's public announcement (PA) system to provide vital information to the men on the ship's status.

It was in September that preparations were made to equip the CGC *Jarvis* with a helicopter to assist in supporting the *Jarvis* mission during Alaska Patrol 1972. Selected as the Senior Aviator for the three aviation detachments in Alaska was LT Ron Huddleston. As stated by the lieutenant, "The Alaska Patrol was a multipurpose operation. It combined the enforcement of United States laws concerning the territorial sea, its contiguous fisheries zone, and its various international treaties and agreements with surveillance functions, scientific data collection, and SAR included."

Coast Guard helicopter HH-52A 1383 was assigned to assist the ship in accomplishing these missions. In mid-September, Helo 1383 was transported to the Coast Guard Air Station in Kodiak for temporary storage, with the pilots and crew arriving September 24th.

Manufactured by Sikorsky Aircraft, HH-52A helicopters served the U.S. Coast Guard for over twenty-five years. The turbine-powered helicopter could land and take-off from the water and had a large cabin to accompany those rescued. Initially deployed in 1963, the aircraft saved over 15,000 lives and $1.5 billion in property loss and damages. Ninety-nine HH-52s were manufactured and served on Coast Guard cutters, air stations, and icebreakers until they were retired in 1989. Often recognized as the backbone of Coast Guard aviation, the official Coast Guard aviation website states: "This little helicopter, a unique assemblage of proven parts, comfortably behind the cutting edge, performed astounding feats in thousands upon thousands of occasions. It became the international icon for rescue and proved the worth of the helicopter many times over. It had an enormous impact on Coast Guard aviation." The HH-65 Dolphin helicopter, with a winch and cable capability for rescues, later replaced the HH-52A.

After arriving October 6th in Kodiak, fueling and minor repairs were completed. An HH-52 helicopter and her crew landed on board two days later, becoming the ship's first Aviation Detachment.

Noteworthy, this was the beginning of a flight deck equipped ship staged in the Bering Sea and the Aleutian Islands. Thanks to an agreement between then-Senator Ted Stevens and the Coast Guard, the Coast Guard would always have a ship with a flight deck and helo in this region, 365 days a year, in support of the Alaskan fisheries.

Flight operations commenced with the arrival of the first National Marine Fisheries Service (NMFS) agent and one observer. Familiarization flights were undertaken including hoisting and lowering them from and to the *Jarvis* as in a real situation; the agent would be lowered to the suspect fishing vessel to check their documents, and to learn the amount and type of fish caught. They would also check the cook's freezer, as sometimes they would feed the crew with banned species. The safety of the inspectors was always a concern and, the agent's toughness admired by the flight crew. Lieutenant Huddleston, the pilot, stated, "I was greatly impressed with the expertise and courage of NMFS agents as I would have been hesitant to go aboard some of those fishing vessels even if moored at the dock."

On October 11th, the *Jarvis* departed Kodiak for ports of call at Dutch Harbor, St. Paul Island, and Ketchikan. After a short layover in Ketchikan, *Jarvis* departed for Juneau, then Anchorage. It was common that while patrolling near these local communities, American crab fishermen would deliver plenty of King crab for the crew to eat. It was the fishermen's way to thank the ship for enforcing the fishery laws by keeping the foreign ship vessels out of the area.

Other communities visited during this trip also fully embraced *Jarvis*. She was the first 378' WHEC (High Endurance Cutter) to visit Alaska and enforce the fishery laws. In every port she entered, the local citizenry would come to tour the ship and welcome the crew, often inviting members to their homes for dinner. Permission was given by the captain for hunting expeditions, although no one ever shot anything. On reflection, Coast Guard members would often rate this time as the best in their career.

Meanwhile on October 24th, *Jarvis* received a call that the M/V *Frisco* was sinking. The helicopter assigned to the ship was returning from Kodiak and diverted to search the area for survivors, but to no avail. The search continued for the rest of the day before the *Jarvis* resumed her scheduled patrol.

Anchorage

In 1972, Anchorage hosted a population of just over 48,000 people, today the citizens number over 294,000. The city itself is Alaska's largest city, located in the southcentral region of the state. The Port of Anchorage is the primary hub of incoming logistical supplies for the entire area.

The 1970s saw a growth spurt of Anchorage with the development of the Trans Alaska Pipeline System, commonly called "TAPS," "Alaska Pipeline," or "Alyeska pipeline." The discovery of vast oil supplies on Alaska's North Slope at Prudhoe Bay in 1968, led to the proposal and construction of a forty-eight-inch pipeline to bring the crude oil 800 miles south to the Valdez Marine Terminal. With the corporate offices located in Anchorage, the city's population grew to over 184,000 by 1980, over three times the size in 1970. Pipeline construction began in 1974 and finished three years later at the cost of over $8 billion.

Toward the end of October, on a beautiful, cold morning, the *Jarvis* was steaming up Cook Inlet toward the city of Anchorage. There, the crew was looking forward to liberty; however, for Petty Officers Bob Loftin and Jerry Sandors, the relaxation before the arrival would be short-lived.

Captain Wooley had decided the ship needed to be at "full dress" [11] when the *Jarvis* tied up at the pier in Anchorage. Normally full dress is for special occasions like the 4th of July or a commissioning ceremony, and not because of arrival to a city. As Chief Herman explained to the two petty officers, "Captain Wooley wants the display and that 'full dress' will be used to build a good image for the Guard."

---

[11] All of the ship's signal flags flying from each masthead, from one end of the ship to the other.

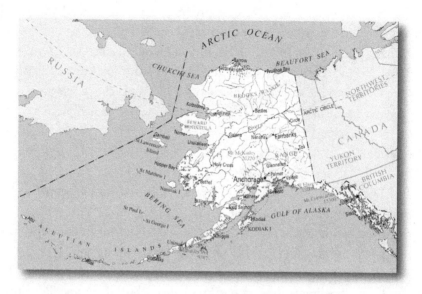

Map of Alaska, showing location in relationship to Russia and Canada.

Loftin and Sandors, along with Petty Officers Tom Looney, Raymond Beaver, and "NOLA" Eaton, immediately went to work on the details. Scaling up the masts, the men attached flags and pennants and snapped them to the cables in proper order. Strapped high up in the relatively calm, but freezing breeze,[12] the temperature felt like thirty below to the men as they worked feverishly to complete the difficult work. Despite the conditions though, all was completed by the time *Jarvis* set the "special sea detail"[13] for anchoring.

The ship made its grand entrance to Anchorage, much to the delight of the local population. As Loftin would later state: "The willingness of these shipmates to take on and complete a tough job is a testament to the character of the *Jarvis* crew." With the ship tied to the wharf, the next few days were spent entertaining special VIP guests and hosting an open house for the community to assist with local Coast Guard recruiting efforts in the area.

On November 6, *Jarvis* departed Anchorage to resume fishery patrols. Shortly after that, the ship stopped in Dutch Harbor for shelter from an approaching storm. It was here that *Jarvis's* troubles began.

---

[12] Anchorage temperatures that week ranged from mid-to-high 20s during the day.

[13] Special sea detail—Everyone has a specific job for the ship entering or exiting the port.

Chapter 5

SEEKING SHELTER

"The Northerly transit had us in the trough the entire way to Alaska, so *Jarvis* was taking heavy rolls the entire time, and being the ship was top heavy, that didn't help. During meals, the captain would put the ship on a smoother course, 'Chow Course,' so we could eat without our food flying all over. After meals, back in the trough! You could definitely feel the seas getting rougher and the climate getting colder the further north we went; this was the beginning of winter after all."

—*Richard Brunke*

Iliuliuk Bay, Alaska
November 11

THE GENERAL CONCEPT of operations for fishery patrols involved the *Jarvis* keeping out of sight while the ship's helicopter conducted surveillance flights to maintain an element of surprise to potential violators. While the flights were taking place, the vessel would anchor or stand off in one of the numerous bays of the Aleutian Islands. Initially anchored in Pavlof Bay, the ship had to relocate on November 11th, due to deteriorating weather, to Left Hand Bay and later on to Balboa Bay, for better shelter.

November 13

On this date, the *Jarvis* passed through Unimak Pass and anchored in Lost Harbor on Akun Island. With instructions from Coast Guard Seventeenth District office in Juneau, the ship was to proceed to a specific area located north of Dutch Harbor and observe foreign fishing activity.

Map showing the Gulf of Alaska, the Bering Sea, and the Aleutian Islands. Courtesy U.S. Geological Survey, Dept. of the Interior, USGS.

November 14
11:45 a.m.

With the ship arriving at Iliuliuk Bay, the Coast Guard helicopter assigned to the *Jarvis*, made two surveillance flights of the area on November 14th. Seeking shelter from an approaching storm, and to also deal with a crewman's dental issues that required a visit to the town of Unalaska, the *Jarvis* anchored at the bay on the east side of Dutch Harbor, with forty-five fathoms[14] of chain to the starboard anchor, in sixteen fathoms of water, described as "muddy bottom." The *Jarvis* had previously anchored in Iliuliuk Bay in almost the exact location on October 15th, just a month earlier, for shelter from the weather. At that time, the winds encountered were up to forty-five knots and the vessel anchored with no issues. This experience, combined with the report from the Board of Investigation (BOI) that Coast Pilot described Iliuliuk Bay as "providing good anchorage," could explain Captain Wooley's decision to seek safety in this bay.

---

[14] A fathom equals six feet, used for measuring the depth of water or chain length.

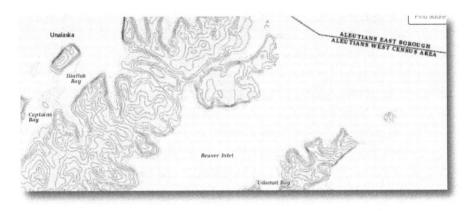

Map showing Beaver Inlet and the surrounding islands. Courtesy U.S. Geological Survey, Dept. of the Interior, USGS.

The day started with clear skies and calm seas but the weather soon changed as the day progressed. Intermittent rain and snow showers quickly affected visibility.

7:00 p.m.

Temperatures began to decline, winds increased, and the ship's barometer readings[15] began to drop. Petty Officer Loftin was on the bridge with Captain Wooley, who kept a personal barograph in his cabin that recorded the pressure with ink on paper wrapped around a drum. The captain mentioned to Loftin that "the bottom fell out of the glass." This expression is used by "old salts" to mean that the pressure drop was dramatic and took place within minutes.

Captain Wooley ordered adjustments to the length and direction of the anchor chain, adding fifteen fathoms as a precautionary measure.

10:00 p.m.

Earlier in the evening, some members of the ship participated in a basketball game with the locals, in town. Returning to *Jarvis* in a small boat

---

[15] A barometer is a scientific instrument on a ship used to measure atmospheric pressure. This pressure can forecast short term changes in the weather.

around 10:00 p.m., they experienced rough water, an indication of what the future would bring.

Relieving Lieutenant Junior Grade (LTjg) Al Sabol as weapons officer for this Alaska patrol, LTjg Paul Barlow was one of the crewmembers who had gone ashore to play basketball against the locals. On their return in a small boat, they encountered worsening sea conditions with the winds starting to increase. Barlow recalled his return to the ship: "Upon arriving on deck, I ran into off-going Officer of the Deck Carl (Schooner) Schramm who said he just had been relieved of duty at midnight and had cautioned the on-coming OOD (Officer of the Deck Eger) to "keep the ship off the rocks." Never thinking another thought, I immediately went to bed."

11:00 p.m.

Around 11:00 p.m., LTjg Schramm contacted the captain to advise him that winds were kicking up to thirty to forty knots with gusts to fifty. Wooley then ordered an additional fifteen fathoms of chain, bringing the total to seventy-five fathoms of anchor chain. Should winds increase, the OOD was to inform the captain. The night orders did not include this written order because the captain expected to be on the bridge throughout the evening, as was his usual practice.

Often, he would sleep on a mattress by the map room near the bridge in case the weather took a turn for the worse, as he wanted to be readily available should the OOD need some guidance.

12:00 Midnight
November 15

Shortly after midnight, Captain Wooley returned to the bridge to do a quick check and reiterate his instructions to Ensign Eger, the current OOD. "Call me if winds increase appreciably," he again told the young ensign. Although inexperienced, Eger was assigned the night shift as the ship was at anchor, and the operations officer wanted to spell the other junior officers who would work the CONN[16] when *Jarvis* was underway. The captain's concern with the ship's vulnerability was that it sat high in the water, with an extensive "sail" area

---

[16] The act of controlling the ship's movement while at sea; to stand bridge watches as the OOD.

making it quite susceptible to high winds. He wanted Eger alert to the situation. The captain observed winds averaging around twenty-five knots with gusts to thirty-five, and he was highly concerned about the anchorage.

Soon after the discussion with Eger, Captain Wooley retired to his cabin, falling asleep immediately, fully clothed on top of the bed. He had been awake for thirty hours.

2:00 a.m.

As the early morning progressed, winds gradually increased, with gusts up to seventy-plus knots. The bursts of winds were playing havoc with the rotation of the radars. The high mountains surrounding the harbor, some approaching 1,000 feet in height, adversely affected the quality of the radar images. Radar ranges provide the data for plotting the position of the ship in the bay.

Just a couple of minutes earlier, Radarman Petty Officer Third Class (RD3) John Moran plotted a fix that showed the vessel had moved north 200 yards. He reported this to the OOD on the bridge. Just before Moran's report, Boatswain's Mate Petty Officer Larson had checked the anchor chain and reported that he could feel no vibration from the anchor chain when he placed his foot on it; therefore, concluded that the anchor must be holding. Unfortunately, Larson would later tell Quartermaster Petty Officer Third Class (QM3) Loftin, the quartermaster on duty, that he did not take into consideration that the anchor was resting in the mud, not rock. With a mud bottom, there would be no sign the anchor was dragging. Loftin, rechecked his radar, considered recent reports that the anchor was holding, and relayed to Moran that they did not concur. Moran erased his work and estimated the position.

Years later, Petty Officer Loftin explained the difficulties of obtaining an accurate radar reading:

> "All I can say is the radar fix that was reproduced under made a triangle on the chart with lengths of about 1/2" on each side. That was the only fix I recall that was plotted under my testimony. There may have been other fixes that were logged. By 0215 (2:15 am), the weather had deteriorated so much that we could not get accurate radar fixes. The wind was stopping the radar antennae as I stated in my recollection. There were no shore lights or visible landmarks that we could use to get a fix with an alledade on the wing of the bridge.

"So yes, I failed to get accurate radar ranges, because the weather rendered the radar useless. You may wonder why I did not notice the wind stopping the radar antenna. The radar on the bridge had a cone-shaped cowling with an eye-opening at the top big enough to accommodate eyeglasses. The cowling was there to prevent light pollution and protect our night vision. Unless you are constantly focusing on the screen, you would miss the beam stopping."

With the wind gusts increasing, the anchors showed a "hard" or "moderate" strain, and they appeared to be holding.

2:30 a.m.

The wind gusts continued to increase to seventy knots, and the seas rocked the *Jarvis*. Falling sleet and snow flurries further affected the radar. Just minutes earlier, Ensign Eger observed the difficulties in plotting the ship's position and took steps to obtain additional radar plotting data. At this point, the ensign determined that the ship had dragged anchors over 175 yards north of their position at 2:00 a.m. Rather than use the PA system to alert the crew, a messenger was sent to awaken the captain.

Within two minutes, Captain Wooley shot to the bridge. He was shocked by what he observed: winds gusting to almost eighty miles per hour. Later, he stated to the Board of Investigation: "I did not feel I'd been called in accord with the orders I had left with the officer of the deck." Regardless, he now had a huge problem on his hands.

He immediately ordered the engines on the line and the setting of the anchor detail, Wooley stationed himself at the radar scope, but he was unable to obtain precise navigational data since the wind was slowing or stopping the radar antenna. Boatswain's Mate Petty Officer Larson was ordered to awaken those critical personnel required for the anchor detail, including Chief Stanczyk, but he forgot to notify Chief Damage Controlman Lowell Montgomery, a key member with years of ship experience.

As Loftin would later recall, it was Montgomery's job to release the anchor brake, not to mention he was intimate with the anchor operations. As the *Jarvis* attempted to heave around, the windlass,[17] used to hoist the anchor, was unable to overcome the strain, and went off the line.

---

[17] A type of winch used on ships to hoist anchors.

Earlier in the evening, LTjg Schramm had been taking radar fixes every few minutes with no sign of ship movement. However, as the winds increased, so did the issues with the radar.

Ensign McCarthy recalled:

> "As I remember it, the ship's radar could not handle the extraordinary winds; that is, the wind would cause the radar screen to 'STALL' as it came fully horizontal to the wind. Now the bridge's radar screen would completely paint part of a picture, but...then would stall, and then would 'race around and blank out the screen with no picture' only to repeat that process over and over. CIC's radar information came from the second radar screen, but the same thing was happening to them. And the time of early morning and weather condition precluded taking visual sightings of where the ship was in the harbor...and the ship as I understand it was dragging anchor. So...what ended up was the ship being 'blown' onto the shallows of the harbor."

David Landis, one of the quartermasters on the *Jarvis*, and with over fifty years sea-going experience, years later explained that "Most radar antennas of that era were good up to eighty-knot winds before they started to what I call chatter, and somewhere around 100 knots they stopped in their tracks."

2:42 a.m.

With the propulsion engines back online, the *Jarvis* crew began maneuvering in an attempt to take the strain off the anchor chain. Those on the bridge were fully engaged: RD3 Moran employed in adjusting the current to the radar antenna drive motor, LT Smith handled the annunciators,[18] and QM3 Loftin was acting as the lone helmsman. along with managing the telephone talker to the forecastle and maintaining the ship log. Any one of these tasks could have been a full-time job. Captain Wooley was observing the radar, giving rudder commands, and working the engine annunciators. This understaffed situation continued for forty-five minutes until more relief arrived.

Working conditions outside were extreme; wind gusts up to seventy miles per hour, freezing rain and snow, even lightning. Combined with the severe

---

[18] A device to order engine speed and direction to the engine control room.

sea swells, walking on the icy deck surface was slippery and hazardous. BMC Stanczyk, in charge of the anchor detail, was having difficulties outside trying to observe the anchor chain and communicate on the phone with his crewman, Boatswain's Mate Third Class (BM3) Larson. The roar of the sea, combined with the howling wind and rain, was deafening. The chief could not adequately determine if the anchor was dragging; the chain was covered in mud, disguising the markings.

The official Board of Investigation would later report:

> "Boatswain's Mate Chief Petty Officer Stanczyk was in charge of the anchor detail, assisted by BM3 Larson on the phones, and several others. The weather conditions were such that both Stanczyk and Larson had trouble keeping their footing, observing the end of the chain, and communicating. Chief Stanczyk had the opportunity to check the anchor prior to the maneuvering of the vessel, and there was no indication that the anchor was dragging. Upon attempting to heave around, the windlass was unable to overcome the strain and went off the line. By keeping the reset switch depressed and operating at low or high speed as the strain allowed, the anchor chain was brought in over a period of approximately thirty-five minutes. Maneuvering of the ship had a minimal effect on relieving the strain due to the inability to bring the bow through the wind and to erroneous reports from the foc'sle....Since the chain was covered in mud, not all chain markings could be seen. No reports were received on the bridge of the one and two shot markings but only of the anchor in sight, the anchor being aweigh without knowledge of either the foc'sle or the bridge."

3:00 a.m.

The chain had been dragged across the bow, making it difficult to raise the anchor, necessary if they were to get the ship underway and away from the reef. The commanding officer commenced backing with a two-thirds astern on both shafts as soon as he observed the anchor was in sight, intending to steer the ship away from its forward anchor chain. It was during this maneuvering that a particularly strong wind gust of seventy mph struck the port side of the *Jarvis*, driving her dangerously close to the reef. Sonar Technician

Third Class Mike Large was on the outside deck when he observed how close the ship was to the coastline and immediately ran to press the General Alarm. Before he reached the alarm, however, General Quarters sounded.

The *Jarvis* had run aground.

Chapter 6

SHIP AGROUND: "THIS IS NO DRILL!"

"Ernie, we're in trouble. We're right on top of the shelf."

—*Captain Wooley to the Operations Officer, LT Ernest Smith*

Rocky Point, Dutch Island
November 15, 1972

3:17 a.m.
ON THE MORNING of November 15th, the Coast Guard Cutter *Jarvis*, struck a reef off of Rocky Point in Dutch Harbor, damaging the ship. On the bridge, Quartermaster Second Class David Landis upon hearing that Petty Officer Moran had recently reported the ship dragging anchor, exclaimed "Bullshit, we're aground!"

The Coast Guard official Board of Investigation would later convey what happened:

"The Commanding Officer commenced backing with a two-thirds bell astern on both shafts as soon as he received the report that the anchor was in sight, there being insufficient sea room to go ahead and bring the bow through the wind. At 0317 (3:17 a.m.), the vessel struck the reef, holing herself in the engine room, and then passed over the reef, causing relatively minor scraping damage, but shearing off the sonar dome and both (sonar) transducers. The starboard propeller struck bottom, causing the starboard diesel to stall and damaging all four blades. The port engine was increased to back flank, with the starboard engine also being backed full after restarting. *Jarvis* backed free of the reef and into the Dutch Harbor entrance and then shaped course out of the confined waters of Iliuliuk Bay."

Petty Officer Loftin recalls Captain Wooley immediately exclaiming, "Son-of-a-bitch. We've run aground!" Crewmember Dave Martin described the scraping a "God-awful noise, rocks grinding against steel—props hitting the rock (*thump thump*)." Immediately seeking shelter from the weather in Kalekta Bay, the crew quickly responded with damage control efforts to stem the flow of the freezing water into the engine room.

When General Quarters was sounded, all hands were alerted to man their emergency stations immediately. "THIS IS NO DRILL" was announced over the PA system to ensure the men understood the gravity of the situation.

"What happened?" Radioman Chief Miltier demanded upon entering the ship's radio room.

Radioman Petty Officer 2nd Class Roy Montgomery, working the radio watch duty, quickly responded: "I think we ran aground!" The chief's quick reaction wasn't surprising; the location of the chief's berthing area is on the lower level of the ship within easy hearing distance of the scraping noise.

Other crewmembers recall their experiences that night. Boatswain's Mate 3rd Class Richard Brunke described it as follows:

"I was the BMOW [Boatswains Mate of the Watch] for the 8-12 underway watch. At the time of the grounding, I was asleep in the Deck Division 30-man berthing [starboard side]. I was awoken by the ship bouncing, and a terrible grinding sound as the ship went over the rocks. Although I did not know what had happened, I immediately knew it wasn't good, and my rack was below the waterline. I jumped out of my rack, quickly dressed and started running to the main deck, that was when I heard the General Quarters [GQ] alarm. My GQ billet was the Fuse Setter in the 5'38" [5-inch/38-caliber] gun mount on the bow. We all mustered and went to the mess deck as the gun crews were needed elsewhere. *Jarvis* headed out to sea to assess the damage and effect repairs. 14th Coast Guard District Operation Center (Honolulu), was advised of the situation and requested guidance."

From ST3 Van Elsberg:

"I had just awakened and was going to go to the head when we ran aground. I remember hearing the sound of the hull striking something and grinding along for a few seconds. I thought we'd gotten underway and hit a fishing vessel. Moments later General Quarters was sounded, and I dressed then headed to the CIC [Combat Information Center] with the rest of the sonar crew. The damage control team had to work hard to stop the flooding, but they were able to deal with it."

Seaman Leo Manipon, part of the working deck force, further commented:

"I think it was early morning of Nov 15, 1972, about 2:00 a.m., when a loud noise that sounds like another ship, rammed us and woke up some of the crew, me included. Seaman Apprentice [SA] Daniel Edwards, whose rack was next to mine, got up and tried to wake me up although I was already awake. He said, 'Leo, I think we ran aground.' I jumped down from my rack and started to put on my dungarees. As I was dressing up, the General Quarters alarm was sounded. I ran to my GQ billet on the flying bridge. I heard from some of the crew that we ran aground."

Senior Aviator Pilot LT John Huddleston was awakened by the sound of the scraping along the hull on the starboard side "for what seemed to be an extensive period of time. Soon thereafter, the emergency klaxon went off, and all hands were to report to their Emergency Stations: 'THIS IS NO DRILL' was announced, which came as no real surprise based upon the noise of the uncharted pinnacle scraping along the starboard side." Huddleston then proceeded to the aviation detachment emergency station where he met his crew to discuss the situation. After meeting with his team, he contacted the Damage Control Central to obtain an update. Once there, he was escorted to the engine room where he observed the crew trying to plug a leak on the starboard side near the bottom of the hull, with water shooting through the hole.

3:22 am

Flooding surged into the engine room with the damage specifically located at frame 241, starboard side, and on either side of longitudinal 9. Compounding the problem was the location of the hole, nearly inaccessible from inside the engine room. Lieutenant Junior Grade (LTjg) Myron Tethal would later testify at a board of investigation that the deck plates were difficult to move, and there was a need for quick-release latches for these plates to accurately ascertain where the damages had occurred. While unable to observe the hole, the only way to identify the size was to lie on the deck plates and feel the hull of the ship with your fingers. Two small cracks were initially identified, roughly four inches by six inches, and later revised to nineteen inches.

Damage control efforts, directed by Tethal and Damage Controlman Chief Lowell Montgomery, immediately went to work with Engineman Petty Officer 2nd Class (EN2) Kacsanek placing wedges and rags into the holes and using other shoring measures as needed. Stopping, or even slowing the leak would prove to be complicated. Kacsanek would recall: "We couldn't get to the hole to set up shoring; we had to remove the deck plate walkway above it. We couldn't unscrew it, had to use a pry bar to pop the screws off, then removed the walkway. Once removed, we stuck plywood over the hole and shored. Pumps were keeping up with the flooding." Over 150 gallons of water per minute was pouring into the ship and continued to do so even after additional patching efforts were complete.

In the *Jarvis* radio room, Chief Miltier directed the watchstander, Radioman Roy Montgomery, to notify CGH Radio Station Kodiak of the General Quarters and the grounding, via Kodiak SAR Sector and RCC Juneau. Later, the ship advised by a radio message that she had struck a reef in hurricane winds, and ruptured the shell plating in the engine room. Flooding now controlled. Inquired by RCC if assistance was required, the *Jarvis* responded with a negative reply. Should the ship request assistance, the nearest Coast Guard asset was the USCGC *Balsam* some 337 miles away.

3:30 a.m.

Directed by Chief Montgomery, the damage control men were using mattresses and any other fibrous materials they could locate. While holding the shoring in place, others poured concrete over the patched areas, keeping the

CGC *Jarvis* engine room. Photo provided by Jack Hunter.

shoring in place until it quickly settled. Twelve minutes later, the ship reported the hole plugged with a temporary patch.

The report on the investigation outlines the ship's status at this point:

"Additional shoring was placed in lower sound to prevent progressive flooding from the distorted cover-plates and proved adequate. Later examination revealed that lower sound had flooded to a depth of three feet. Careful soundings were taken of all tanks, and it was determined that no tank had been ruptured so as to contaminate fuel supplies. The starboard shaft when operated, and it was determined that there were no vibrations in the shaft operated at least at two-thirds speed with no difficulties. Portable pumps and hoses were laid out for dewatering purposes and continuous watches set on the engine room patch."

After General Quarters sounded, crewmembers began a stem-to-stern to check for additional damage. Over the PA system, an announcement directed all damage control personnel (DCs) to report to the engine room for the response. On arrival, SNGM Randy Kerr and FN Silva were directed by DCC Lowell Montgomery to inspect the magazine compartment for damage. Upon inspection of this section, the duo felt pressure on the vertical water tight door, a clear sign of a problem. Kerr and Silva then removed the deck plates to allow access to the sonar dome plate. They observed water leaking around the plate, itself bent upwards in the middle, no longer flat, thereby allowed water to flow into the magazine. Sonar Technician Chief (STC) Valerga removed the existing bolts to the plate and replaced each nut with hemp, stopping 99% of the leaks. The water level was reduced using different pumps at different times. A bucket brigade would soon be in commission. According to the duty GM, the water level in this room had been controlled and never exceeded eighteen inches.

4:00 am

The watch changed over at 4:00 a.m., at which time QM3 Loftin went to the mess deck[19] to retrieve a much-needed cup of coffee. Here he was confronted by members of the deck force and the glare of BM1 Greene. Petty Officer Ferron Suljeman, sitting next to Greene, exclaimed, "It's all your fault, Loftin! You're cashiered!" With that remark weighing heavily on his mind, Loftin returned to the bridge to assist QMC Herman and QM2 Landis wherever he could. On arrival, Landis explained to Loftin that he felt it was a williwaw that had struck the ship. He further described it as a

---

[19] Dining hall on board a ship.

gust of wind that comes down the side of the mountain and, because Dutch Harbor is a protected bay, the wind takes on a spinning effect.

It was during this period that Captain Wooley relayed an order to Gunner's Mate Chief (GMC) Jack Hunter to have everyone not directly involved in the damage control efforts to form up and start a bucket brigade. The chief's personal opinion of the need was that the captain wanted everyone busy and contributing to the effort. There was also a concern to keep the ammo dry in the magazine room above the sonar dome; emptying this compartment would ensure the water height would not increase up to the next level.

The brigade worked for a few hours and consisted of at least twenty crewmembers, both officers and enlisted. The crewmembers would fill the bucket and pass it up the fifteen-foot ladder through the forward cargo hole, and over the side. With the rough sea conditions rocking the ship, everyone got drenched as they pushed and pulled the buckets upward. Interviewed later by the newspaper *Honolulu Advertiser*, Electrician Technician Jerrold Sandors recalled dumping a bucketful of cold water over crewmember Ray Christianson's head when the latter handed him a bucket too full of water. With the "bucket brigade" operation now completed, a small pump with a hose was positioned, to dump the remaining excess water from the magazine room into a deck drain.

Others went to their emergency General Quarters stations. Seaman Ray Christianson reported to the bridge to work as the helmsman. Christianson, despite being an E-3, had previously served in the same position aboard the CGC *Rush*. Captain Wooley was a true believer in having crewmembers work at jobs they qualified for, regardless of their rank.

Fireman Bill Sewell reported to the Damage Control (DC) shop where later he would work to maintain the pumps on the main deck in cold, frigid weather conditions.

The admin staff had their emergency billets as well. Yeoman Third Class Mark Carter was assigned as the Port Bearing Taker,[20] but was also involved in the bucket brigade and other cleaning details as required.

---

[20] The bearing takers on each bridge wing take a bearing on landmarks and aids to navigation (lighthouses, etc.), and report them simultaneously to the Quartermaster Navigation station on the bridge interior. The Navigation Station is between the main bridge and the Combat Information Center (CIC). The quartermaster takes these reported bearings and plots them on a navigation chart. Along with radar bearings reported to the Navigation Station from the bridge and CIC, these plots confirm the current location of the ship. (Mark Carter)

Some crewmembers did not have an emergency position due to the ship circumstances. Sonar Technicians Mike Large and Joe Borosh, along with Ensign Jim Nagle, were somewhat unemployed due to the loss of the sonar dome. These three, along with another sonar technician volunteered to work in the cold and wet confines of the engine room. Petty Officer Large had a unique skill that would greatly assist the *Jarvis* in these times, that of a scuba diver. As a youth, he trained as a diver at the Pentagon swimming pool where his Air Force officer father had a pass. During his father's tenure there, Large lived in the water. Later, he attended high school in Alexandria, Virginia. The movie *Remember the Titans* featured the same high school he attended; he had been the captain of the football team the year before the timeline of the film.

Enlisting in the Coast Guard, Large jumped at the chance for assignment to the *Jarvis*. With the ship homeported in Hawaii, it was a scuba diver's dream.

With a strong faith in God and quiet confidence in his abilities, Large's friend Joe Borosh would serve the *Jarvis* well in this time of need. Six-foot-tall with a slender build, a full beard and brown hair, twenty-one-year-old Borosh was part of the team that had wired the entire ship in the development stage. Therefore, he had an intimate understanding of the vessel and her nuances. His best friend on board was ST3 Eddie Donaldson, who would also play a pivotal role in the recovery efforts.

Once the submersible pumps[21] started operating, a problem immediately arose; the P-250 pumps stopped functioning. Petty Officer Mike Large retrieved his diving equipment and once outfitted in the engine room, dove into the freezing, oily, greasy water to check out the issue.

Rags and other material, used to plug the hole, had been sucked into the hoses. Large removed the obstructions, and the pumps resumed operation. Petty Officer Joe Borosh, standing in the freezing water as well, assisted Large in gathering the loose material out of the water. However, due to the amount in the water, Large had to repeat this diving process seven or eight times throughout the entire ordeal. Eventually, the polluted water would destroy his scuba gear. Sonar Technician Robert L. Van Elsberg would later comment

---

[21] Submersible pumps work underwater while the P-250 works on the deck.

that Large "was one tough guy and when we needed him most he stood up to the challenge." Of Large, fellow crewmember Leo Manipon said, "This guy I could tell was so tired, but he kept on diving just to install the patch and shoring." The icy water conditions did eventually take a toll on Petty Officer Large, as he was later medically evacuated and admitted to an Anchorage hospital, suffering from pneumonia.

7:52 a.m.

Having experienced unpredictable wind gusts from thirty to sixty-five knots, the *Jarvis* entered Kalekta Bay, and maneuvered to the leeward side[22] of the mountains. Later in the morning the decision was made to replace the patch over the hole, a decision met with disbelief by some of the junior engineer staff.

A new foam rubber mattress pressed over the rupture failed to decrease the 150-gallons-per-minute rate of flooding. Consideration of other flood control measures included the recommended procedure of installing a concrete patch, but that was discounted due to insufficient cement on board the ship. Nor was there a capability to conduct underwater welding to construct a steel patch, as those recreational divers on board were not Navy qualified as required by Coast Guard Commandant's directives. One hour later winds had increased on the leeward side of the mountain from eighteen to forty knots, with the *Jarvis's* unit logs noting "experiencing strong williwaws."

9:30 a.m.

Soundings of the ship's tanks showed no contamination of the fuel supplies. Activation of the starboard shaft revealed no vibrations in the shaft or the reduction gear. The conclusion reached by the officers was that they believed the ship could operate to at least two-thirds speed with no difficulties. Portable pumps and hoses were laid out for dewatering purposes. Continuous watches were positioned to monitor the engine room patch.

With the examinations and patching now complete, LTjg Tethal and CWO Strickland recommended to the captain that the ship was now prepared to depart for the open sea. The water level in the engine room had

---

[22] The leeward side of a mountain is the side protected from the prevailing wind.

stabilized between three and four feet below the deck plates and had caused no damage to any of the equipment or engines. Captain Wooley reviewed the situation along with the recommendations of his officers and decided to proceed to Honolulu where repairs would take place.

12:30 p.m.

Pilot LT John Huddleston met with Captain Wooley on the bridge and relayed his desire to fly the HH-52 helicopter back to Kodiak air station. The captain agreed with Huddleston's assessment. Both did not desire to have the aircraft on board in these weather conditions.

Shortly after meeting with Huddleston, Captain Wooley, and Captain Mathieu from the Seventeenth CG District discussed the options regarding the HH-52 helicopter, the aircrew, and the Marine Fisheries Service agent still on board the *Jarvis*. Wooley relayed his request to send the air assets to Kodiak Air Station. Captain Mathieu denied the request, outlining the difficulties that were involved in flying the craft such a distance from Dutch Harbor to Kodiak. These challenges included the lack of range for the single-engine HH-52 helicopter to fly this distance. This would require a C-130 fixed-wing aircraft acting as an escort to carry fuel, and also require the necessity of adequate airfields for refueling purposes. Unofficially recognized as the workhorse for Coast Guard aviation, the C-130 fit the service needs for long-range search and rescue and fishery patrols. The C-130 in the 1970s could fly up to fourteen hours and cover 2,600 nautical miles in low-altitude flight. The aircraft also featured a loading ramp and door in the tail that enabled easier cargo loading. The cargo bay was large enough to load a small vehicle.

Other challenges discussed included dangerous icing of the helicopter at altitudes for which she would fly, the natural hazards (wind, rain, snow) of the environment, and lastly, no real operational advantage to transit from Dutch Harbor versus Seattle or Honolulu. Captain Wooley listened to the reasoning and agreed. The conversation ended with a discussion of the local weather environment and concluded that the best conditions would lie to the south.

1:00 p.m.

Water continued to pour into the *Jarvis* at a rate of 300 gallons per minute but was contained with the use of three submersible pumps and one eductor in the engine room. Shoring efforts continued with wedges, rubber, and anything else at hand. Conditions inside the engine room were described as "wild" with waves sloshing around. The crewmembers were often knocked down in the freezing water as they continued to work on the containment of the flooding.

2:00 p.m.

At this time Captain Wooley initiated a phone patch to Captain Mathieu to relay that repairs were proceeding positively, and that he would soon be ready to put the *Jarvis* to sea. A review of the weather conditions confirmed that the best weather was to the south. Weather forecasts from the Fleet Weather Central in Pearl Harbor and the Anchorage Weather Service predicted an intense storm north of Dutch Harbor. Also brewing were storms between Dutch Harbor and Kodiak or Seattle, with a smaller system expected between Dutch Harbor and Adak within twelve to twenty-four hours. Swells were expected to exceed thirty feet.

Captain Mathieu relayed his approval for transit to Honolulu. It was granted on conditions that repairs were satisfactory, and that *Jarvis* had adequate fuel. With final permission from the District office, the Coast Guard Cutter *Jarvis* exited Dutch Harbor at 2:30 p.m.

3:10 p.m.

The *Jarvis* departed and arrived at Akutan Pass with no issues or problems encountered. Winds at that time in the pass ranged from fifteen to twenty-five knots with light seas. The vessel proceeded at the standard speed of fifteen knots then at two-thirds ahead (eight knots) when she approached open water.

4:30 p.m.

As *Jarvis* entered the open seaway, the rate of engine room flooding increased. A third submersible pump was placed in action to compensate for the rise. The water level in the engine room decreased, and the pump was taken off-line.

Akutan Pass
6:00 p.m.

Once *Jarvis* exited Akutan Pass into the open seas of the Pacific, you could see the "mountainous" waves on the horizon and the fair weather. Smooth sailing conditions quickly deteriorated. The XO, Commander Ken White, would later write: "Just as we cleared the Aleutians, we entered the most tremendous seas I had ever seen, with snow, wind, and rain. The ship started to sink." Winds from the southwest increased significantly from forty-five to fifty knots, with gusts over sixty knots. The ship began to immediately pound and pitch from the terrifying seas, with the patching material being pushed back into the vessel. There was a noticeable increase in flooding in the engine room, resulting in General Quarters sounding five minutes later.

With huge sea swells, severe winds and freezing rain, not to mention an engine room flooding, Wooley was facing many challenges at the same time. It was now pitch-black outside as the captain attempted to come about and return to safer waters. He was unable to view the dangerous wave conditions. While make the turn, *Jarvis* was immediately rocked by thirty-foot plus waves, thus experiencing a sixty-degree roll that would have capsized most ships.

Radioman Second Class (RM2) George Fewell vividly remembers the roll: "As the seas were already pretty bad, going that far over was not a huge shock, it was just a little more than what we were already experiencing. I do remember when it happened because I was up in radio and remember almost walking on the bulkhead and wondering what was going on."

Seaman Wayne Debord remembers it as follows: "When the ship was rolling down off one wave, the ship would roll beyond forty-five degrees, I would stand on the downhill wall of the ship and look through the bridge window below me as the next wave approached. This was of course on the windward side, on the downwind side, I could watch the wave that just passed."

The General Quarters alarm was announced at 6:05 p.m. The captain directed that all personnel not on watch, proceed to the engine room. Those working in the engine room faced extraordinarily difficult conditions. By now it was apparent the patch had failed to hold. The freezing Alaska waters were rushing in uncontrollably. The engine room crewmembers were pounded as they fought to save the ship.

Seaman Joel Cortez, one of those fighting for the ship's survival, had the responsibility of ensuring that the suction hoses on the submersible pump were free of obstructions. After donning his wetsuit, Cortez accidentally cut his hand while working. Not wanting to leave the scene, he explained that he merely stuck his "hand into the freezing water and the bleeding stopped." The ship continued to roll severely, and the engine room personnel were

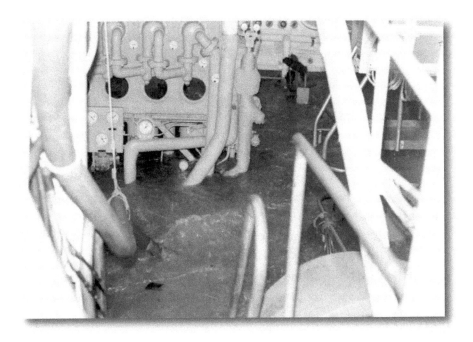

CGC *Jarvis* engine room. Photo courtesy Jack Hunter/Hank Lipian.

getting soaked, bruised, and extremely cold. Later, with electrical sparking lighting up the room and conditions worsening, Cortez was ordered to "get the hell out of the engine room."

Others were operating the P-250 pumps and continued to do so even in the freezing elements.

Seaman Edwards played a dual role during the incident, working the pumps and fixing food for the crew as a cook striker. He recalls working the P-250s with ST3 Donaldson, on the starboard side of the ship and seeing how close the waterline was to the main deck. Later, he would take food below deck to the engine room where he observed the intense looks on everyone's faces. "You didn't have to ask anyone about how serious it was…it reflected in their faces. Crewmembers were quoted regarding the lack of fear. Things were happening too quickly to even think of fear because we all knew what had to be done to save the *Jarvis*," he would later recall.

Response efforts by other crewmembers continued outside in the harsh weather. In desperate times, emergency response attempts may get to the point of trying anything. Petty Officer Large recalls one such measure when the deck force put together a tarp with each end weighted and thrown over the side trying to cover the hole from the outside. Unfortunately, the effort failed when the tarp and ropes got sucked into the engine room.

Radioman Third Class Robert Craig was another crewman pressed into action to operate one of the pumps. "I was working on a P-250 pump, threading a discharge hose and did not have a spanner wrench.I reached out and grabbed the first leg running by and said (loudly due to all the noise) that I needed a spanner wrench. In less than a minute LTjg Sasse came back with the needed wrench."

Described by his fellow crewmembers as quiet, but extremely strong (most likely from lifting weights), Seaman Tim Lawler explained his work on the deck of the ship, while wholly drenched from the rain and the waves crashing over him. "Each wave would cover the pumps, killing them instantly. I would have to restart each time while freezing. I took a break to change my clothes; then the pumps ran out of gas." He would further describe swells as big as the ship that caused several fifty-five-degree rolls.

Despite the ship's design to be watertight (i.e., watertight compartments), maintaining watertight integrity was impossible when the need was to use the hoses to get the water out. This required the hatches to remain open. Engineman Ken Wenner would comment on the use of the hoses and the difficulties:

> "At this time, we were realizing that in our haste to pump the engine room, we had multiple hoses on top of each other going up the only steps from the engine room, and down the only hallway to an open hatch on the leeward side of the ship. P-250s (pumps) were getting swamped on the 01 deck as the ship rolled and water flooded the deck, shutting them down and thereby preventing hoses beneath them from removing water. Peri-jets pump one gallon in to remove two gallons out as I recall. Well, we were pumping one gallon in with nothing coming out."

Lieutenant John Huddleston, hearing the GQ alarm, mustered his aircrew together to discuss the current status and then proceeded to Damage Control (DC) Central where he encountered LTjg Doug Phillips, an Assistant Engineer. Believing the *Jarvis* condition to be quite safe with a probable quick trip back to Dutch Harbor, Huddleston jokingly quipped, "How high is the water, Douggie?" Phillips immediately became quite visibly and vocally upset. It was at this time that the pilot realized how precarious the situation was.

Phillips was monitoring the water height in the engine room with grease pencil lines on a TV remote in DC Central. The level was rising very fast as the ship's pumps could not keep up with the flooding.

The lieutenant returned to his aviation detachment with the news that there was a real possibility the *Jarvis* could sink, and they needed to think about abandoning ship. He further explained that the helicopter was the best lifeboat on the vessel, which would be a real asset should the crew need to leave the *Jarvis*. At that time, they were experiencing forty-degree rolls and fifty-knot winds. The conditions were unsuitable for launching. Unfolding the blades manually also seemed an impossible task. Aviation crewmembers Hawes and Lawson felt they could do it if they waited for a lull and timed the unfolding between gusts. "I told them to brainstorm it and, if they could do it safely, Bill (Wolfe) and I would fly it off the deck," Huddleston would later recall.

6:48 p.m.

With the water level quickly rising in the engine room, the command wanted to secure the electrical power panels on the lower deck but needed to keep the bilge pumps working. The worst fear of those working in the engine room was electrocution. Electrician's Mate (EM2) Ken Wenner was assigned the task to shut off all non-essential uses of power. He worked in waist-deep water trying to shut down selected breakers. The main switch had to stay on to keep the pumps running, but the rest had to be shut down, one by one. Wenner recalls, "As water swished back and forth, I was knocked off my feet and dragged across the deck plates, holding on to get as much electric power secured, as I could. At one panel, the water was two inches below the buss bars in the panel while I frantically shut down circuits."

Despite utilizing all available pumps on the *Jarvis*, the situation became further dangerous when she lost its fire pumps, resulting in the loss of three eductors,[23] and making a bad situation even worse. The water level continued to rise to four feet, causing a progressive failure of engine equipment.

---

[23] Eductors are used as emergency water pumping devices.

The official Board of Investigation report outlined the difficulties of controlling the flooding. Noting the dewatering capacity of the ship's pumps was just at 1,350 gallons per minute, reducing the water level proved very difficult. The ship had an insufficient length of hoses required, and there was a lack of access space to reroute the hoses out of the engine room. An attempt was made to use the main diesel salt water pump which would have added 800 gallons per minute to the dewatering process, but this proved unsuccessful, most likely from the presence of air in the engine's cooling water intake caused by the rolling of the vessel. Despite some of the problems, the water level was decreasing slowly until the loss of equipment occurred.

Things were now progressively getting worse. The ship was experiencing sixty-knot winds and seas estimated at thirty feet in height. Non-rate fireman Leo Griffin's General Quarters assignment was to operate the number two generator. He split his time between operating the generator and working with the other engine personnel in trying to patch the hole. "The water was coming in real bad and flooded the whole engine room," he would later recall.

At 6:51 a.m., the *Jarvis* lost fuel pressure to the number two turbine as a result of the number two generator going down due to the flooding. The emergency generator automatically came online at that time.

However, the lights in the engine room were so dim with this emergency generator's power output that an electrician had to string extra lights across the room's ceiling so the crew could work. The flooding increased, and small fires broke out. Several times, the damage control and firefighting crews evacuated the space due to the dangerous circumstances, and then returned soon to continue their missions. They were "working like dogs," as Petty Officer Montgomery explained. The ability to effectively deal with the flooding continued to deteriorate as a film of oil now floated on top of the water. This left a layer of slime on the walkways as the crewmembers moved about, making any movement on the surface quite hazardous. The discovery of a rupture of the fresh water tank was quickly identified when Petty Officer Denny Strutton grabbed a cup of coffee and took a swig, gagging on coffee brewed with salt water.

At this time, the water level had reached a point where it would soon touch the hot operating parts of the main diesel engines. Significant damage would occur with continued operation. The decision was made to kill the engines.

At 6:54 p.m., the Coast Guard Cutter *Jarvis* lost all propulsion. The ship was now dead in the water.

Chapter 7

DEAD IN THE WATER

"My first thought…is that it was the only time I'd been on a ship/boat in heavy seas that I wasn't seasick; didn't even give it a thought so apparently the thought of sinking overcomes any other inclinations. I can remember thinking that I sure longed for an air station that tied up at the same power pole every night. May not be able to go ashore, but I could see it and touch it."

—*Richard "Tiny" Lawson*

East of Akutan Island
November 15, 1972
6:54 p.m.

THE *JARVIS* GROUNDING was now in its second day. Many, if not all, of the crewmen, had not slept during the entire time since GQ was first sounded. While the officers and chiefs had one or two men assigned to a room, petty officers were fifteen to a berthing space, and those below that rank berthed in thirty-man rooms. Unfortunately, the vacuum transfer pump that was utilized to flush the toilets was not working. When someone used the "head"[24] above the main deck, the sewage would exit in a commode located in the large berthing area below. Urine and feces flowed throughout the sleeping area and was not exactly conducive to obtaining a good night of sleep.

The lack of heat and the ship's severe rolling only exacerbated the problem. Still, some members did find places to sleep where it was somewhat warm.

---

[24] Naval terminology for bathroom.

Electrician's Mate Howard Jensen, familiar with the ship workings, slept on the floor where the emergency generator was situated. The generator was located in the aft steering section[25] of the ship and produced enough heat to warm the space. Wearing "Mickey Mouse" ear pads to protect against the noise, the petty officer was better off than most.

With the whole world watching, Coast Guard Public Affairs was busy keeping the press up-to-date on the condition of the ship. In no small degree, accurate reporting by the media was achieved. There were a few isolated instances of inaccurate reporting, including at least four reports, that the ship had sunk, with all hands lost.[26]

One such occurrence was with Petty Officer Brunke's father, residing in Chicago, IL. Hearing on the news that the *Jarvis* had sunk in the Bering Sea, his father contacted senior Coast Guard officials in Washington to obtain more information on his son. While tight-lipped with providing much detail, they did assure him that the ship had not sunk. In those few instances of false reports, Coast Guard families were put through heart-breaking trials trying to obtain more information on the *Jarvis*. When contacted, the Coast Guard assured those families that the situation was stable but continuing.

Crewmembers' families and friends were highly concerned as news of the *Jarvis* mishap was becoming national headlines. Over in Pennsylvania, Petty Officer Ken Wenner's high school classmate was viewing the new show *Good Morning America*. With an emergency announcement that the *Jarvis* was without power and in danger of sinking in Alaskan waters, Wenner, was given "two lines of fame" with the local man theme in the local newspaper.

Back on the home front in Hawaii, concerned family members stayed by their radios and televisions to hear the latest news of the *Jarvis*. Mrs. Carol Herman, wife of *Jarvis's* Chief Quartermaster James Herman, explained, "I think they've convinced us that our husbands are in no danger, but not being there and not knowing for ourselves, we still worry. We're all trying to hold our own, but all we can really do is wait." Mrs. Herman went on to say that in her husband's sixteen years, he had never experienced such an event. "I've been with him for fourteen years, and I've never spent a day like this."

---

[25] Toward the stern (rear) of the vessel.

[26] Families of AD1 Lawson, BM3 Brunke, (all hands lost), PO Strutton, SA Debord.

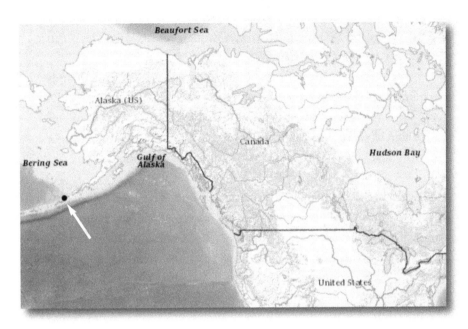

Map showing location of Akutan Island. (U.S. Geological Survey, Department of the Interior/USGS.)

Captain Wooley's wife, Margaret, had similar feelings. "It's kind of a help-less feeling—just waiting for information," she said. "We're pretty sure that they're all right, but naturally, until you know there's a tow line on, you're concerned. When your husband goes to sea most of his life, you know some problems like this may come up, and you learn to weather it."

With *Jarvis* homeported in Honolulu, the local newspapers were reporting daily updates on the status. Upon her return to Honolulu, the *Honolulu Star-Bulletin* interviewed both the XO, Commander Ken White, and Ensign James Richardson. As reported by the newspaper, Ensign Richardson recalled:

"We were in seas 35 to 40 feet high. A 70-knot wind was off our starboard quarter. We were rocking with a tilt of about 35 degrees. Our bridge is 44 feet high, but the tops of the oncoming waves appear to be up to our feet. The engine room was flooded. We were adrift. We were taking a pounding, and a lesser crew would have seen it go to the bottom. All through this, there wasn't a single complaint from anyone in the 170-man crew, even though most worked eighteen hours a day for a three-day stretch.

"The ship's executive officer, Commander Ken E. White of Honolulu, said: 'The ship was down on its knees.'

"Both White and Richardson painted a picture of a gallant crew and captain laboring under tremendous stress. The cutter had been caught by high winds while riding at anchor in Dutch Harbor."

Now powerless, the *Jarvis* was drifting toward the dauntingly rocky cliff of Battery Point, on the south side of Akutan Island. As temperatures dropped inside the ship to near freezing; crewmembers recalled seeing their breath when talking or breathing. Parkas and heavy weather gear were worn inside the vessel, along with heavy boots even when resting. Those sleeping in the upper bunks found themselves thrown from their beds due to the severe ship rolls.

Crewmembers in the lower bunks resorted to tying themselves onto the racks to prevent being thrown out.

It was so cold one crewmember reported seeing icebergs outside earlier. The freezing temperatures, and in many cases the wet condition of the members, existed for days. In the entire time, the ship rocked with forty to fifty-knot winds and huge swells. At 6:57 p.m., the water level rose over the deck plates in the engine room and all available pumps were ordered into use.

On the island of Akutan, the village of Akutan, with a population of just over a thousand people, is the principal village. One of the busiest fishing ports in the country, it has no roads, only boardwalks that can get you anywhere in the community. Businesses, mostly run by the Akutan Corporation, include a small hotel, one bed-and-breakfast, a café, and a small supply store.

Trident Seafoods is located about one-quarter of a mile down the beach from the town and has the capability of processing over three million fish per day. Akutan recently completed a small harbor that will accommodate fifty-eight vessels up to 165 feet long. Additionally, a new runway was constructed seven miles away on nearby Akun Island that offered helicopter service back to Akutan. Nature tourism is popular on the island with hiking amidst the wildflowers and berries on the hills and mountains. Akutan also hosts an active volcano with steam emissions and an occasional dusting of

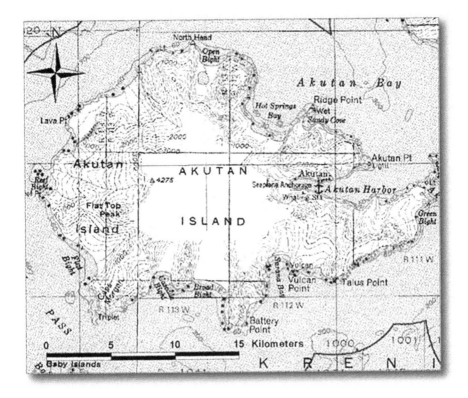

U.S. Geological Survey map of Akutan Island, Alaska.

volcanic ash. Wildlife consists of only a few foxes, there are no bears on the island. Between the Trident factory and the village of Akutan, no other population resides on the island. Much of the island remaining unexplored.

Akutan Pass, in which the *Jarvis* began to have serious problems, is known for some of the largest halibut that are caught. It is also well known for its treacherous waters. Former *Jarvis* member and experienced mariner Dave Martin years later would comment, "Akutan Pass is a terrible place to pass through—strong currents, an ebb current runs into huge seas."

Coast Pilot, an official United States publication that is issued yearly to supplement nautical charts of the United States, states the following regarding Akutan Pass:

"In Akutan Pass the currents have an average velocity at strength of about 5.5 knots; however, velocities of nine knots may occur. The tide rips in Akutan Pass are strong during the periods of largest tides. With a heavy northwest wind, the rips are menacing in the vicinity of the fifteen-fathom spot just south of Cape Morgan. They are confused and make a vessel very uncomfortable; they are dangerous for small craft. However, the strongest rips are not generally found in the middle of the pass. With a current setting north, the rips will be strongest in the north entrance, and with a current setting south, the strongest rips will be found at the south entrance to the pass. When the current setting north is opposed by a strong north wind, the tide rips in the north entrance to the pass are dangerous, and it is advisable not to use this pass in a gale. Under ordinary conditions, when there are no strong winds, this pass can be used by full-powered steamers at any stage of the current but sailing vessels should not use it except at or near slack water. It is said that the most dangerous rips occur at the north entrance to the pass."

Akutan Island's Battery Point is composed mostly of rugged cliffs facing the sea. Writer and frequent visitor Myra Scholze described Akutan Island thus: "thin strips of accessible beach cling to steep rocky cliffs. The island is volcanic, and there are some pretty cool columnar basalts on the beach near town. The whole island feels like a creature that's hunkered down to wait out a storm, which, indeed, is much of what it does in the winter. Lots of jagged rocks, windswept tundra, and dramatic landscapes." She further writes: "the beach becomes rockier and less accessible, and often slippery with ice. Going west from Trident, the beach is only accessible at exceptionally low tides. There is a trail straight up the mountain behind the processing plant, but it doesn't turn west, so from there you're just following erratic ridgelines in the tundra."

Had a ship gone upon the rocks and some crewmembers somehow survived the initial grounding, it is doubtful they could have endured much longer in the winter weather. With practically no beach to rest upon, and with cliffs surrounding the area, the ability of survivors to trek to the nearby village of Akutan would have been nearly impossible especially in severe weather con-

Battery Point, Akutan Island, Alaska. Photo by Bob Webster (bob@xpda.com).

ditions. The harsh sea environment of the rocky shoreline and the crashing waves would have prevented small rescue boats from coming ashore.

7:00 p.m.

Lieutenant Huddleston recalled that within the engine room, all diesel propulsion engines, dewatering pumps, and main circuit panels were flooded entirely. With the loss of all mechanical and electric power, "*Jarvis* was adrift without power in heavy to mountainous seas up to thirty feet, winds gusting in excess of sixty knots, blowing snow and freezing temperatures." Any power that remained rested with the GE-T58 jet turbine engine, similar to the one that operated the Coast Guard helicopter on deck. This was providing emergency electrical power to the ship, enough to at least run the ship's radios, bridge, and flight deck lighting.

Out on the deck, the crew was taking a pounding from Mother Nature. Communicating with each other was extremely difficult or impossible in the harsh environment; crewmembers had to rely on training and instinct to perform their jobs.

7:04 p.m.

The water level in the engine room was the same as outside, all engines were dead. With no fresh water available, there was very little cooking. Combined with the exhaustive and lengthy working conditions in the filthy water, the lack of hot water, and heat, crewmember sanitation needs were severely lacking.

Captain Wooley surveyed the situation: the engine room was flooded, power was lost, high seas and gale force winds were pounding the *Jarvis*, freezing working conditions had caused several of the crewmen to show signs of sickness, and the ship was drifting toward a rocky coastline. Running aground there would destroy the ship and probably kill most of the men.

With the ship in peril, Captain Wooley ordered an emergency message be sent to the Seventeenth Coast Guard District Office requesting Coast Guard assistance. The message read in part:

Z 160459Z NOV 72 FM USCGC *JARVIS* TO CCGD
SEVENTEEN JUNEAU AK COMPACAREA COGARD SFRAN
CA I NFO CCGDFOURTEEN HONO HI KODIAKSAR-
COORD KODIAK AK BT UNCLAS DISTRESS POSIT
53-42N 165-50W **MOUNTAINOUS SEAS LOST MAIN
PROPULSION LOST GENERATORS. REQ ASSISTANCE.** BT

Radioman Second Class George Fewell, who went on to later retire as a chief warrant officer, notes the message begins with "Z," the first letter always signifying the importance of the message. The letter "R" is for Routine, "P" is for Priority, "O" is for immediate and "Z" is for Flash, the highest importance. In his thirty years of service, Fewell had only seen "Z" used twice; once during the Vietnam era and this message.

Within minutes, the District office replied there were no Coast Guard assets near enough to provide immediate assistance.

At 7:04 pm, for one of the few times in Coast Guard history, a MAYDAY call for help would come *from* a Coast Guard vessel.

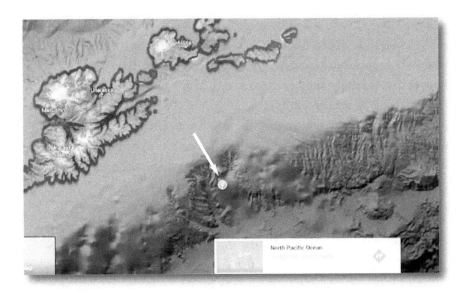

Location of the CGC *Jarvis* MAYDAY, southeast of Akutan Island. Courtesy of Jack Hunter

Southeast of Akutan Island
7:04 p.m.

Initially mistakenly sent as an "SMS" instead of the correct "SOS," the message was immediately corrected and resent. Within minutes of the SOS transmission, over twenty-two vessels responded by establishing contact with the *Jarvis*. As later reported in the official Coast Guard Board of Investigation, the closest ship was a Russian stern trawler, but that vessel either was unable or refused to assist. Two Japanese fishing vessels did respond positively: the 336-foot *Koyo Maru No. 3* and the *Haruna Maru*. Both ships immediately proceeded toward the *Jarvis*.

Those working in the radio room were faced with many challenges as they labored to complete the numerous tasks happening at the same time. Chief Miltier was handling the Morse code circuit, RM1 Dupree working the voice communications and the rest of the radiomen working as directed. The SOS message, to be passed via voice and Morse code, was written for the captain's approval. Numerous messages had to be received and sent out at the same time; RM2 Thomas Franke quipped about the "teletype going crazy" throughout the incident. The radiomen were working ten-to twelve-hour shifts, as Franke further commented, "We were so busy, we didn't have time to think about the sinking."

Radioman Franke was tuning the MF transmitter, while fellow crew-member Montgomery was activating the middle position, monitoring frequency 500 KHZ, and starting a radio log. Petty Officer Montgomery explained further his duties and what was occurring:

> "My major job was to write the positions down and give them to the Chief (Miltier) and he would relay them to RM3 Beaver on the bridge for plotting and to see who was the closest to us. A ship that was below the Equator actually replied to our SOS. Tom told the vessel thanks, but she was a tad too far away for assistance. The craziest part of the night was a Soviet ship answered our SOS and when asked for his position he gave it. His position was written down, confirmed, and sent to the bridge for plotting. Apparently, he was about twenty-six miles from us and was told to come at full speed to our position. He replied that his plot showed him to be fifty or sixty miles away from us. He was asked to reconfirm his position and he gave the same one. It was again confirmed and sent to the bridge and again, the request to head to us at best speed was made and again, he stated he was too far away from us. Being in radio, most of us didn't know what was going on. I had since moved to the radio-teletype position to send and receive messages from NOJ. During this time, it became clear that we were going to stay afloat but, we were drifting northeast towards, I think it was an island. We had between two and four hours before we went aground. Apparently, the number of casualties estimated upwards of 75-90% if we had to go into the water."

Should the ship end up on the rocks, Montgomery's job was to destroy as much of the classified material as he could, including the crypto machines. With the weather and sea conditions as they were, he felt his chances of survival would be between slim to none. Only twenty years of age, he felt some comfort at what his father, a former coxswain in WWII, would often tell him: "Son, when it's your turn to go, you can hide under a rock, and if it is your turn, the rock will fall on you!"

With the SOS sent, the executive officer, Commander White, immediately ordered the senior aviation officer, LT John Huddleston, to the bridge. There, White explained the command's plans to abandon ship. The combined effects of the sea swells, the large sail area of the *Jarvis*, the extreme wind conditions, and the attached helicopter, all contributed to heavy rolling. There wasn't much the *Jarvis* could do about Mother Nature, but there was something they could do about the helicopter: drop it off the side. He further explained they were desperately running out of fuel for the generators and a Coast Guard C-130 airplane was on the way to drop off fuel barrels onto the deck. The plan was to lessen the weight of the ship and to clear the flight deck for parachute drops of fuel barrels. The helicopter had to go. Huddleston returned to discuss the orders with his crew. Despite the inherent dangers of severe winds and heavy seas, they all agreed to attempt to launch the helo.

At 7:10, the engine room reported to the bridge that flooding was not under control, and twenty minutes later indicated that the water had risen to five inches over the deck plates. "All modes of propulsion inoperative, only power is the emergency generator. Report of equipment shorting out in engine room due to water splashing." During this period, a fire was reported in the engine room, but was immediately extinguished. Petty Officer Ken Wenner explains the challenging work conditions in the engine room:

"We had been underway bound for Hawaii when we flooded. With no power, and without the constant groaning of the engine room you would think it would be quiet. But P-250s were running topside, people were hustling everywhere, and at the mercy of the sea [no power] we were rolling pretty hard. Crashing and banging was everywhere especially in the galley. I don't remember quiet. I guess we were too busy to notice. Too busy trying to stand upright and perform tasks. In the engine room, it was the constant sloshing of tons of water as the ship rolled."

Upon notification of the *Jarvis* distress message, Coast Guard District Seventeen directed a Coast Guard C-130 aircraft to circle the ship and provide a direct communications link. Others involved with planning response actions included the Coast Guard Air Stations Kodiak, Alaska; Barbers Point, Hawaii; Coast Guard High Endurance Cutter *Winona*, homeport in Port Angeles, Washington; and the Coast Guard Buoy Tenders *Balsam* and *Citrus*. These three ships are an integral part of Coast Guard history.

The 255-foot, Coast Guard Cutter *Winona* was initially built for military service during World War II. The construction of the ship was completed shortly after the war ended and then assigned to other missions. It was not until the Vietnam War that she saw military action. The ship carried ten officers, three warrants, and 130 crewmembers.

Of historical military note, the *Winona* was assigned to Coast Guard Squadron Three in South Vietnam from January 25 to October 17, 1968. She was part of a Coast Guard contingent with missions of search and rescue, aids to navigation maintenance, port security, and attacking cargo movements and forces over the water. When the war ended, over 8,000 Coast Guardsmen would have served in Southeast Asia.

Winona's assignment was as part of a joint blockade effort by the U.S. Coast Guard, U.S. Navy, and the South Vietnamese government to undertake prevention of personnel, munitions, and equipment from being delivered to North Vietnamese forces. The United States and South Vietnamese ships enforced their authority of the twelve-mile restricted zone from the coast to stop and search any vessel in this area.

Shortly after arriving in Vietnam on March 1st, the ship encountered a fishing trawler that failed to yield after the firing of warning shots. The trawler opened fire on the *Winona*, and the ship returned fire; the suspected ammunition loaded ship exploded in a massive fireball, with several pieces hitting the Coast Guard cutter, but with no damage. As one crewmember commented years later, the only remnants left of the trawler was part of a human skull that floated by.

The *Winona* was scrapped in 1974; the Coast Guard Cutter *Jarvis* escort would be one of the ship's final significant missions.

The CGC *Balsam* was a 180-foot buoy tender and had served in WWII in the South Pacific. Her future homeports would include Astoria, OR; Eureka, CA; Honolulu, HI; and finally in Alaska. She was decommissioned in 1975 and sold to a private company.

The CGC *Citrus* was also a 180-foot buoy tender built in 1942 to assist in the war effort. Assigned to Alaska after a short tour on the Great Lakes, the ship was armed to protect the Aleutian Islands recently liberated from Japanese forces.

Stationed at Ketchikan until 1964 and later Kodiak to 1979, the *Citrus* spent her time escorting Soviet fishing vessels out of U.S waters, towing disabled fishing boats back to port, medevac'ing injured crewmembers, assisting with the search for missing planes and conducting maintenance of the numerous buoys through their Aids to Navigation missions.

For two months in the fall of 1975, she assisted with providing icebreaking escort for fifteen tugs and barges to bring vital supplies to the new oil fields of Prudhoe Bay, thereby averting delay to this national development. As a result of her efforts, the ship and crew were awarded the Coast Guard Unit Commendation with the Operational Distinguishing Device.

Later in the 1980s, the *Citrus* and two other 180-foot tenders were painted white and converted to medium endurance cutters, to be used in search and rescue missions and law enforcement missions. This conversion led to her assignment to Coos Bay, OR, where she remained for fifteen years, enforcing maritime law as required. Of particular note during this period, was the boarding of a Panamanian-flagged ship M/V *Pacific Star* on January 1, 1985. As reported from the U.S. Coast Guard Historian's Office:

> "When the boarding team attempted to board the vessel, the master set the *Pacific Star* on fire and commenced to scuttle the vessel. In a final act of deterrence, the master turned his vessel and rammed *Citrus* on the starboard side. The boarding team did get on board and located a large quantity of Thai marijuana in the vessel's forward hold. As the vessel sank, more than 3,800 pounds of marijuana were recovered as it floated to the surface and the seven-man crew was arrested."

On September 1, 1994, after fifty-one years of service, the CGC *Citrus* was decommissioned and later sold to the Dominican Navy.

News of the *Jarvis* predicament spread like wildfire throughout the country. Jim McDonough was working in the Atlantic Area Rescue Coordination Center on Governors Island, just across from Manhattan and Brooklyn in New York City. While the Center had no actual involvement in the incident response, they closely monitored the situation, noting that the *Jarvis* ground-

170 Aboard Flooded Coast Guard Cutter

Article that appeared in the *Honolulu Advertiser*.
Courtesy of Jack Hunter and Dan Edwards.

ing was "big." Steve Wiezorek from the Rescue Coordination Center (RCC) in Juneau, AK, was immediately informed of the situation when he assumed the watch. "One of the first things myself and the duty officer did was to review the file notes, brief senior staff officers concerning past and future operations and endeavors."

At the Radioman school in Petaluma, California, student Terry Tolentino was kept abreast of the grounding daily by his instructors. Soon after being assigned to the *Jarvis*, his fellow crewmembers would call him "SOS" Tolentino. Another radioman, serving at a remote station in Alaska would recall reporting to duty and being made aware of the SOS and the *Jarvis*. "Which ship called into the *Jarvis*?" he asked, and his supervisor replied, "No, it is not another ship; it is the *Jarvis* calling the SOS!"

Crewmember Ensign James Nagle was attending the Search and Rescue (SAR) school on Governors Island when the grounding occurred. He recalls waking up in the morning, and hearing news of a cutter in trouble up in Alaska. Nagle immediately got dressed and quickly walked over to the Rescue Coordination Center (RCC) office where they confirmed it was the *Jarvis*. For the next few days, he would be in constant contact with this office to keep abreast of any updates.

Jarvis, faced with dwindling fuel for the portable pumps, soon requested additional gasoline. Only a six-hour supply remained on board. The Seventeenth District then began planning to meet this request.

As the Japanese fishing vessels were coming on scene, measures began in earnest to prepare for the towing of the *Jarvis*. Eight-inch towing hawsers had to be broken out from below deck by the towing detail. As the vessel was taking forty- to fifty-degree rolls, carrying the line up two levels of the ship was extremely challenging. According to BM3 Brunke:

> "The ship was rolling so severely that it was almost impossible to stand up and walk, we did a lot of work while crawling. At times, we were rolling so severely, I thought the bridge wings were going to hit the waves. Our greatest fear was not of capsizing, but of drifting on an island that was only a couple miles away. If we would have run aground on the island, *Jarvis* certainly would have been lost, and I am certain many of the crewmembers, if not all, would have lost their lives."

Soon after, the hawser was deemed too dangerous to use with the current weather conditions and it was carried back below deck. Brunke continues in explaining:

> "It was very cold, windy, and slippery. When we tried to stand up, and the ship rolled, we were thrown across the deck and into the lifelines [three steel cables along the entire deck].
>
> "Even when we were crawling, when sliding into the lifelines, we had to grab them so we would not be thrown overboard. The ship

was rolling so badly, that when we rolled port or starboard, the ocean water (not waves), came right to the knife edge of the main deck."

Back at the *Jarvis* homeport in Honolulu, the Coast Guard Cutter *Mellon*, another 378-foot cutter moored at Sand Island, was directed to respond. The command later advised district that it would be at least twenty-four hours before the ship could get underway. Other Coast Guard assets ordered to assist included a Coast Guard C-130 aircraft out of the Coast Guard Air Station in San Francisco to ferry in pumps and equipment. U.S. Navy assets as well were involved including CINCPACFLT, Pearl Harbor, and divers from the Navy Salvage Tug and Salvage Team (HCU-1), also from Pearl Harbor.

The Coast Guard C-130 would be utilized to bring in hoses, pumps, and additional emergency equipment as requested. The C-130 is an extended-range airplane often used for search and rescue missions, fisheries patrols, pollution observations, and as a Coast Guard platform to bring in supplies and personnel. When used for training missions to Japan from Hawaii, golf clubs would often accompany the crew and officers. A Volkswagen Beetle, affectionately known as the "bug," fits somewhat snugly inside the Coast Guard workhorse for those members transferred from Oahu to another island.

With the U.S. Coast Guard, U.S. Navy, and other agencies assisting as requested, it was "All- hands-on-deck."

8:00 p.m.

The CGC *Balsam*, the closest Coast Guard ship, messaged the *Jarvis* to inform they would be on scene to render assistance in twenty-eight hours. The two Japanese fishing trawlers, *Haruna Maru* and *Koyo Maru No. 3*, were still proceeding toward the *Jarvis's* last known location to assist as needed. The *Haruna Maru* was further motivated to support rescue efforts as the *Jarvis* was instrumental in a medevac of their injured crewman during a fishery patrol the previous month.

As the *Koyo Maru No. 3* would be on the scene first, the Coast Guard advised the *Haruna Maru* their presence was no longer necessary. The *Haruna Maru* acknowledged the information but notified the Coast Guard they would continue until they could visually confirm the safe towing of the *Jarvis*. At 8:12 p.m., the *Koyo Maru* gave an estimated time of arrival to the *Jarvis* of 3:30 a.m. Unfortunately, for all concerned, that was thirty minutes after the time that the *Jarvis* was predicted to hit the rocky shoreline.

9:00 p.m.

At this time, helicopter pilot LT John Huddleston and co-pilot Bill Wolfe, went to the bridge to discuss the helo situation with commanding officer and the executive officer. There, Huddleston requested permission to launch to both save the aircraft and, if necessary, to transfer as many of the 170 men as possible to dry land. The goal was to fly to nearby Akutan Island to initially drop off his three crewmen where the men would light a sizeable fire to serve as a beacon for the helo. Wooley was extremely reluctant to consider such a mission due to the hazardous conditions, but, after reviewing all points of the argument, he granted permission for the pilots to launch. Should adverse circumstances occur in the attempt, Huddleston and Wolfe agreed to abort. This launch was a one-shot deal, Wooley relayed. If the helicopter failed to take-off, then it was going over the side.

Meanwhile, Coast Guard command had provided a C-130 airplane from the Kodiak Air Station to serve as a communications platform for the *Jarvis*. Pilots LT Chuck Hughes and LT Denny Morrissey were directed to provide whatever aid was necessary and to direct any available vessel aid to their rescue while flying overhead in the severe weather. Flying weather conditions were considered to be "extreme"; Coast Guard safety guidelines normally do not allow flying under any circumstances when "extreme" is forecasted. In this case, the rules were bent as our own people were in grave danger. The pilots carefully picked their way through the bad weather cells as depicted on their radar as they began their descent to get under the system. With the worst turbulence and potential icing at higher attitudes, they navigated their way through the storm and arrived on scene above the ship. The flight was extremely bumpy with the anti-icing and de-icing equipment working as advertised.

Throughout the entire period of this incident, the galley continued to operate 24/7, preparing hot and cold meals as best as they could. Sandwiches and soup were served, although very few full meals. Petty Officer Lawrence Baker commented, "That was the biggest thing the guys wanted. And the cooks were fantastic." There was a limited supply of water and crewmen were dipping cups into five-gallon canisters for their drinking water. There were no hot showers.

Coffee was an invaluable commodity in the harsh, cold conditions. When interviewed later, Petty Officer Bill Webster sarcastically quipped, "The ship's store ran out of candy."

9:45 p.m.

In radio discussions with the Soviet trawler, the CGC *Jarvis* relays that she will go aground at 3:30 the next morning if no assistance arrives. The Soviet trawler refuses to assist.

At 9:45 p.m., preparations began to launch the helo. Pilots Huddleston and Wolfe, along with their supporting aircrew, were faced with considerable challenges in departing from the ship.

Weather conditions were such that snow and hail were falling, huge sea swells were striking the vessel, severe winds with unpredictable gusts, and temperatures in the twenties. All conditions attributed to an extremely high-risk takeoff for a helicopter; the odds were against success. As stated later in the official Board of Investigation, "The launch was made under wind and sea conditions which far exceeded the parameters of safe helicopter operations."

Aviation crewmembers AD1 Hawes, AT1 Lawson, AD2 Page, AM 2 Hicks, and AE2 Robertson removed the protective cover from the aircraft and prepared to unfold the main rotor blades. Co-pilot LT Wolfe guided efforts on the unfolding of each blade as everyone waited for a lull in the weather. One man was to operate the blade crutch while the other two aviation crewmembers were on the rotor head wearing safety harnesses.

Disaster almost struck while preparing to insert a bolt into the rotor head hub connecting the blade cuff. A gust of wind tore the blade out of the crutch where it flew up, then down to the flight deck. At six feet, five inches tall, and 240 pounds, Petty Officer Richard "Tiny" Lawson[27] caught it as it drove him to his knees. The blade spar hit the deck edge coaming. Inspection of the blade revealed a visible dent; it was immediately smoothed out and attached. With the other two rotor blades unfolded, the helicopter was declared fit to fly.

Pilots Huddleston and Wolfe had decided to launch in an unprecedented manner: all tie- downs would remain on while they started the engine and the rotors.[28] Some of the deck crewmembers were somewhat skeptical that the helo

---

[27] Lawson's wife while driving her children to school, heard that morning that the *Jarvis* had sunk with all hands.

[28] A similar take-off was completed in December 2004 with a CG Helo H-65 and the CGC *Alex Haley* in the same region involving sinking of the Malaysian cargo ship *M/V Selendang Ayu*.

could take off safely, and they had secretly taken bets on its success. Despite their doubts, LT Wolfe, an ex-Army pilot with three more years of stick time than LT Huddleston, was told to take the lead in the take-off. Removal of the secondary tie-downs commenced by the aircrew, after which they boarded the helo. The LSO (Landing Signal Officer), BM1 Charlie Greene, and the ship's tie-down crew were the only personnel allowed on the flight deck at that time.

The LSO must ensure the safe landing and take-off of the helicopter from the ship through the use of signals to the helicopter pilot. To qualify for this position, the crewman must perform these signal tasks during the day, then do the same at night. It requires the use of flags during the day and at night, the use of flashlights. Standing on the forward part of the flight deck, aft of the balloon shack, he directs the chopper's approach by passing signals for a safe landing. After the aircraft lands, the LSO signals the six crewmembers assigned to tie- down the helo. For take-off, as in the case of the *Jarvis*, he signals for the detachment of the tie downs. Timing this can be tricky in high winds. The lee side is removed first, then the windward, while at the same time monitoring the ship roll. The LSO has to exercise independent judgment and coolness under pressure.

Commander White, the XO, took charge of the flight deck as the Helicopter Control Officer, working out of the Balloon Shelter forward of the flight deck. Before departure, White handed LT Huddleston a ship's roster with those names selected to be evacuated first upon the helicopter's return to the *Jarvis*. Those crewmembers chosen to be flown out were men who were single and the youngest. He chose these criteria for selection because "they had not experienced much in their lives yet, and they deserved to get more of a chance to live."

The goal for the launch was to time the height of the swells and to release the tie-downs at the highest point. But before they would leave, LT Huddleston relayed a message to Chief Stanczyk who was in charge of the deck crew, stating that once he dropped his aircrew on land, he would return to begin evacuations of the ship's crew until everyone was safe or until he ran out of fuel. With the top swell approaching, Huddleston signaled for the release. Unfortunately, one of the tie-downs was challenging to handle and failed to release, resulting in the helo skidding toward the side but stopping short.

Reattachment of the main tie-downs commenced immediately along with preparations for a second launch. But before this attempt, LT Huddleston motioned for the tie-down crew to come over to his cockpit window. With him shouting in a loud voice due to the deafening noise from the helicopter's engine and the sea swells, Huddleston relayed a simple message: "If the tie-downs fail to release at the same time, the helicopter will flip over, killing the aircrew AND those on deck!"

On the next try, with the engine screaming and the rotors fully engaged, the tie-downs were released simultaneously, and the helo shot upward off the deck of the *Jarvis*. The second attempt at the launch of HH-52 was successful at 10:09 p.m. with destination for Akutan Island. Both Chief Stanczyk and BM3 Richard Brunke would later remark that the helicopter sprung up like a spring, five feet straight up. Quartermaster striker Dave Martin, a lifetime mariner in his career after the Coast Guard, and Radarman Third Class John Moran, both remember the helo starting to skid off the deck after the tie-downs were released before it shot into the air. Martin stating, "Amazing it took off, once the tie downs were released; the helo started to skid off the helo deck, skimmed to the edge of the water as it took off." All this was accomplished in severe weather conditions of wind and rain, in erratic and extreme sea rolls, and in the pitch-black night.

Perhaps the most gripping recollection of the take-off comes from the LSO, BM1 Charlie Greene:

> "During the ordeal after supplies started to come and go, I did most of the landings and takeoffs, being the junior LSO I guess, plus it was cold. The night of the ordeal, my heart was in my throat, I think a few other organs were there too. A vessel not under power tends to wallow in the trough thereby taking the wind off the beam. At the given moment, everyone was at his station; the chopper was up to power with downward pressure applied to hold it when tie-downs were released: leeward came off first, [then]as soon as the windward ones were released, I gave the signal to take off. Between my signal and the pilots' reaction to lift, the chopper slid across the flight deck due to the wind, and the front wheel hit the very short coaming that goes around the deck; at that moment it lifted off and disappeared into the black night. I have speculated many times what would have happened if that small coaming wasn't there, would there have been another disaster."

Earlier, the names of personnel to be flown off the ship were announced and they were directed to get prepared for departure. Not everyone who had been chosen jumped at the chance; BM3 Brunke, when notified, declined the offer and told the officers to select a married man instead. He preferred to stay with the ship, not to mention, as often the case with young men, felt he was "young and invincible."

For those remaining on the *Jarvis*, preparations would soon begin for evacuation by lifeboat. Personnel and pay records along with other vital documents were boxed and covered with plastic sheets in anticipation of departure. "Mae West"[29] life preservers were broken out and issued.

Some crewmembers changed into their undress wool blues uniform as that offered the best protection from the weather. Crewmembers emptied lockers of snacks and other food items in the eventuality of abandoning ship.

---

[29] "Mae West" life vests inflate when carbon dioxide is released when the cords are pulled. Because the front air pockets fill completely, the wearer would resemble the look of a shapely woman, thus the name. Mae West was a singer, actress, comedian, and sex symbol whose career spanned seven decades.

Chapter 8

ABANDON SHIP

"I was trained under QM2 David Landis, excellent mentor, still very good friends to this day. I remember being dejected on the ship due to the incident going on, sitting in the corner of the bridge. Dave told me to get my ass up and start writing in the logbook. He knew it was important to keep busy in this situation and not dwell on my fears and thoughts."

—Dave Martin

East of Akutan Island
10:10 p.m.

SOON AFTER HH-52 left the *Jarvis*, LT Huddleston received a radio message stating: "Is that you Bill? Did you guys really take off from the ship?" The caller was referring to the copilot LT Bill Wolfe. It was a C-130 airplane pilot who had previously worked with LT Wolfe at another air station.

Huddleston then asked the C-130 pilot for a vector to the nearest suitable site for landing the helo. There he planned to drop off his crewmen, and head back to the *Jarvis* to pick up as many of the members as possible. The plane pilot replied with a compass heading and directions to Broad Bight beach on Akutan Island.

Flying north into severe winds and blowing snow, Huddleston flew on instruments at 140 feet, with the hover lights off and the nose light on, in case the helo engine iced up. Flying at that altitude would give him a second or two more to land safely, rather than at the routine forty feet.

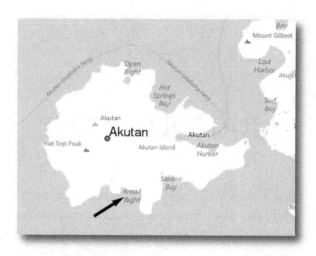

Map showing the location of Broad Bight beach on Akutan Island.

10:30 pm

With the possibility of abandoning ship, Captain Wooley led a small group of crewmen in prayer. While not particularly religious, he was a very spiritual person. He and the crew held hands in a circle and prayed for the safety of the *Jarvis* and their fellow crewmembers. The prayer conducted was short, sweet, and to the point.

"Some went down to the sea in ships,
doing business on the great waters;
they saw the deeds of the Lord,
his wondrous works in the deep.
For he commanded and raised the stormy wind,
which lifted up the waves of the sea.
They mounted up to heaven;
they went down to the depths;
their courage melted away in their evil plight;
they reeled and staggered like drunken men
and were at their wits' end.

Then they cried to the Lord in their trouble,
and he delivered them from their distress.
He made the storm be still,
and the waves of the sea were hushed."

—*Excerpts*, Psalm 107:23-29 *(English Standard Version)*

Captain Wooley explained how the crew would proceed to abandon ship if necessary. Those selected for the HH-52 would commence toward the flight deck in groups of twelve crewmembers, for air lift one group at a time. Those not chosen would evacuate the ship via the life rafts. Those selected for the life rafts met the news with disbelief. With weather conditions as they were, most, if not all, felt that leaving the ship would be a death sentence. There was no way they could survive the monster waves, freezing temperatures, and severe winds. If they did manage to reach land, the shoreline was extremely rocky, surrounded by cliffs. If the water did not kill them, attempting to land on the coast would. Several of the men had already decided they were staying on board the vessel, regardless of the conditions. They felt it was better to remain on the ship and die at sea, than to die of hypothermia in a small life raft, or to drown in the rough surf. Many felt the possibility of even reaching land without capsizing, were slim to none. Overall, the odds were better in staying on the ship.

With orders from Commander White, Chief Stanczyk directed his crew to prepare for departure. "Go on deck and help the boatswains mates tie the life rafts together," Petty Officer Strutton recalls the chief telling him, adding, "This is the first indication I had of how bad the situation was."

The boatswains mates were gathered together with instructions from Chief Stanczyk to start bringing the life rafts to the flight deck, in case they were needed to abandon ship. The men knew help was on the way; the problem was that they didn't know if it would arrive before the *Jarvis* crashed and broke apart on the rocks.

The liferafts were stacked three high in cradles, and they were designed to automatically release and inflate when the sinking ship reached a certain depth. Waiting for the ship to submerge to get access to the rafts would not be very helpful in the freezing conditions. An initial examination of the life rafts revealed that the release clasps were frozen on the straps. Seaman Ron

Vergeer was instructed to cut the straps so the boats would be ready for deployment. However, because of the *Jarvis's* extreme rolling, the deck force was unable to release the life rafts out of the cradles. Another attempt was made using a different approach, but that failed as well. While they did manage to get one life raft down, the effort was deemed too dangerous to continue. While retreating into the confines of the vessel, Petty Officer Brunke glanced over at the Balloon Shelter. There sat a very depressed lone crewman with his life jacket on and a hopeless look upon his face. Brunke would later comment that the member "had zoned out waiting for the ship to sink."

Broad Bight Beach
November 16, 1972

Flying through severe winds, HH-52 with LT Wolfe at the controls, he finally located the surf line and then the rocky coastline of Broad Bight Bay, which was situated on the southern coast of Akutan Island, west of Battery Point. Once sighted, LT Huddleston took the controls of the helicopter. LT Wolfe aimed the nose light as they searched for a sandy beach large enough to land the helo.

At the same time, LT Hughes was flying overhead in the C-130, providing vector information to the helicopter pilots. The plane was on its last orbit over the HH-52 when the plane crew suddenly observed a flash of light and a huge explosion. Immediately the pilots and the entire aircrew believed they were going down with the plane, however after a few seconds, they soon realized they were still flying. Pilot Chuck Hughes explains further what happened next:

"We all realized that we were still alive and the aircraft was still flying. I was flying the C-130 on auto pilot, and my first instinct was that I was going to have to handle an extreme control situation. I flipped off the auto pilot but immediately realized I was blinded and couldn't see the instruments so I re-engaged the auto pilot and started an immediate climb away from land. Slowly we all started regaining our vision and I noticed that everything on the instrument panel looked fine. We restarted the outboard engines. We started inquiring with the rest of the crew including those in the rear cargo area to look over the aircraft and report anything unusual. Nobody really saw anything to report. Flying over water south of the Aleutians, lightning did not cross our minds. None of us had encountered lightning under these circumstances so we were wondering what, on the aircraft, could have blown up. We were all amazed that we were still in stable flight and under control. Eventually we noticed that we had no radar. We were in radio control with our Operations Center and we all concurred that it could have been lightning but none of us were entirely sure. The decision was made that we needed to leave scene and proceed to the nearest airstrip [Cold Bay, Alaska] in order to check what damage had been incurred."

The HH-52 soon landed on a sandy beach and discharged three of the crewmen, who immediately established a base of operations for the helo. Once the crewmen, the pallets of supplies, gasoline, and a hand-held survival radio were all off-loaded, the pilots informed the *Jarvis* and the C-130 of the beach's location. With the news relayed, Huddleston and Wolfe prepared to return to the ship to evacuate as many of the men they could, and as the remaining fuel would allow.

With one plane suffering unknown damages, another C-130 plane soon headed out from Kodiak to assist *Jarvis*. Chuck Hughes and his C-130 crew flew on to Cold Bay to inspect the damages to their plane. After landing during a snowstorm, they climbed to the top of the plane and immediately saw the damage: a hole in the radome,[30] approximately one foot in diameter. They also spotted some burnt lightning arrestor wicks on the trailing edges of the control surfaces. The lightning strike had entered on the wing tip and exited on the radome. Everyone was extremely tired from the lack of sleep and the order was given to "hit the rack" for some much-needed rest. However, after only two hours of sleep, all were awakened to immediately support another air mission to airdrop vital dewatering equipment to the ship. After another six- hour mission of support to *Jarvis*, the pilots and crew finally got some rest.

---

[30] A dome or other structure protecting radar equipment.

Back on the ship, a concerted effort was being made to find a way to slow the vessel. The *Koyo Maru*, even though speeding to the *Jarvis*, might arrive too late to save the ship from drifting onto the rocky coast of Akutan Island. It was imperative that the crew slow the *Jarvis* down, and to slow it down soon.

12:45 a.m.

Lowering the bow thruster and placing the rudder hard over slowed her somewhat, but more was needed. The deck crew analyzed the situation and attempted to construct a "sea drogue" for use as a makeshift sea anchor. It was roughly six-foot square in size when completed, and it was dropped over the stern in hopes it would slow the vessel down. Meanwhile, the engine room water level rose to thirteen feet and forced the evacuation of the men from that compartment.

The compressor flat was shored to ensure against rupture and further flooding.

1:40 a.m.

Minutes later, to the great delight of the crew, and despite the rolling seas, sleet and rain hindering vision, the navigation lights of the Japanese fishing vessel broke through the darkness. "I was on deck, wearing a hooded jacket, and googles because of the sleet. When we saw the lights coming toward us, we threw up our hands and cheered and yelled and jumped up and down," crew member Petty Officer Wager later would recall.

Help was on the way!

1:55 a.m.

Since the receipt of the distress call from the *Jarvis*, Coast Guard response preparations had been actively planning how best to provide the necessary fuel for the pumps on board.

Supplying fuel by boats was discounted due to the severe weather conditions in the area; the only other option available was by air. Advance preparations included obtaining the fifty-five-gallon fuel drums and then rigging cargo parachutes onto the drums, something that had not been done before. A C-130 airplane, piloted by LT Rick Gallien and LT Bill Jacobs, was now arriving to drop off much-needed fuel for the portable pumps. When the SOS had originally been relayed, *Jarvis* had six hours of fuel remaining; those six hours were almost up.

With the *Jarvis* dead in the water, landing of the fifty-five-gallon barrels of fuel directly onto the vessel had to be precise. Under the leadership of Chief Stanczyk, the deck crew prepared for the fuel drops.

The first attempt of the C-130 ended with the first barrel missing the deck by 1,000 feet. Lieutenant Junior Grade Paul Barlow would comment: "I'll give every accolade possible to the HC-130 pilots dropping those supplies to our stricken ship. With winds approaching seventy knots, they were able to make recovery possible. Under these adverse conditions, their drops were close; close enough that the first drop had the parachute ride up along the side of the ship. We were unable to retrieve it because it drifted by too fast."

Approximately every ten minutes another flyover by the C-130 would attempt delivery of the fuel barrels, and each met with failure. The second attempt fell twenty-five yards short off the starboard bow, the third, 100 yards down range. The fourth also fell 100 yards off the starboard side. An hour later, another was attempted. It landed 500 yards off the fantail.

Now approaching 3:00 a.m., the decision was made to clear the flight deck and the Balloon shelter,[31] and to have the plane fly over the stern of the ship. The barrels would bounce off the surface of the vessel and then slam into the safety net. It didn't take a genius to figure that that was pretty dangerous. Paul Barlow explained their plan of action:

> "However, we were ready for the drop, and those pilots were perfect! The chief, myself and the deck force were stationed in line on the flight deck, holding hands, ready to retrieve the drop as it made its way towards the floundering ship. The HC-130 crossed the T as we saw the parachute perfectly deploy heading straight downwind to us. In no time, we realized, this was not such a good idea as we saw a parachute holding a fifty-five-gallon drum full of gasoline heading for us at seventy knots. I'm not sure who yelled, but we all dispersed as the fifty-five-gallon drum hit the starboard side of the flight deck, sparked across the width of the flight deck and landed safely in the safety net on the other side. Needless to say, we terminated this method of recovery."

---

[31] Dave Martin: "It was used to prepare radiosonde weather balloons for launch while the ship was out on Ocean Station patrols. A National Weather Service meteorologist on board would launch these balloons every twelve hours or so. It was also used to stow the helicopter crew gear."

With the barrel successfully retrieved out of the net, Seaman Dave Martin noted the barrel was dented and leaking fuel. Although it had crossed the deck in "a shower of sparks" before landing in the net, surprisingly it had not caught fire or exploded. While observing this flight that had successfully dropped the last barrel, Petty Officer Brunke remarked that it appeared the pilot was so driven to be successful and on target, that "I thought they might hit our mast." Later, the C-130 pilot, in discussion with Chief Stanczyk, told the chief, things could have been somewhat dicey in the air after dropping the last barrel.

Wanting to ensure the drop was on- target, the pilot was temporarily blinded by the lights on the flight deck when he looked back at the *Jarvis.* Flight engineer Tom Scoggins recalled that toward the end of the air drops, both pilots had developed temporary vertigo [32] while flying at an altitude of 1,000 feet and diving at 500-feet-per-minute. Scoggins immediately set the plane on autopilot and obtained a heading away from the mountains from the navigator. The pilots soon recovered and the last shipment of fuel was delivered. The plane was never in danger, but those additional factors added to the overall excitement. Additional deliveries of gasoline would terminate once the *Koyo Maru No. 3* arrived on the scene.

In the meantime, RM2 Roy Montgomery was copying replies to the *Jarvis'* SOS message when the *Koyo Maru* communicated with him their position and to assure the ship she was heading at top speed to the *Jarvis's* location. Montgomery conveyed to the Japanese trawler that in ninety minutes they would run aground on the nearby rocky coastline.

South of Akutan Island
November 16, 1972

3:00 a.m.

At this time, the PA system announced that the deck crew was to report to the foc'sle [33] to receive the tow line from the *Koyo Maru.* Communication with the Japanese trawler had just conveyed the heaving [34] signals necessary

---

[32] Vertigo can be described as a sense of spinning dizziness and can be caused by fluctuations in cabin pressure.

[33] The forward, upper deck portion of the ship.

[34] Heave is a nautical term meaning "to move to a certain position."

for the safe approach of the ship to the *Jarvis*. One blast was to *heave* around, two was to *avast,* or to stop movement. Weather conditions were such that the men had trouble standing, let alone to try and connect the tow line to both ships. Waves described as sixty-foot in height, combined with freezing rain and snow, and strong winds were battering both ships and the men aboard. At 3:00 in the morning, visibility was extremely challenging with only the moon, stars, and the lights of the arriving ship to help guide the *Jarvis* crewmembers to the towing tasks at hand.

Minutes later, the *Koyo Maru* moved alongside the ship in preparation for the passing of the tow line. Understandably, the arrival of the *Koyo Maru* was met with much relief by the crew of the *Jarvis*. The appearance of the Japanese trawler "was a beautiful sight," Chief Stanczyk would recall as the fishing trawler began preparations for the tow.

3:05 a.m.

About the same time, the base camp for the helicopter support had been set up at Broad Bight. Pilots LT Huddleston and LT Wolfe proceeded back to the *Jarvis* to begin evacuation of the crewmen. Soon after take-off in a torrential hail storm, LT Huddleston was advised by Captain Wooley to disregard the return, as the Japanese trawler had arrived on scene to take *Jarvis* in tow. Huddleston was relieved as he felt that "landing on a moving ship in a storm was more dangerous than taking off from a moving ship." He planned to return to the camp to pick up his crewmen and fly to Akutan Village on the north side of the island; there they would spend the night.

Flying back under foul weather conditions, Huddleston located his crew by a fire that had been set as a marker to assist the pilots. The lieutenant would also comment later, that the Aleutian Islands all look the same at night, which added to the challenges. Upon the retrieval of his aircrew, they began slowly heading east along the rocky coast to the end of the island. There, they ran into trouble as Huddleston would relate:

> "When we tried to turn the corner to the north, we ran into the full force of the storm, with horizontal wind-blown snow causing us to lose visibility and start to ice up. Having difficulty simply making forward progress, we decided to abort and return to Broad Bight to land and spend the night. We informed *Jarvis* and began the trip back with Bill (Wolfe) piloting and me controlling the nose light."

Landing back on Akutan Island, Huddleston, Wolfe, and the aircrew would soon begin settling down for the evening. After notifying the appropriate parties of their position, status, and communication contact information, the crewmen commenced preparations for the night. Despite being on a freezing helicopter on a desolated beach in Alaska, the pilots and crew were quite happy with the current situation versus remaining on the *Jarvis*.

With only four sleeping bags available for the six people on board, the two pilots volunteered to sleep in their cockpit seats, while remaining crewmembers used the bags. Due to the size of the helicopter, two of the aircrewmen decided to sleep outside underneath the helo until Huddleston pointed out that "they would make a nice snack for the Kodiak bears," at which time the two decided sleeping inside in cramp quarters wasn't such a bad idea. Huddleston and Wolfe also found out that when you sweat inside a wet suit, the condensation turns to ice. The sun couldn't come up soon enough for these two, so they could get the engine started and turn on the heater.

At 3:30 a.m., the line-throwing gun from the *Jarvis* was brought out with the *Koyo Maru* maneuvering for the exchange of the towing line. With the rough seas, members of the *Jarvis*, and probably the *Koyo Maru* as well, understood that this would be an extremely difficult shot at connecting the towing line. Retired Coast Guard Captain Terry Grant, an experienced mariner, explained the towing procedures:

> "To get that heavy hawser passed from one ship to another involved passing a succession of lines (ropes) back and forth, starting with a light line that can be thrown by hand (not possible in *Jarvis's* situation) or pulled across by a projectile fired from a line-throwing gun—a specialized rifle. The crew on the receiving end connects that line to a little larger line—a small rope, and was called the messenger. The messenger can't be too heavy because it has to be pulled back to the first ship using the light line that now connects the two ships. This back and forth, increasing the size and strength of the rope continues. Eventually the vessel providing the hawser [*Jarvis*] will fasten the end of it to a rope that is used by the other ship to pull the hawser to it. [As the ropes get heavier, capstans or winches are typically involved.]

"The process of taking a vessel of any size is fraught with hazards and requires many hands and applied skill. Those men on both ships were tested that night. I get emotional just picturing in my mind what they accomplished and how critical the timing was. That was deliverance!"

The passing of a tow line between both vessels proved to be quite difficult. Both ships were severely rolling from the rough seas, with very little visibility to help guide the efforts.

Compounding the problem were communication challenges outside as the Americans didn't speak Japanese and the Japanese crewmen didn't speak English. The *Koyo Maru* attempted to fire the line over to the bow of the *Jarvis*, but missed three times because the lines ended up in the mast or the radar. The *Jarvis* then attempted to pass the line. Chief Gunner's Mate Jack Hunter, with GM2 Nylen standing by, took the line gun. Because of the rough seas and the cold temperatures, he had to fire from his knees. His attempt was successful and the messenger[35] line was passed to the *Koyo Maru*. The *Koyo Maru* quickly returned the messenger and the towing commenced. However, the line broke at 4:25 a.m. and another attempt was made to exchange the messenger. As they approached the *Jarvis*, the master of the *Koyo Maru* skillfully did a "crossing T" starboard-to-port maneuver near the bow, close enough that one crewmember thought for sure they were going to collide. As both ships passed each other, the *Koyo Maru* threw over their messenger line to the *Jarvis*, which was immediately attached to their towing bitt at 4:37 a.m.

Boatswain's Mate Brunke, on the scene for the entire time, explained the episode:

"I believe the first shot from our line throwing gun went into their rigging and therefore had to be detached [parted]. Our second shot from the line throwing gun was successful and our messenger was passed. We had the tow line attached to our tow bitt at about 500 feet so if we lost control on our end, the entire line would not go overboard. We had no power to the capstans so all we could do was

---

[35] A messenger is a tow line.

feed the tow hawser over the side. If it needed to be adjusted, we did that while underway on our end, but the main concern was to get connected to the *Koyo Maru* and away from the danger."

The *Koyo Maru* immediately came to a "hard right" to take the slack out of the line,[36] which now put them in the trough.[37] The Japanese trawler now found itself in a precarious position, having to fight the wind, seas and the dead weight of the *Jarvis*, trying to tighten the tow lines and maneuver the bows of both ships into the wind and sea. Captain Minami, in charge of the *Koyo Maru*, and his crew, valiantly fought the extreme elements and succeeded in the safe towing of the *Jarvis*.

Terry Grant further adds some clarity to the passing of the lines:

"While these lines are being passed, *Koyo Maru* had to stay close enough to *Jarvis* for the exchange but also maneuver to stay clear of *Jarvis's* bow. Both ships are in motion relative to each other while men are handling the lines and trying not to go overboard. The master on *Koyo Maru* and the line-handlers are desperately trying to keep the lines from going slack and getting caught in the screw [prop]. This is a tense time in the best of situations. When the tow line is passed and secured on the towing bitt, *Koyo Maru* must then gradually put a strain on the line to get *Jarvis* moving and headed into the wind.

"Then the problem becomes adjusting the length of the tow line so that the pitching motion [up and down] of both ships is synchronized. He doesn't want the tow line to ever become a straight line [*sproing!*] because it then could break."

When asked on what was going through his mind with the ship coming dangerously close to the rocky shoreline, Petty Officer Brunke replied:

"I never thought about the inability to think. We were all on autopilot getting things done. It was so windy, even by yelling to each other, we could not communicate. We all just knew what to do and worked

---

[36] The tow lines were made of double braided nylon; strong and will stretch under tension.

[37] The depression between two waves.

as a team to get it done. We were being thrown about so severely; we always had to hang on to something for fear of going over the side. There was truly no room for error. We all felt great relief when we could feel the tow line get taut and *Jarvis* begin to be pulled out of the trough, we were underway again, under the power of another vessel. We all had hope now and knew everything would be okay. It was a display of great seamanship on the part of the Japanese vessel's captain and crew."

Years later, Brunke would still marvel at the seamanship of the *Koyo Maru's* captain and his ability to tow a disabled vessel in such dire weather conditions.

The November 17th edition of the Hawaii newspaper, Honolulu Advertiser would recapitulate the towing of the *Jarvis*:

"The Hawaii-based Coast Guard cutter *Jarvis* was taken in tow yesterday by a Japanese vessel after hurricane winds and high seas threatened to batter the flooding, powerless ship against an island in Alaska's Aleutian chain. A local Coast Guard spokesman said the rendezvous with the 336-foot Japanese fishing boat at 3:30 a.m. yesterday ended eight perilous hours during which mountainous seas drove the flooded ship within three miles of the rocky coast of Akutan Island. The *Jarvis* was about twenty-five miles south of Akutan Island when she began sending SOS messages. By the time the *Koyo Maru* arrived, she had been driven twenty-two miles back toward the island. 'We were lucky that the fishing vessel got there when it did,' a Coast Guard spokesman said."

The towing of the *Jarvis* commenced with the destination of nearby Beaver Inlet, just southwest of Akutan Island and located between Unalaska Island and Sedanka Island. An hour later en route to Beaver Inlet, it was noted that the flooding in the engine room had increased to twelve and a half feet of water above the keel.

Much like the elation and joy experienced by the whalers in the summer of 1898 when they were rescued by David Jarvis, these feelings cannot be fully understood or appreciated by those who have not been through similar

Article from the *Honolulu Advertiser* dated November 17. Provided by Jack Hunter/Hank Lipian.

times of desperation and hopelessness. Many of the *Jarvis* crewmembers were greatly elated when the drifting *Jarvis* soon began to move under the control of the Japanese fishing vessel. The *Koyo Maru* had arrived with less than an hour to spare before the *Jarvis* would have struck the nearby Battery Point rocky shoreline located just three miles away. Crewmember casualties had been predicted at over ninety percent with any survivors unlikely to endure the harsh winter environment for any length of time.

God willing, the danger was over.

Daybreak
November 16

As the bitter cold Aleutian sun rose, the crew of the HH-52 commenced preparations for departure from the Broad Bight beach. The snow was still falling, but the wind had slackened. With the campfire now extinguished, the crew began their preflight checklist.

Preparing to lift-off, Huddleston communicated with the *Jarvis* who advised him of their destination in Beaver Inlet. Further instructions from the

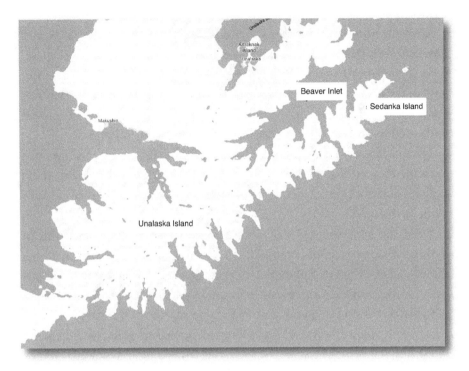

Map showing Beaver Inlet, Unalaska Island and Sedanka Island.

vessel advised them to proceed to Dutch Harbor and to wait for future directions. Taking off from Broad Bight, the HH-52 encountered blowing snow and potential icing conditions; the decision was made to fly along the coastline to the west versus flying over the mountains. Thirty minutes later, the helo and the aircrew landed at Dutch Harbor Airport.

Upon landing at Dutch Island, LT Huddleston contacted the *Jarvis* and relayed that he intended to inform the airport manager of the ship's present condition and to ask for material and communication support. Huddleston volunteered to take responsibility as the Coast Guard representative, and he assured the manager of reimbursement for all expenses. The manager readily agreed to the arrangement and made plans made for fuel, parking, and maintenance at the Dutch Harbor airport.

11:50 a.m.

With the wind and sea waves moderating, the arrival of the *Jarvis* and *Koyo Maru* to Beaver Inlet was without incident. The ship began preparations for repair. At noon, the anchor detail was set with the current water level in the engine room topping off at the maximum amount at fifteen feet above the keel. Using the bow thruster, the ship was able to maneuver to set both anchors and to bring her bow into the wind at 12:20 p.m.

The tow line was returned to the Japanese fishing vessel, but she remained on scene to assist if requested. She furnished the stricken vessel with some supplies and even some sake, which Seaman Ray Christianson would later quip, "was used."

While the *Jarvis* waited for Coast Guard assistance to arrive, personnel in the engine room were still attempting to stop the flooding. Diver Large continued to dive in an attempt to plug the hole and keep the hoses free from obstruction, Seaman Joel Cortez assisted Large as needed; both later would receive official awards for their actions. Chief Montgomery still led the damage control efforts, with many others working as directed. Several crewmen would end up in the hospital within a day or two, suffering from colds, pneumonia, and or other injuries incurred during the hazardous and freezing response. The rest of the crew went to work in whatever jobs they could contribute to saving the *Jarvis*…and their lives. By now the entire ship knew how dire the situation was. The *Jarvis* still endured with no heat and was bitterly cold. To further compound the problem, there was a limited amount of extreme cold weather clothing aboard, and it, understandably, went mostly to boatswains mates and other crewmembers who had to work outside in the freezing weather.

Media coverage of the entire incident was extensive throughout the country. *The New York Times* on November 17th reported the arrival of the *Jarvis* to Beaver Inlet on Sedanka Island after a nine-hour ordeal. The article went on to describe the Coast Guard assets that were en route, including three Coast Guard cutters with the assistance of CG aircraft. As reported, when asked if the *Jarvis* was safe, a CG spokesman declined to affirm, but did comment, "She's in better shape than she was."

In Billings, Montana, the local newspaper, the *Gazette*, briefly described the weather upon the ship's arrival: "Rains driven by winds up to sixty miles an hour and heavy seas buffeted Beaver Inlet on Sedanka Island where the disabled cutter took refuge Thursday under tow by the Japanese ship."

The *Honolulu Advertiser* reported the same day that a snowstorm with winds up to seventy miles per hour was expected to pass nearby south of the area. The unrelenting weather, combined with the flooding of the engine room, took a toll on the men as they fought to keep their ship afloat. Captain Wooley reported that his crew was near total exhaustion. Captain Donby Mathieu, Chief of Operations at the Seventeenth Coast Guard District in Juneau, summarized the current state of the *Jarvis*: "This experience put the mettle of the entire crew to the test. Being adrift without propulsion is a trying and harrowing experience for any mariner. You feel helpless; you're at the mercy of the seas."

Engineman First Class Lawrence Baker would comment that as the men struggled against the waves in the engine room trying to stop the leak, they became oblivious to the time. Baker himself had worked through the night and was surprised when he went topside, that morning had broken. He further described that as the men would get off their shifts, the ship's cooks had hot soup waiting, a luxury they quite appreciated. "That was the biggest thing the guys wanted," said Baker in an interview with the local newspaper. "And the cooks were fantastic." With a limited supply of fresh water, the crewmen would dip their cups into five-gallon canisters for their drinking water. Since there continued to be no hot water for showers and given the filthy working conditions, this created even more challenges for working with your close shipmate.

Coast Guard assets were on the way to assist the *Jarvis*. The *Honolulu Star-Bulletin* reported on November 18th, that "…a fleet of five cargo aircraft and three helicopters flew through winds gusting to fifty knots to reach the staging center, while the 378-foot, high-endurance cutter, hole at the very bottom of her hull, rode out the storm at nearby Sedanka Island in her day of misery yesterday." The Coast Guard Cutter *Balsam*,[38] a sea-going buoy tender, was on the way to assist as well.

The procurement and delivery of supplies to the *Jarvis* was assigned to the Coast Guard Air Station at Kodiak by the Naval Engineering Branch at the Seventeenth Coast Guard District, with the air station at Cold Bay as the alternative dependent on the environment. Should weather conditions

---

[38] The CGC *Balsam* was decommissioned in 1975, sold to a private company, and later converted into a crab fishing vessel.

dictate, the Cold Bay air field would be easier to access as it is 180 miles northeast of Dutch Harbor while Kodiak's distance is over 800 miles.

The process was for the air station to deliver the supplies to Dutch Harbor on C-130 airplanes, and for the helicopter to deliver them to Beaver Inlet. These flights did come with some danger as there were some landing and lightning damages along the way. With some sources of supply as far away as Ohio, many Coast Guard units acted to expedite procurement and transportation.

Out of Juneau, the Coast Guard released a message outlining the agency's efforts to assist in the *Jarvis* repair:

> "Coast Guard ships and aircraft are staging large amounts of materials to assist in the repair of the high-endurance cutter. In addition, naval engineering personnel are being flown in from the ship's district at Hawaii to direct the operation. The Cutter *Balsam* from Adak, Alaska ,is expected to arrive on scene at midnight tonight; the Kodiak-based Cutter *Citrus* will rendezvous late tomorrow night; and, in addition, the Cutter *Winona* has departed from Port Angeles, Washington, to assist. The HC-130 patrol aircraft from Air Station Kodiak will continue 'orbiting' the *Jarvis* until the ship is safely anchored."

12:51 p.m.

The *Jarvis* continued to list five degrees to port side. The CO sent a message to the Seventeenth Coast Guard District office requesting divers to inspect the hull for damage.

1:15 p.m.

The Coast Guard C-130 airplane arrived and airdropped one P-250 pump to assist with dewatering efforts. Within the hour, other planes would drop additional pumps, hoses and fuel. Seaman Manipon would note that during this period, he saw "some of my shipmates with tears in their eyes" as they struggled to save the ship; many were physically sick. Petty Officer Van Elsberg, wanting to view the rescue team parachuting into the water from the C-130, came out on the deck for the observation. There he noticed that the ship had gone from fifteen feet of freeboard to only five feet or so. "When I saw that, I realized just how bad off we were," he said, "and it sent a chill through me."

With these new assets, by late afternoon it was determined that the flooding in the engine room had reduced considerably, and the water level had dropped.

2:48 p.m.

The *Jarvis's* remaining supply of gasoline for the portable dewatering pumps was running dangerously low. Communicating with pilot LT Huddleston, helo CG 1383 obtained the fuel but had to contrive a delivery technique. As Huddleston would explain, "We did not have an external cargo sling available, so my aircrew jury-rigged a sling to hang from our external hoist with ropes. A fifty-five-gallon barrel of gasoline weighs in the neighborhood of 400 pounds, and the external hoist was stressed for around 600 pounds, so we decided to take two full barrels at a time, one in the cabin and one on the hook." The first two barrels were delivered to *Jarvis* shortly, onto the flight deck.

The port list had now increased to eleven degrees, adding to the ship's woes.

4:06 p.m.

Within the next four hours, several helicopter air drops of supplies, known as vertical replenishment (VERTREP),[39] were completed to the *Jarvis*. Also arriving by helo were Navy divers from Naval Station Adak, who dived and installed a canvas patch over the hole of the vessel. With the repair cover in place, along with the extra pumping capacity, the water level continued to decrease. By 7:10 p.m., the seawater was three feet above the keel and remained so until 10:00 p.m. when it was even lower at one foot.

The Coast Guard helo 1383, piloted by LT Huddleston and LT Wolfe, had now completed two flights (sorties) delivering 220 gallons of fuel to the *Jarvis*. Preparing to shut down for the evening, Petty Officer Hawes advised the pilots that due to the harsh weather, parking the helo outside would not be such a good idea. He suggested that an old abandoned WWII hanger next to the runway would provide excellent protection for the helicopter. Following Hawes, Huddleston then taxied the helo into the hangar, made a 180-degree turn to face the opening, and shut down the aircraft.

---

[39] VERTREP is a method of delivering cargo to maritime vessels by helicopter.

6:05 p.m.

Damage Control Central reported to the bridge that the water level had been reduced six feet in the engine room because of additional pumps and the use of a canvas patch.

10:05 pm

The Coast Guard buoy tender *Balsam* arrived, and soon after the cutter *Citrus* also arrived on the scene. With the arrival of the Coast Guard vessels, the *Koyo Maru* was released to continue her voyage; however, five minutes later that message was modified to request that the fishing trawler remain to provide additional aid, if needed, to which they agreed.

The water level in the engine room at this time had been reduced to one foot, four hours earlier it had been seven feet.

11:17 p.m.

Preparations began for the *Balsam* to come alongside, but first, the *Jarvis* had to bring aboard the Navy divers who were attempting to patch the hole at frame 241. The *Balsam* stood off 5,000 yards while the divers came aboard utilizing the *Jarvis's* "Jacob's ladder."[40]

11:30 p.m.

By this time the engine room had been completely dewatered. Although a canvas patch had been attempted before the tow while drifting, it was not completely successful. As stated in the investigation conducted after the incident: "The tenuousness of a canvas patch was illustrated by the fact that one was partially washed clear in Beaver Inlet when the *Balsam* turned over her propeller, while moored alongside."

November 17
1:17 a.m.

The CGC *Balsam* moored alongside the *Jarvis*. An hour and a half later, the *Jarvis's* emergency hawser was passed to the other ship through the starboard bow chock, for better stability between the vessels.

---

[40] A portable rope ladder hung over the side of the ship.

Balsam soon provided hot food and men to relieve the exhausted crew of the *Jarvis,* many of who had not slept much since the grounding some sixty hours earlier. Crewmen from the *Balsam* operated the pumps and other positions, relieving tired men on the *Jarvis.* These men made their way to the visiting ship where they could enjoy hot food, heat, and coffee, not to mention some well-earned sleep.

5:45 a.m.

Almost as daylight began to break, the weather started to kick-up winds with gusts to sixty knots. The *Jarvis* maneuvered itself, using the *Balsam* to hold anchorage. The *Balsam* soon disconnected from the *Jarvis* and kept her distance for the remainder of the day, until weather conditions calmed down.

With the wind gusts came more flooding even though all pumps were fully utilized. At 6:37 in the morning, the General Quarters alarm was sounded again for all men to get to their emergency stations. The *Koyo Maru* was notified and requested to maneuver to the port side of the ship and to standby. Thirty minutes later, Navy divers on-scene reentered the water to install an exterior hull patch that had been created. With this completed, the water level at 7:40 a.m. was at one foot above the keel, with the flooding decreasing. Ten minutes later it stopped altogether.

Throughout the morning and into the afternoon, winds were erratic, with some gusts up to fifty mph. The wind conditions resulted in some flooding, up to 150 gallons-per-minute, but the *Jarvis* crew managed to keep it in check. By 10:30 a.m., two holes had been patched by the Navy divers with work commencing on the third hole. This third patch was installed by 11:07 a.m.

The Navy dive team soon discovered additional small holes and those were repaired. Petty Officer Lawrence Baker, when interviewed a few days later in Honolulu, would comment about how even the professional Navy divers had challenges determining the exact amount of damages, due to the weather, cold water, and sea conditions that severely limited necessary work time.

One diver, taking a metal plate with him to jam against the hole, stated that the suction from the hole in the ship forcibly took the plate out of his hands and "just ate it up."

Media interest was still very intense, but no more so than in Juneau. M. Joseph Leahy, a journalist for the local newspaper, the *Juneau Empire,* would write on November 17th:

"The Coast Guard Cutter *Jarvis*, crippled by a ruptured hull and no means of propulsion, is standing up to a raging windstorm in Alaska's Aleutian chain. With winds gusting to fifty knots, the Cutter *Balsam* and a Japanese merchant vessel are standing by to assist if needed. The 378-foot high-endurance cutter has fought for its stability since early Wednesday morning following a grounding at Dutch Harbor, Alaska. An initial survey of the *Jarvis*' [s] hull indicates that the ship has sustained one 4 x 6-inch hole and another smaller. High winds and fast water currents caused by the hard-hitting southeasterly storm are causing a delay in the installation of temporary patches. When installed, the *Jarvis* will be towed from its present position in Beaver Inlet to Dutch Harbor, a distance of twenty-four miles. There, a large workforce and materials have been staged to effect additional repairs to the ship. Meanwhile, the de-watering process is continuing, with about two feet of water remaining in the ship's engine-room. Portable pumps airlifted to the scene by Coast Guard aircraft and carried by the *Jarvis* and the *Balsam* are being used to pump out the ship's flooded spaces."

Late in the afternoon while anchored at Beaver Inlet, *Jarvis* was loading supplies and equipment for the divers from a small boat tied up next to the vessel. Now operating in calm waters, the crew was utilizing a davit crane to hoist the material aboard when a freak wave struck. The davit swung around, hitting BM3 Lester Bruch and throwing him into the cold water. Seaman Mike Campbell, observing what was happening, immediately dove into the water, almost hitting the water at the same time. Grabbing Bruch, he heaved him into the small boat and pulled himself in as well. Campbell was wearing a PFD (personal floatation device) while Bruch was not; due to the thick clothing Bruch was wearing, there was a good chance the crewman could have died in the freezing waters. Chief Stanczyk, standing on the deck and watching the entire episode, marveled at how quickly Campbell jumped in and how he easily tossed Bruch into the small boat. "He was a strong crewman," he would later quip.

The patches consisted of cementing the holes and at 4:30 p.m., another 600 pounds of cement was dispatched from helo CG 1383. This cement patch work continued for another three hours. The final hole at frame 241 was repaired at 7:40 p.m.

At 8:17 p.m., the CGC *Balsam* prepared to get underway due to the heavy sea conditions.

While *Balsam* was tied next to the stricken vessel, a raging storm had flattened her port running light and inflicted some cosmetic damages to the boat davits. The swiftness and severity of the storm led many to believe a williwaw had struck the ship.

9:22 p.m.

Chief Hospital Corpsman (HMC) Jerry Walker, a close friend to Captain Wooley, and who had previously served with him on another ship, grew concerned about the captain. The captain had not slept throughout the entire ordeal and was showing signs of exhaustion. After administering a dose of 100 mgs of the sleep agent Seconal to the CO, the chief wrote in the unit logs that it was "absolutely essential for captain to get some sleep at this time."

Back on the mainland, the Coast Guard was taking immediate steps to investigate the incident. It had been announced by the Coast Guard Public Information Office (PIO) out of San Francisco, that a formal Board of Investigation (BOI) into the circumstances surrounding the *Jarvis* grounding would soon assemble. The Board would be convened by Vice Admiral Mark Whalen, Commander of the Coast Guard's Pacific Area and headed by Rear Admiral Joseph McClelland, Commander of the Thirteenth Coast Guard District in Seattle. The other member of the board announced, was Captain William Tighe, Chief of Engineering, Twelfth Coast Guard District from San Francisco. Commander Henry Haugen, the legal officer from the Thirteenth District, would act as the recorder.

Chapter 9

ROAD TO RECOVERY

"Meanwhile, the storm that had hampered repair efforts on the *Jarvis* passed and seas were calm in a quiet rain. Two Alaskan-based cutters are attending the *Jarvis*. They will accompany the commercial tugboat now scheduled to tow the stricken vessel to Dutch Harbor tomorrow. Eight Coast Guard aircraft were flying materials between staging areas in the Aleutians while two other cutters were providing the *Jarvis* with close-in support."

—Honolulu Star-Bulletin *newspaper, November 19, 1972*

Beaver Inlet
November 18

S UPPLIES AND PERSONNEL continued for days to flow into Beaver Inlet and to the nearby staging areas for the *Jarvis* response. The Coast Guard Cutter *Citrus* arrived this day, and the Cutter *Winona* was scheduled for arrival on November 21st from Port Angeles, Washington. Divers from the Coast Guard Cutter Staten Island also dropped in to assist mid-morning.

Lieutenant Commander (LCDR) George Buffleben arrived at the ship by helo shortly after 9:00 a.m. and resumed his duties as *Jarvis's* Engineer Officer. Buffleben, who had been absent due to family leave, provided vital leadership to the ship's rehabilitation efforts in Dutch Harbor. He immediately took to the task of cleaning the engines for the return trip to Honolulu. In the early evening, a message was sent to the Fourteenth CG District office by *Jarvis*, requesting that crewmember Engineman Dale Hoosier's leave be cancelled and he be issued temporary orders to serve on *Jarvis's* repairs. As the chief engineman aboard the ship, he would be instrumental in the recovery efforts.

Air assets contributing throughout this period consisted of Coast Guard helicopters and C-130 aircraft from the air stations at Barbers Point Hawaii; Kodiak, Alaska; and San Francisco, California. Other military assets included a Navy P-3 aircraft from Kodiak and an Air Force helicopter escorted by a refueling plane from Anchorage. Air Station Kodiak again provided a C-130 piloted by Chuck Hughes. He and his copilot John Cullens, were again pressed into service because of the shortage of qualified pilots. They flew to Los Angeles where their latest cargo included barrels of rust preservative, vital to the engine recovery of the *Jarvis*. Hughes, now coming down with a cold from the lack of sleep and continuous flying, was scheduled to arrive around midnight and advised of severe weather in the Kodiak area. Earlier, many planes had been diverted to Elmendorf AFB in Anchorage and Hughes planned to follow suit. However, due to the maintenance requirements that could only be completed in Kodiak, the Commanding Officer ordered Hughes to land at Kodiak "at all costs." This presented severe challenges in that Barometer Mountain sits at the end of the primary runway and rises vertically to about 2500 feet above sea level. With hills on both sides of the approach, there is no go-around should problems arise on the touchdown. Against his better judgment, Hughes followed the orders. As Hughes later recalled:

> "The approach and landing was one of the most harrowing of my career. I knew I had to land close to the end of the runway in order to get stopped at the other end [fighting the forty-knot tailwind and the hydroplane effect of the driving rain on the runway]. Right at the minimums of the instrument approach I saw the runway lights, pulled off the power and pointed the nose right toward the approach end of the runway. I literally planted the C-130 at the end and immediately used max reverse and max brakes to get stopped, using up about 3/4 of the runway in the process."

Pilot Huddleston and his helicopter crew continued to bring personnel to *Jarvis* from Dutch Harbor. This included vital Navy diving personnel from Adak, led by CWO Honer and his three divers, along with 800 pounds of diving equipment. Supplies were also delivered including some gravel and 500 pounds of cement.

Later in the day Coast Guard helo HH3F-1481 from Air Station Kodiak relieved Huddleston and his crew. Led by pilot LCDR Jack Denninger as the Aircraft Commander, this larger helo continued vital air supply operations to *Jarvis* until the ship's departure for Honolulu in three weeks. Pilot Huddleston and his aircrew were on crew rest until November 23rd, at which time they departed to Cold Bay, Alaska, only to be delayed for four days due to inclement weather. Finally, with a departure on November 27th, HH-52 1381, escorted by a Coast Guard C-130, landed at Port Heiden, Alaska.

Huddleston recalls the sorties flown:

> "From the 16th through the 18th of November, additional sorties were made delivering fuel, food, blankets, District and Headquarters Damage Control experts, diving gear, divers, and cement—all brought to Dutch Harbor Airport by CG C-130 aircraft. On return trips, we evacuated sick and injured *Jarvis* crewmembers and treated them to barbecued hamburgers, hot dogs and beer—that also was delivered by C-130 from CGAS Kodiak. The *Jarvis* crewmen were then flown to area hospitals for treatment of their various ailments."

The weather and work conditions of the previous few days had taken a severe toll on the crew, and many of the men required immediate hospitalization. Ensign Eger was the first to be evacuated by helicopter to a medical facility at Dutch Harbor. Later in the day, eighteen more crewmembers suffering mostly from cold-related illnesses, but also a few back and arm injuries, were airlifted to the medical facility. All but two were cleared medically within a day or two; those other two remained in the hospital for additional medical treatment. Those medically evacuated from *Jarvis* were later flown back to Honolulu. Dave Martin recalled the C-130 aircraft flying in from Barbers Point, Hawaii, and seeing the evacuees board the plane for the trip home. The flight itself was eight-and-a-half-hours, during which the men sat in uncomfortable paratrooper-style web seating along the sides of the cargo bay. The cargo bay itself was loaded full of hoses, pumps, and other emergency gear that had been previously sent to *Jarvis* for the response.

The Coast Guard buoy tenders had insufficient towing power for safely moving *Jarvis* from the Inlet to Dutch Harbor, so the Coast Guard contracted the tug Richard Foss out of Seattle for the task. She would depart immediately and arrive early the next morning.

To complete the repair patch, over 1,000 pounds of quick-drying cement was used. A pipe was encased in the concrete to allow controlled flooding while the concrete hardened.

Then, with the pipe firmly capped, preparations began for towing to Dutch Harbor.

Dutch Harbor
November 19

In the background, the Seventeenth Coast Guard District, along with Headquarters support, was communicating with numerous districts, commands, and agencies to ensure all logistical needs of *Jarvis* were met. The ship had to be seaworthy for the long 2,200-mile trip back to Honolulu. Navy damage control experts were requested, medical supplies and salvage gear ordered, and fuel and oil barrels delivered. Coast Guard cutters *Winona*, *Citrus*, and *Balsam* were assisting along with numerous Coast Guard aircraft. In Honolulu, the Coast Guard Cutter *Mellon* prepared to get underway for Alaska, in case her assistance was needed. Chief Stanczyk, in charge of the deck crew, would later comment that so much was being sent to help with the repairs that there was a surplus and some supplies were returned.

At 1:00 a.m., preparations began for towing by the tug Richard Foss with the actual towing commencing four hours later. *Jarvis* exited Beaver Inlet and entered Unalga Pass ninety minutes later. At that time the flooding was controlled at less than 100 gallons per minute. The weather for the trip was finally cooperating with winds subsiding to twenty-five miles mph and seas at twelve feet; temperatures reached a balmy thirty-nine degrees later in the day.

For those crewmen not evacuated, fatigue was finally catching up with them. Seaman Leo Manipon, on watch at the helm of the ship, was found lying on the deck of the vessel after falling asleep at the wheel. The Officer of the Deck (OOD) woke him up, and asked him how much sleep he had had since the initial grounding. "Zero," he replied. He was immediately relieved of duty and told to get some sleep. As he explained, "The reason I did not get any sleep was I was afraid I might go down with the ship if it sinks and another reason was the berthing area stinks. It was about midnight when I went to sleep on a vacant rack on the main deck berthing area."

11:00 a.m.

Later in the morning, the setting of the anchor detail was completed with anchoring in Dutch Harbor shortly after noon. At 12:39 p.m., *Jarvis* moored on the port side to Bally-hoo Pier in the harbor. Coast Guard Cutters *Balsam* and *Citrus* remained on scene. Coast Guard Air Station Kodiak continued to provide logistical support for *Jarvis*. Radioman Montgomery commented that when they arrived in Dutch Harbor, the weather conditions were a mess: "Rain, sleet, snow, and wind." Not exactly the best working environment to perform emergency work.

The Coast Guard-owned Bally-hoo dock is frequently used by Coast Guard vessels who stop at Dutch Harbor. It is not recommended for mooring as it would be imprudent to tie-up at the dock in adverse weather because of the poor state of the pier. Lacking other docking facilities, Coast Guard vessels don't have a choice. Those who do tie-up at this facility often followed tradition by painting the ship's name on a rock, water tank, or makeshift board near the pier. "*Jarvis*" now appears among the names of Coast Guard vessels written on the old water tank that sits near the dock.

The harbor and bay are both relatively well protected from the elements, surrounded both by high mountains and low-lying land areas. This can change dramatically in the winter months when storms can strike with very little warning, particularly with williwaws. The existing airstrip dated back to World War II. In 1972, the airstrip was unpaved and utilized by Reeves Aleutian Airlines.[41] It was used by Coast Guard C-130s only in an emergency. As for port services in the region, there were none that could assist with the *Jarvis* recovery. If the ship were to sail to Honolulu, the crew needed to complete the repairs themselves, aided by experts flown in from elsewhere.

Divers from the CGC *Staten Island*, Naval Station Adak, and the U.S. Navy Hull Construction Unit One surveyed the damage to the hull and then began welding on underwater patches. The divers started by constructing an external cofferdam.[42] The construction of the steel cofferdam proved labor-intensive and required six days to complete. There also existed concern

---

[41] Reeves Aleutian Airlines, headquartered in Anchorage, ceased operations in the year 2000.

[42] A cofferdam is a watertight enclosure pumped dry to permit ship repair work below the waterline.

concerning the accumulation of hydrogen and oxygen gases created by the welding.

Therefore, a two-inch long gap was not welded to avoid the possibility of creating excessive pressure from gas generated in attempting to completely close the cofferdam.

The Navy divers continued fabricating a metal box on both sides of the punctures, with holes to hold cables. Seaman Manipon was assigned to assist and to observe the procedures, and he was curious and impressed with how they could weld while under water. As Chief Stanczyk remarked, "The Navy dive team from Pearl Harbor did a hell of a job with a new patch."

As noted in an official Coast Guard report issued later, the *Jarvis* crewmen had "worked in near exhaustion levels in the initial stages of the incident and the vessel was without heat, regular meals, or pressure on the on the domestic water and sanitary system for several days after the flooding of the engine room."

The weather had subsided November 19th, and allowed for the air transfer of nineteen sick crewmen, suffering mostly from colds and fevers, to Elmendorf Air Force Base. There, they were given a complete medical examination. Two men required hospitalization; later they were flown to Kodiak, then on to Honolulu. A list was drawn up of non-essential crewmen who also would be sent. That list was welcomed by some, but not by all. Some personnel wanted to stay on the ship, to see her complete this mission, while others just wanted to go home—cold, tired, and stressed by the ordeal. New personnel from other Coast Guard units were also now being assigned as "temporary additional duty" (TAD) to the *Jarvis* to fill critical positions. Among these was Senior Chief Electrician Mate (EMCS) Werley who proved invaluable in repairing the ship's electronic equipment, which had been damaged by sea water.

The fresh water system on *Jarvis* was not operable. Junior officers Paul Barlow and Doug Phillips—along with a few "deckies,"[43]—including BM1 Charlie Greene, BM3 Richard Brunke, and SN Tim Lawler—decided to rectify the problem by obtaining water from the side of the mountain adjoining the harbor. The men found a small stream 300 feet up the moun-

[43] Members of a ship's deck crew.

tainside, then laid out all the fire hose they could find to pipe water down to the ship. To funnel water into the hose, they hooked a "rat guard" to it at the stream entrance. This rig worked well the first day, but unfortunately the night temperatures froze the water line. The men had to take the hose apart and bring it back to the ship to thaw. Once thawed, the men re-rigged the project, but this time they used baseball bats on the hose to break the ice every thirty minutes throughout the evening. This job was not entirely successful, but credit for ingenuity was warranted.

To get themselves down the mountain quickly (and probably more to the fact they were young men willing to do anything sounding dangerous), some of the crewmen engineered a cardboard sled. On this they could slide down the mountain at high speed into the pitch-black night. Surprisingly, this feat was accomplished without injury—if you don't consider the extreme fear experienced by those who had never gone sledding before. However, as is often the case, in resolving one issue they created another: the use of the rat guard. These guards are placed on mooring lines to prevent rats from coming on board; now the ship lacked that protection on one line. The absence of this shield thus required the active use of a gun detail throughout the night.

"Elephant Snot"
Dutch Harbor
November 19-28

While *Jarvis* was undergoing temporary hull repairs, rehabilitation of the critical engine machinery damaged by the sea water was required. Without flushing of the main-engine parts, corrosion would have occurred from the salt water. This lengthy process was extremely laborious and took nine days to complete. Some parts were flown to Anchorage for commercial repair. Once the water was removed from the engine room, a complete teardown of the machinery commenced.

A challenge was how to move the large engine parts down the passageways and up to the flight deck for cleaning. Brass rods were found and cut into two-foot sections, then placed on the deck to serve as rollers. The engine parts and other heavy engine room equipment were then placed onto the rods and moved much like "how the Egyptians moved huge rocks for the pyramids," as Seaman Lawler would attest. After the parts rolled down the passageway, they were then tied onto a block-and-tackle system and lifted up to the flight deck. There they were disassembled, cleaned, and reassembled. The final step was to reverse the process by reconstructing the parts and moving them back into the engine room. Most of the involved crewmembers worked grueling twelve hours on, then twelve hours off.

Every electric motor, motor controller, switch, panel, and circuit breaker was disassembled, cleaned by spraying with an industrial solvent, and then given a final wash in a sonic cleaner. Once cleaned, they were then "baked" to remove all moisture. Drying of the parts took place in either the ship's galley ovens or in a shack on the flight deck. This shack itself was routinely used for the crewman on watch to use as a shelter to get out of the weather. The shack utilized a kerosene heater that provided the hot temperatures necessary to dry the electrical parts. After drying, the components were reassembled and reinstalled.

The amount of work to be done in the engine room was so massive, the word was spread that all personnel not on watch were to proceed to the engine room. Many of the deck personnel volunteered even after their regular work shifts were over. Upon reporting in the engine room, the men were issued wiping rags and coveralls and told to wipe down any equipment covered with grease. This task took almost a full day to complete. The working conditions were extremely filthy. Any of the greasy mix and insulation that dropped onto their head, neck or hands proved to be quite itchy. Seaman Leo Manipon remarked that by the end of the work shift, many of his fellow shipmates were unrecognizable because of the oil that covered their bodies. Those who dived to repair the patch and work the shoring were covered entirely, including Petty Officers Large, Borosh, and Kacsanek. Tired and exhausted, many of the men fell to sleep immediately on their bunks, too tired to get out of their clothes.

Chief Dale Hoosier was in charge of the crew cleaning the engines. Chief Hoosier explained the process:

> "All water was out when we started cleaning. The problem was getting rid of insulation and muck in the engine room. We formed a bucket brigade of about a dozen crewmembers with five-gallon buckets, and they worked at night. If you didn't have a job, you worked the bucket brigade—operations people, storekeepers, cooks, electronic technicians, seamen, firemen—all lower enlisted.

"Unofficial name, some called it 'mucky shit' or 'elephant shit,' [others called it elephant snot]. We had to clean bilges and get rid of the slime. Not sure if there was a lot of asbestos—that had been replaced by a different product."

The cleanup was messy, smelly, and mucky. As mentioned above, most crewmembers called the slimy, oily water "elephant snot"; it was as if "an elephant stuck his trunk in the engine room and blew his nose," LTjg Rick Sasse would comment, adding:

"If I recall we were working twelve (hours) on/twelve off. We went through a lot of CRC[44] or a product to displace water. Over the next year, we would find that connectors which had not been cleaned had corroded and caused circuitry problems. The planning by CWO Bill Strickland, ENCS Cox, ENC Hoosier, ENC Bateman, BT1 Stoppelmoor (I'm sure there were others) was to flush out the engines and reduction gears and to work up plans for making fresh water. This was a once-in-a-lifetime event, and they responded extremely well."

Numerous Coast Guard C-130 aircraft were continuing to bring in pallets of lubricating oil to the ship for the cleaning of the engines. One of the three Coast Guard helicopters from Air Station Kodiak picked up two barrels at a time, and flew them to the *Jarvis* flight deck, where the ship's crewmembers detached the barrels. The barrels were moved onto the fantail so more helos could approach and deliver additional oil. This impressive operation continued for several days due to the amount of lube oil required to flush the two diesel engines. The salt water had destroyed the two gas turbine engines, rendering them useless for the trip home. In total, over 3,000 gallons of oil were flown in to flush the engines. In the Honolulu newspaper, Ensign Richardson stated that the crew's efforts toward flushing the engines probably saved the government over a million dollars.

Jarvis remained docked at Bally-hoo pier until November 29th, performing the same duties daily. Navy divers worked underwater, completing repair

---

[44] CRC is an electrical parts cleaner.

work on the hull. Crewmen continued to disassemble, scrub, and clean engine and electronic parts, then reassemble and install them back into the ship. Helo CG 1481 continued to off-load fifty-five-gallon drums of oil and pick up empty barrels for the return trip while Coast Guard C-130s brought in supplies and more lube oil. The two Coast Guard buoy tenders, *Citrus* and *Balsam*, remained on scene as well.

During this period the initial investigation into the grounding and near-sinking began.

Several days after the Navy salvage team arrived, members of the Board of Investigation—a vice admiral and a captain—came aboard to start the inquiry. Observing their arrival, Petty Officer John Moran, while standing with Petty Officer Robert Loftin, attempted humor in the situation and quipped: "Portsmouth Naval Prison won't be so bad. They have color TV and sliding weekends."

Off and on, heavy winds rocked the ship and the tug *Richard Foss* assisted by holding her in place until winds died. The divers worked in freezing conditions. Engineer Officer Buffleben described the divers' work as "amazing," noting the divers would weld underwater for short periods, then come back on board with their skin a blue tint due to the coldness of the waters.

Those in the engine room were still working in oily, greasy, cold, and filthy conditions.

The nearby Coast Guard cutters offered hotel services to the *Jarvis* crew. Some chose to sleep on the buoy tenders; some remained on *Jarvis*. Those remaining continued to sleep in their oily clothes, not only due to exhaustion but also because there were no clean clothes available. The filthy conditions, combined with the lack of fresh water for washing or showering, led to very inhospitable conditions. Those who wanted took a "sea shower" which consisted of rinsing one's self from a small sink of cold, icy water and then wiping down.

Coast Guard Cutter *Winona* arrived on November 21st to escort *Jarvis* back to Honolulu once she was seaworthy. The same day, other members of the Board of Investigation arrived in Dutch Harbor to view the damages and the current status of the ship. As noted in the official report, "the vessel was actively engaged in repairs, and no testimony of witnesses was taken." Three days later, the Board reopened at the Seventeenth Coast Guard District Office in Juneau for the taking of testimony.

On November 22nd, the eighteen crewmembers flown to Kodiak earlier in the week departed aboard a C-130 aircraft for a trip back to Hawaii. Several of the men were suffering from the flu, bronchitis, or common head colds caused by exhaustion or exposure to the cold elements.

Additional members were flown back later.

On Thanksgiving Day, November 23rd, the crew was surprised with a Thanksgiving dinner supplied by some generous people in Anchorage who had taken up a collection for the ship. The dinner, including all the trimmings and cranberry sauce, was flown over by a Coast Guard C-130 and off-loaded for the vessel. To the crew's delight, the meal included beer.

The dinner was served on paper plates with plastic utensils due to no fresh water being available; the men had grown accustomed to the inconvenience. Before arriving in Dutch Harbor, the men had been forced to use paper plates and plastic silverware because of the lack of water. However, even those items were in limited supply. Petty Officer Wenner commented, "For a while, we ate from paper plates and plastic utensils. As they ran out, you would look for a friend who was just finishing his 'eat' as you entered the mess and he would give you his used plate and utensils. And you watched when you were done to share your reused stuff with a buddy."

With more oil soon to arrive, the crew had one hour to eat before having to reset Flight Quarters.

Starting Friday, November 24th and continuing throughout the week, wind gusts of up to fifty knots struck the ship while docked, routinely bringing Captain Wooley to the bridge. Wooley communicated with the tug *Richard Foss* during these periods so the tug could relieve the strain on the mooring lines. The next day, November 25th, hogging lines[45] were attached by Navy divers, and the hull was "deemed seaworthy for the voyage" back to Honolulu. Late on November 27th, the sanitary system was back in operation, much to the great relief of the crew.

The engineers worked tirelessly to restore the diesel engines. Getting them running was, as Chief Hoosier stated, a matter of pride. "We didn't want to be towed back," he said.

Throughout the ordeal, over 3,000 gallons of lubricating oil had been used to clean the engines. On November 28th, the engines cranked and smoke billowed out of the smokestacks. Preparations were now underway to depart Dutch Harbor on November 29th. A skeleton crew of 118 was

---

[45] Hogging lines are temporally used to hold an object close to the side of a ship.

selected instead of the full complement; those chosen to ride included three Navy divers who were available to assist if required. Petty Officer Martin was one of those not selected and remembers unhappily, "…dragging my seabag in the snow from the ship to the Dutch Harbor airport to await the C-130."

The XO, Commander White, was quoted in the local Honolulu newspaper as saying, "This crew saved the government $500,000[46] in overhaul costs by doing the job of fixing the engines that normally would have been done in a shipyard."

It was time to go home.

---

[46] Calculated in 2019 dollars, the cost would be roughly just over $3 million.

Chapter 10

THE RETURN HOME

"It was an interesting couple of nights and some long days. What I saw was a lot of Coasties doing their absolute best in saving a ship and lives. Nothing occurred by a single person's actions; it was a team: a team that saved the ship and got the helo off. If one member of the team didn't give their all, it wouldn't have been the success that it was."

—*AT1 Richard (Tiny) C. Lawson, Sr.*

November 29, 1972
Departure from Dutch Harbor

AT 9:09 ON THE morning of November 29th, *Jarvis* was in tow by the tug *Richard Foss*, departing Dutch Harbor with Captain Wooley at the conn[47] and the XO as "navigator" on the bridge. Once outside the harbor, the tug was released and soon began her journey back to Seattle. The eleven days of tug service cost the Coast Guard $60,000.

Accompanied by the Coast Guard Cutter *Winona*, *Jarvis* began her 2,200-mile voyage back to the Coast Guard base, located just across the harbor from the city of Honolulu. The only issue with the *Winona* escorting *Jarvis* was that she was a bit slower, so *Jarvis* had to slow down occasionally to allow the *Winona* to catch up. *Jarvis* was manned by a skeleton crew that included several sick members who could have left the ship earlier, but chose to stay on board for the simple reason "it's our ship."

Except for some minor glitches, the trip back was comparatively unevent-

---

[47] The navigation term "conn" is the act of controlling a ship's movement while at sea.

ful. Engineer Officer LCDR Buffleben remembers that the remnants of the "elephant snot" continued dripping onto the hot engines and "smoking like hell" all the way home. Fireman Bill Sewell, part of the engine crew, remembers the trip back to Honolulu as being "on one engine; no fresh water for laundry or showers, and being escorted home by another ship from Oregon, that had only been home from Ocean Station November[48] for a few hours. What a long strange trip it's been."

A second vessel assigned to the escort was Coast Guard Cutter *Storis*, recalled on short notice to assist. One of the oldest ships in the Coast Guard, with a distinguished career, the 230-foot *Storis* was commissioned in 1942 for the primary purpose of icebreaking duty. She served off the coast of Greenland during WWII. After the war, *Storis* was assigned to Alaska to conduct routine fisheries patrols and to be a Search and Rescue (SAR) resource. It was during one of these patrols that the great Alaska earthquake of 1964 struck, registering a massive 9.2 on the Richter scale.

The vessel was directed to break ice in Cook Inlet to provide a critical path for the inflow of logistical supplies into Anchorage. Seven years earlier, the ship traveled through the Northwest Passage and returned home through the Panama Canal. Thus *Storis* became the first United States vessel to circumnavigate the continent. Commander Wood, the Commanding Officer of the ship, would state to a friend: "We were able to gather—for our [military] forces—more hydrographic information about these waters than had been amassed in the last 400 years. It's a good feeling to have had a part of something like that."

As a historical note, in 1975, *Storis* participated in the ice-breaking patrol in Prudhoe Bay, located on the North Slope of Alaska, where the starting point of the Trans-Alaskan Pipeline. The ship's capabilities allowed for the tugs and barges to deliver tons of construction material for the pipeline. In 1989, the *Storis* served as command and control vessel for the clean-up operation following the massive Exxon Valdez oil spill where an estimated eleven million gallons of oil spilled into the pristine Alaskan waters.

On October 1, 1991, the Coast Guard Cutter *Storis* officially became the

---

[48] Ocean station between Hawaii and California providing weather information, radio communication and to assist with search and rescue as needed. Often scheduled for weeks at a time, the *Jarvis's* first Ocean Station November was for twenty-one days.

Coast Guard Cutter *Storis,* 1962. Photo courtesy of Terry Grant.

oldest commissioned vessel in the Coast Guard. She surpassed the previous record-holder Revenue Cutter *Bear* as the longest serving ship in the Bering Sea. A plaque was issued granting the *Storis* National Historic Place Designation. The ship was decommissioned in 2007; she was later put up for auction but failed to meet the reserve bid. The "Queen of the Fleet"—having traveled over 1.5 million miles, saving over 250 people and twenty-five vessels—was later unceremoniously scrapped in Mexico.

On November 29th, the same day that *Jarvis* sailed with her escorts from Dutch Harbor, Coast Guard aviation technicians prepared to dismantle the helo HH-52A 1383 for the trip back to the Coast Guard Air Station in Elizabeth City, North Carolina. Flying back on a CG C-130 airplane, the pilots and aircrew had to remain in the cabin of the helo due to non-availability of seating in the cargo bay itself. Also on board was a Coast Guard admiral and his party. Upon landing in Mobile, Alabama, LT Huddleston instructed the aircrew to get their gear and proceed on liberty. Wolfe then advised Huddleston that the commanding officer wanted the crew and the pilots to attend a reception in the wardroom. Huddleston declined, preferring to spend time with his wife; besides who would notice his absence? Shortly after, Huddleston found out the reception was hosted by the admiral, who wanted to recognize him and his crew for their efforts in Alaska. Somewhat embarrassed, Huddleston recalled a line that a friend often quoted, "...to assume means making an ass of you and me."

The Coast Guard did not forget the rescue of the *Jarvis* from the rocks of Akutan Island. On November 29th, a message was sent from Captain Durfee of Coast Guard Headquarters in Washington, D.C., to the State Department representative, Mr. R. A. Ericson, Jr. In Captain Durfee's letter, he writes:

> "The Japanese fishing vessel *Koyo Maru No. 3* owned by Hokusuisan aided the Coast Guard Cutter *Jarvis* and her crew on the night of 16 November 1972 from a position of great peril off the Aleutian Islands Alaska.
>
> "*Jarvis* was drifting helplessly toward the beach in high winds and heavy seas. The *Koyo Maru* responded willingly and in the highest spirit of the tradition of the sea to the distress call of *Jarvis* and took her in tow. The *Koyo Maru* demonstrated superb seamanship in successfully towing *Jarvis* to safe anchorage. The *Koyo Maru* stood by *Jarvis* until Coast Guard Cutter *Balsam* arrived on scene. The professionalism and dedication of Captain Toshimasa Minami and crew are greatly admired and highly commended.
>
> "The Commandant U.S. Coast Guard will present a Distinguished Public Service Award plaque at the Japanese embassy for the *Koyo Maru* in early December.
>
> "It is requested that the Japanese government be asked to present award and USCG gift at an appropriate ceremony in Japan at which U.S. Embassy officials and USCG Representative Captain J.E.B. Stewart might be present to express deep appreciation and thanks to Captain Minami and crew for their gallant performance. In addition, it is desired that Captain Minami be advised as early as practicable of award and gift from USCG.
>
> "Request further Commandant USCG be advised of Japanese response to this proposal and prospective date of ceremony."

After a couple of days at sea on the trip back to Honolulu, *Jarvis* had to temporarily shut down the starboard shaft because of vibration issues caused

KOYO MARU NE 3 / JDXF
STERN TRAWLER
336 FT LONG
CAPTAIN TOSHIMASA MINAMI - MASTER
HOKUYO SUISAN KK - OWNERS
TOKYO - PORT OF REGISTRY

Intercepted JARVIS distress call and
proceeded to scene.
161445Z NOV 72 - took JARVIS in tow
enroute Beaver Inlet
162215Z NOV 72 - anchored JARVIS in Beaver
Inlet.
171033Z NOV 72 - BALSAM arrived Beaver Inlet.
172300Z NOV 72 - KOYO MARU NE 3 departed
Beaver Inlet.

HARUMA MARU / JKJL
STERN TRAWLER
328 FT LONG.
CAPTAIN T. DEGUCHI - MASTER
NIPPON SUISAN K.K. - OWNERS
TOKYO - PORT OF REGISTRY

Proceeded toward scene on receipt of

Koyo Maru No. 3 master notes.

by the damaged propeller blades. Shortly after that issue was resolved, *Storis,* located 2,700 yards off the port quarters, was having engine trouble, forcing her to slow to just over eleven knots per hour, thereby forcing *Jarvis* and *Winona* to slow their progress. Further taxing the crew, a storm afflicted the vessels with high swells, twenty-five to forty-degree rolls, and winds of forty knots. The trip was not going smoothly.

December 1st saw the arrival of another storm in the north Pacific and the ships again experienced forty-degree rolls and reduced visibility because of fog. Earlier in the day, the CGC *Storis* was released from escort duty to head for Cold Bay. At 4:35 in the afternoon, a brief fire occurred in the engine room. Although quickly extinguished, it was determined that the cause was an overflow of lube oil residue on an exhaust manifold. The next day, *Jarvis* continued to suffer from thirty-five-degree rolls, and around 9:00 a.m., both main diesel engines briefly stopped because of the loss of fuel oil pressure.

The ship continued for the rest of the voyage with some minor engine and radar problems; small swells and fog were experienced off and on throughout the rest of the trip. As the ship approached the Hawaiian Islands, the seas became calmer and the air warmer. With the moon shining brightly on moderately tranquil waters, the view was breathtaking at night. Combined with the purring of the engines and the quietness of the evening, one could take a break from the recent memories of Alaska and pause to think about other matters. Ensign Carl Schramm gazed out over the Pacific waters while standing deck watch during the trip home and recalled a sense of sadness that night while on midwatch. "Sadness because, at that moment, I realized nothing would ever be the same again," he said. "I realized the magic was gone—that once we got back to port, we would all eventually go our separate ways and what we had between us would be lost forever. And of course, that's exactly what happened over time."

Similar feelings were expressed by other crewmembers as well. In times of traumatic events, those directly affected will often come together and forever be a "band of brothers."

December 7, 1972
Honolulu, Hawaii

Finally, on December 7th, the men of *Jarvis* saw the first of the Hawaiian Islands. First, Kauai emerged on the horizon. *Jarvis* continued on, en route to her final destination, Honolulu. Around 6:30 p.m., the ninety-five-foot cutter *Cape Newhagen* pulled alongside to transfer mail and ship personnel, CWO Lape and Yeoman Chief Hess, to the *Jarvis*. With Barbers Point, Oahu, in view three hours later, the CGC *Winona* was released from escort duty to proceed back to her home base in Port Angeles, Washington. At 10:12 p.m., Captain Wooley relieved the conn, and nine minutes later the special sea detail was set.

Jarvis would soon be home.

It was now early evening of December 7th as the CGC *Jarvis* entered Honolulu Harbor. Petty Officer Loftin would recall the scene as memorable. "We passed Diamond Head in the afternoon, then Waikiki Beach. Next was Aloha Tower on the starboard and Sand Island Coast Guard Station on the port. The shore was filled with the families of the crew," he would recall. Upon entering the harbor, the harbormaster communicated with Captain Wooley, and offered tug service for the ship; Captain Wooley declined.

Petty Officer Robert Van Elsberg recalled the communication:

> "My proudest moment in twenty-two years of service was when we rounded Diamondhead, and the harbormaster offered a tug to take us in tow. Captain Wooley told him we brought our ship all the way back from Alaska and we would bring her back to her dock. All of us heard that, and I remember standing extra tall on the deck as we came back into port. Whatever you or anyone else might say about him, I would have followed him to the gates of hell. That is the kind of respect I felt for him."

He would add later, "We'd saved the Coast Guard's newest 378-foot cutter from nearly sinking in the cold waters of Alaska. We'd earned the right to be proud."

Regardless of the communication, two commercial tugs came out to tow *Jarvis* to the Coast Guard Sand Island Pier. The arrival of the tugs was met as an insult by the crew and the captain. *Jarvis* had sailed over 2,000 miles without assistance, and therefore there was no need for the tow. The tugs came alongside and tossed the heaving lines; they were immediately thrown back off the ship into the water. This response from the crew did not go over well with Commander White, the XO, who yelled from the bridge, ordering the men to take the lines, which they did. However, as requested by Captain Wooley, the tugs escorted *Jarvis* to the dock but did not tow.

At 10:33 p.m., the Honolulu pilot came aboard *Jarvis* at the fantail and was to be escorted to the bridge to assist with navigating the harbor. Deck force non-rates and best friends Joel Cortez and Travis Deleon, both invaluable to the *Jarvis's* recovery, immediately volunteered to Chief Stanczyk to help escort the pilot to the bridge. While initially agreeing to the offer, the chief grew suspicious as their volunteering for the detail seemed "too easy." Chief Stanczyk quickly went to the fantail where it appeared the two were preparing to launch the pilot overboard into the harbor. The chief advised them the potential errors of their ways and the ship continued to the pier—with the pilot.

At 10:48 p.m., the mooring lines were thrown to dockside base personnel, and *Jarvis* was tied up at the Coast Guard pier on Sand Island. The ship's return from a patrol was usually a festive event, but this night there was no band and no crowd to cheer, only family and a few crewmembers who had arrived home earlier. Lieutenant Junior Grade Rick Sasse commented, "You could have heard a pin drop as we came in and moored."

Crewmember Seaman Quartermaster (SNQM) Keith Fawcett, one of those who had an excused absence for the *Jarvis* trip to Alaska, was on the pier when the ship docked. He observed:

> "As the ship struggled to stabilize and repairs were made, I followed the news as best I could and went out to Sand Island the night the ship came home. I stood there on the dock knowing I was part of the crew but at the same time not part of the crew because I did not share the danger of the grounding. That bond was different and tighter than an ordinary crew bond. The ship pulled alongside the pier, and in the dim light she looked beat, scarred by the rubber fender marks, chaffed and scraped up. The brow went up on the ship, and the exhausted crew came down into the arms of family and friends. And they walked off into the Hawaiian night."

December 18, 1972
Drydock
Honolulu, Hawaii

Ten days later, on December 18th, the CGC *Jarvis* was pulled into drydock for repairs at Dillingham Shipyards in Honolulu. The estimated cost to repair the damages was $400,000[49] with an estimated timeline of three weeks to complete restoration. Lieutenant Junior Grade Sasse was on the scene when the ship entered the drydock. As the water was pumped out, Sasse and others got to see first-hand the damage to the vessel, including the chipped propeller

---

[49] Equivalent to $2.3 million in 2019.

and the missing bow thruster. It was apparent that the *Jarvis* repair crew had done its job well to secure the hatch and stop the engine room flooding.

Later, the Coast Guard official Board of Investigation further described the damages in their final report:

> "Drydock examination of the rupture of the hull plating in the engine room revealed that the plating had been dished in with an L shaped rip twelve inches by eleven inches between longitudinals 8 and 9. Because longitudinal 9 had been separated from the plating, it appeared during damage control efforts that there was a fracture outboard of longitudinal 9 from the ingress of water, but such was not the case. The shape and location of the hole was such as to make it extremely difficult to determine its size by feel alone, and it was not one particularly suited to patching with wooden wedges. Based on NAPSHIPS Technical Manual, the approximate area of the gash at the particular depth involved (fifteen feet) and its shape gives a flooding rate of 1,200 gallons per minute which would require somewhat in excess of six hours to free flood the engine room. The vessel's estimated flooding rates were generally twice that of the computed values."

The *Honolulu Advertiser* reported the initial examination of the ship revealed no additional damage that was not known, that the temporary steel-and-concrete patch placed by the Navy divers was still in place, and that the ship's two huge propellers were badly nicked. The patch was removed on December 18th and work began on removing the propellers.

Other repair measures begun as well. The two large diesel engines and the two gas-turbine engines had all been damaged by the grounding and the flooding. The diesel engines were cleaned while in drydock at Pearl Harbor; the jet engines were dismantled and shipped to California for renovation. (The difference between the two types is simple; *Jarvis* cruises on the diesel engines while the jet engines drive the propellers faster and are utilized for special rescue missions when speed is essential.)[50]

Lieutenant Commander George Buffleben, Engineer Officer aboard the

---

[50] The primary differences are 1) Horsepower and 2) Fuel consumption. The diesels power the ship at a reasonable speed relatively economically. The gas turbines have a lot more power, use more fuel, and provide a high-speed capability.

Photos showing extent of damage to *Jarvis's* propellers.
Photos courtesy Jack Hunter and George Thomas.

Jarvis, spent his time assisting the Fourteenth District Office in overseeing the repair efforts. Working with Commander Ed Parker from the district, who Buffleben describes as "a brilliant engineer," they spent countless hours and days working on the repair, which Buffleben called, "the longest days of my career." An especially challenging job was moving the gas turbine engines up to the dock for further transfer to California. This was accomplished through the use of steel plates that had been attached to the engines and then lifted up through the ship and transported to their destination for repair.

While the repairs went according to plan, there were occasionally minor blips. Buffleben recalls LTjg Rick Sasse working on top of the starboard free turbine engine to reinstall it. "He dropped a small crescent wrench. It landed on the top strut which is hollow to allow air flow to cool an internal bearing. The wrench managed to slide all the way down into the bearing housing. Luckily, we were able to get to the housing and remove the wrench. In basketball, that would have been a three-pointer," he would quip later.

The standard tour of duty for personnel on the *Jarvis* (and most cutters) was two years, and many of those in the crew were now approaching that anniversary. While the ship was in drydock, the transfer of many crewmembers commenced. Those remaining departed on leave or liberty to spend the Christmas holidays with their families.

Upon taking command of *Jarvis* from Captain Wooley in May of 1973, Captain Hollingsworth (later admiral) remarked that there was "almost a complete turnover of wardroom personnel when I took over. Only some of the warrant officers remained." The turnover was so complete, that when the new crew reported under Captain Hollingsworth the following year, many did not know the story of the grounding. Those crewmembers who had not transferred did not know the complete story, only their small participation of the event.

During the incident, coping with the rolling sea, freezing working conditions, and severe weather, *Jarvis* crewmembers devoted their full efforts to saving the ship and with it, their lives, each working on the specific emergent need at the time. As former members related, they did not have time to roam the vessel to get the complete picture of what was going on. Later, when the ship docked in Honolulu, there was no group setting to review and discuss what had happened; the timing was such that many of the members were either assigned to temporary duty or transferred. Those members involved later in the official Coast Guard hearings of the accident had some insight after the fact, but they had only a partial view of the investigation.

Richard Brunke, a third class petty officer aboard the ship during the grounding, was also unaware of the total picture of the events that had transpired. As he commented:

"Later in my career while attending Prospective Commanding Officer School to prepare for orders as commanding officer of USCGC *Conifer*, the case study of the *Jarvis* grounding was what we studied for stability. I was shocked to find out that *Jarvis* was taking rolls up to sixty degrees, well beyond its designed ability to stay afloat and not capsize. I must say, in my entire thirty-three-and-a-half-year career, I had never seen, or been in conditions so severe."

Of those transferred, some remained in Hawaii while others were sent to other assignments throughout the country. Several of the chiefs requested to stay on board, including Jim Herman, Walt Stanczyk, Jack Hunter, and Lowell Montgomery; their wishes were granted.

Those remaining on board would be working what the Coast Guard calls "tropical hours," which run from 7:00 a.m. to 1:00 p.m. Radioman George Fewell and other members would work on administrative matters and training. After a couple of months, Fewell was sent to the Communication Station San Francisco, out of Pt. Reyes, California. Seaman Dan Edwards, qualifying for the commissaryman (CS) rating, felt a sense of loyalty to the ship and elected to a one-year extension on board *Jarvis*. "We were a band of brothers, especially after what we had just gone through in Alaska," he said.

Led by the chiefs, many of those remaining were instrumental in the recovery of the *Jarvis*. Engineman Second Class Kacsanek remained on board to assist with engineering repairs including replacing the starboard propeller and restoration of the pumps, not to mention countless other minor mends and fixes. Fireman Bill Sewell contributed as needed in the engine room until his transfer to Engineman school in the fall of 1973. Sonar Technician Denny Strutton, Chief Stanczyk's right-hand man, stayed on board to help with the change out of the sonar dome. Later in the year with his rotation due, he was sent to a sonar system school. The *Jarvis*'s second commanding officer, Commander Bobby Hollingsworth, much appreciated those who chose to remain on board past their standard tour of duty. As he commented later, those who remained "were important parts of the recovery efforts to return *Jarvis* and its crew to fully operational status."

One of the more difficult recovery jobs was the repair to the electronics of the ship. Electrician's Mate (M2) Ken Wenner had to de-solder all military connectors to anything that had been underwater, which was pretty much everything. As he relates:

"There were hundreds of them[connectors], some with three wires, some with a hundred. It was impossible to set up with a de-soldering vacuum, solder gun, solder feed, and associated tools because there were workers everywhere and most of my work was done on a narrow deck plate [in a] passageway constantly used by them. I volunteered to work nights to get the job done without interruption."

Electrician's Mate (EM3) Howard Jensen also acknowledged the challenges encountered upon return to Honolulu. While the difficult task of taking apart every single electrical component to dry and reassemble, had taken place at Dutch Harbor, the cleaning had to be repeated because of water seeping down onto the engine room equipment while sailing home. "I sat for days with my back to the wall, taking the components apart," he said. "The ship was never the same."

Most of the crew, however, were transferred. Lieutenant Junior Grade Rick Sasse soon departed and continued his Coast Guard career until retirement, as would LTjg Paul Barlow who eventually retired as captain. Leaving *Jarvis* for the Coast Guard buoy tender *Planetree*, QM striker Dave Martin, was then sent to the U.S. Navy Signalman School on Ford Island in Pearl Harbor; upon his graduation, he returned to the *Jarvis*. Seaman Ray Christianson soon left the Coast Guard and enrolled in college. Seaman Tim Lawler promoted to boatswains mate third class and transferred to the "Garden Island" of Kauai. Most of the other crewmen finished out their Coast Guard careers on the mainland.

Perhaps the best gig following the *Jarvis's* grounding belonged to BM3 Richard Brunke. After arriving in Honolulu, a transfer sent him to the Fourteenth CG District on a detail for "special assignment" to the U.S. Army at Fort Shafter, located just up the road from Honolulu. Fort Shafter has the distinction of being the oldest military base in Hawaii, having celebrated its 100th anniversary in 2007. Since the Coast Guard did not have any funding to support its sports program, the Coast Guard District Commander decided to supply a full-time Coastie to assist the Youth Activities Coordinator in running the military sports programs year-round. Brunke's uniform was shorts and a blue shirt that read "Special Services." He had a military vehicle assigned to him, and he was responsible for thousands of dollars of sports equipment. His only issue during this assignment was that the Military Police (MP) on the base stopped him almost every week for some "offense," then said they would let him off if he provided them with some sports equipment. Once he figured out the reason, he passed the word that if they submitted a list to the main gate, he would ensure they received whatever they requested. After that, the MP stops ended. This job, if one could call it that, was an excellent way to spend a couple of years.

January 1973
Dillingham Shipyard
Honolulu, Hawaii

Once shipyard repairs were completed, *Jarvis* was towed to the Coast Guard base at Sand Island on January 12, 1973. The ship was not yet seaworthy as repairs were still being completed in the engine room and would continue while moored at Sand Island. Captain Wooley resumed duties as the Commanding Officer on January 15th, but was relieved by Commander White ten days later.[51]

With the Board of Investigation findings looming before him, Captain Wooley wrote the closing statement in the *Jarvis* book, *The Wake Behind Us*:

"The first year of the *Jarvis* has been both monumental in the goals obtained and traumatic. The ships grounding in Alaska was a terrible thing and a shock that most of us will never recover from. The eleven months preceding this tragedy proved we were ready to fight our ship back to life during our eleventh hour, and the lessons learned will serve us forever.

"We have made many friends and have shared our lives with many fine shipmates. The spirit of *Jarvis* will live on and those following us will accomplish greater goals. Let us never forget: 'The *Jarvis* has returned.'

"A sincere 'well done' and an appreciative thank you for your tireless efforts and gallant performances during this first year."

---

[51] The *Jarvis* ship logs show the last signed entry by Captain Wooley to be March 26, 1973. It would appear that between leave and temporary active duty, he served intermittently as CO of the *Jarvis* from arrival to Honolulu up to his change of command ceremony.

Chapter 11

THE INVESTIGATION

"In my thirty years, I've never seen anything like this or such dedication by a crew, not one man of which got hurt—and I was aboard the *Lexington*[52] when it was torpedoed."

—*Executive Officer/Commander Kenneth White*

Board of Investigation
Honolulu, Hawaii

HAVING FLOWN BACK from Alaska, the Board of Investigation (BOI) met again at the Fourteenth Coast Guard District Office in Honolulu on December 11th. A week later, *Jarvis* was put into drydock at which time Captain Tighe was designated to view the underwater damage to the ship, taking notes and photographs.

Just a few days before, the *Honolulu Advertiser* reported on the pending investigation:

"The $17 million *Jarvis*—one of the Coast Guard's newest high endurance cutters—was the subject of the service's first ship's commissioning ceremony on Oahu in August. The inquiry into the *Jarvis* incident is the first of its kind and size to be held in the Honolulu district in more than a decade, a Coast Guard spokesman said."

---

[52] The USS *Lexington* was critically damaged by Japanese forces on May 8, 1942, and scuttled by the U.S. Navy due to the damages.

The Board met from December 11th to the 14th to interview witnesses and take testimony. At this time, the members consisted of Commander Henry Haugen, as recorder and legal counsel for the Board, with parties involved including Rear Admiral James Palmer, of the Seventeenth Coast Guard District; and Captain Donby Mathieu, Chief of the Operations Division, from the same district. *Jarvis* crewmembers included Captain Frederick Wooley, with his legal specialist Commander F. D. Hunter; and LTjg Myron Tethal and Ensign Martin Eger, both represented by legal specialist Commander Christopher Holland. Additional *Jarvis* members testified throughout the three-day hearing.

All sessions of the Board were open to the public, and there was a vast media interest; daily reports were sent to newspapers and television outlets throughout the country.

The report first outlined the initial grounding of the incident and included timelines of the entire phase for both the grounding and near-sinking. Next, the report detailed the backgrounds of the primary participants:

Rear Admiral James Palmer, Commander of the Seventeenth Coast Guard District in Juneau. The Admiral was a 1941 graduate of the U.S. Coast Guard Academy and had an aviation career background. As stated in the BOI: "Admiral Palmer made or was immediately advised and concurred in every significant decision made by the Seventeenth Coast Guard District during this incident."

Captain Donby J. Mathieu, Chief of the Operations Division of the Seventeenth CG District. Donby's career had begun in 1941, with eleven years of sea duty including commanding six CG vessels; but no sea time in the Aleutian Islands. He previously worked at Coast Guard Headquarters in Washington, D.C., as Chief of the Military Readiness Division where his responsibilities included supervision of the pre- commissioning training for the *Jarvis*.

For the USCGC *Jarvis*, the following members testified during the hearing:

Captain Frederick Wooley, the Commanding Officer of the *Jarvis*. Wooley's background included ten years of sailing in the Merchant Marine, during which he served as Master of four vessels in the United

States Lines. Commissioned in 1951, he served on three Coast Guard vessels including as Executive Officer aboard the CGC *Boutwell*; however, he had never sailed in Alaskan waters. As stated in the BOI: "*Jarvis* had earned a reputation as being particularly well-manned, a fact known to both Admiral Palmer and Captain Mathieu."

Lieutenant Junior Grade Myron Tethal was the most senior engineer officer to testify. A 1970 graduate of the Coast Guard Academy, he had been assigned to the *Jarvis* pre-commissioning detail in 1971. With several engineering training courses and details under his belt, Tethal served as the Acting Engineer Officer during the incident due to the approved absence of the assigned Engineer Officer, LCDR George Buffleben. Buffleben did return to Dutch Harbor during rehabilitation efforts.

As for describing the ship repair challenges, LTjg Myron Tethal testified on the fourth day of the hearing about the difficulties encountered in trying to make temporary repairs to the *Jarvis*. As reported in the *Honolulu Star-Bulletin*, Tethal summarized the response issues: Water was sloshing around, fifteen feet deep in the ship's bottom; there were not enough 2-½ inch hoses on the vessel; the location of the deck plates made it difficult to move them to make repairs; there existed a need for quick-release latches on the deck plates. As he stated, "The only way to get at the damage was to lie on the deck plates and feel the hull of the ship by my fingertips."

Chief Warrant Officer (WO3) William Strickland served as the main propulsion assistant and was present at all critical damage control phases during the incident. His career stretched over seventeen years of engineering sea duty, going back to 1949, when he was an enlisted man in the U.S. Navy. During the construction of the *Jarvis*, he worked at the Resident Inspection Office (RIO).

Other members involved with the damage control efforts included ENCS Harold (William) E. Cox, ENCS Charles C. Bateman, DCC Lowell Montgomery, EN1 Eugene F. Wnorowski, EN2 James C. Wimbley, and EN2 Andrew J. Kacsanek III.

Commander Edwin Parker,[53] from the Fourteenth Coast Guard District

---

[53] Edwin Parker retired as captain in 1980 having served thirty years in the Coast Guard. He passed away in March of 2011 on Whidbey Island, Washington.

Engineering Branch, was also called to testify concerning his presence on the ship during the repair efforts at Beaver Inlet. He had arrived on November 18th and remained on board until the ship moored back in Honolulu. Several senior electricians mates accompanied him.

For those on the deck force, serving both on the bridge or on the anchor detail, numerous crewmembers were called to testify:

Lieutenant Ernest (Ernie) Smith was the Operations Officer on board the ship and present on the bridge during the grounding.

Lieutenant Junior Grade Carl Schramm stood the watch immediately preceding the grounding and arrived at the command center soon after the ship went aground.

Fresh out of the Academy, Ensign Martin Eger was the Officer of the Deck (OOD) during the incident and a key participant. Those on watch with him included RD3 Bill Pigman, RD3 John Moran, QM3 Robert Loftin, and BM3 Tim Larson. Chief Boatswains Mate Walter Stanczyk testified as well, having been in charge of the anchor detail on November 15th.

Quartermaster (QM3) Loftin stated his testimony during the BOI:

"The crucial point of my testimony was when I was asked to approach a table with a chart of Dutch Harbor. Then I was asked to take a compass and plot the ranges from landmarks we had logged that would indicate the ship's position in the bay. It was a miracle. The ranges I plotted somehow crossed, not perfectly, but in a small triangle. The plotted position was close to the position we recorded when we dropped anchor on the afternoon of November 14th."

The report continued to clearly outline the purpose and duties for the CGC *Jarvis*, along with information regarding Dutch Harbor:

"The Alaska Law Enforcement Patrol is the subject of an extensive Seventeenth District Operation Order under which the Coast Guard and joint patrols in the North Pacific Ocean and the Bering Sea to fulfill enforcement obligations dictated by statue and several international treaties regarding the conservation of fishery resources. Surveillance is maintained of foreign fishing fleets and the vessels assigned to the patrol are instructed to additionally transit areas of U.S. fishing activities and call at outlying fishing communities to assure domestic interests that enforcement patrols are being conducted.

"CGD17 assigns large patrol areas to the patrol vessel, relying on the Commanding Officer and embarked NMFS agent to develop the best coverage as the situation dictates.

"The *Jarvis*, a Fourteenth Coast Guard District vessel, was assigned by Commander Pacific Area to the Seventeenth Coast Guard District for deployment on the Alaska Patrol during October and November 1972. CGD17 exercised operational control during all periods that the vessel was in Alaskan waters. The Fourteenth District exercised administrative control which includes such things as personnel matters, repairs, and routine engineering support."

Testimony of Captain Wooley

During the hearing, Captain Wooley provided the most crucial information about the grounding. In testimony given on December 13th, Wooley stated that if his orders had been followed properly, his ship "might not have gone on the rocks." His instructions to the OOD on watch were to notify him if there was "a radical change in the weather." He continued in his testimony of being told by old-timers that winds in the area were often "treacherous and sometimes went from ten to 110 knots within fifteen minutes." The local newspaper, *Honolulu Star-Bulletin,* continued his recollection of events during the hearing:

"The *Jarvis* had put into Dutch Harbor because a crew member needed to be taken ashore by the ship's helicopter for oral surgery. The weather had become fierce, visibility was poor, black clouds filled the sky and the winds began rushing down from the mountains with terrific velocity." Wooley said he had been warned about the winds in that area but chose Dutch Harbor to ride out the storm because he had done so once before on this patrol and had found it relatively calm.

"Captain Wooley continued. 'Perhaps someone who'd been there longer would have acted differently. But in my experience, it seemed a good place to ride out a storm. As the day went by it looked less and less like a good place to be. The wind was a high- pitched screaming.' The ship was heeling, and he became apprehensive. After nearly thirty hours on the bridge, he became so tired shortly after midnight that he left orders with the OOD and collapsed on his bunk, still dressed, for a nap."

Regarding anchorage, the BOI further referenced the *Coast Pilot* description of Dutch Harbor as "exposed to the strong winds which may be encountered in the area. Violent williwaws are experienced during gales, especially from the southwest."

The *Coast Pilot* edition published in 2019 references Iliuliuk Bay as "good holding ground," but also mentioned the possibility for "the anchor to drag"; it is unknown if this information was available in 1972:

"Iliuliuk Harbor is small but landlocked with good holding ground and has general depths of 5 to 9 fathoms. There is sufficient room for backing and filling in turning a moderate- sized ship. Violent williwaws are experienced with south gales. Vessels under 200 feet in length have ridden out gales here, but the short scope of chain allowable usually causes the anchor to drag. Because of the limited swinging room, an anchorage in Dutch Harbor or Unalaska Bay is recommended during severe weather."

Captain Wooley further continued his testimony as reported by the *Honolulu Star-Bulletin*:

"At 2:25 a.m. he said he was awakened and informed that 'the OD (officer of the deck) thinks the anchor is dragging.' Wooley said he went immediately to the bridge and was shocked to find the wind registered more than seventy knots on the anemometer. He couldn't see the lights at Dutch Harbor, he said, but the ship seemed out of position and alarmingly close to one of the islands. He ordered the anchor brought up but the anchor detail couldn't raise it; the chain was caught under the ship's bow and straining with the weight. Wooley said he reversed the starboard engine, trying to turn the ship.

"Within seconds, Wooley said, he heard the ship run aground. He ordered both engines on full and steamed out of the shallows, but the ship had a hole through the hull and the engine room started flooding.

"Wooley was asked later by the investigating board, Rear Admiral Joseph McClelland of Seattle and Captain William Tighe of Washington. D. C., whether he had considered cutting loose the anchor, and if not, why not.

"At first, Wooley replied: 'No I didn't think of it. I don't know why,' but later added it would have been dangerous. The chain was under such tension that it would have killed the man who let it out. Later, with the damage patched, the *Jarvis* headed for Honolulu, but in the heavy seas the patch opened and the hole in the ship's bottom became larger. The crew rushed to fill the hole, but water kept pouring in, he said. Soon the engines were completely flooded, and the ship's electrician shut off power. At that point Wooley said he sent out an SOS."

The newspaper story continues:

"Captain Wooley was also asked by the board if he had not received orders to proceed to Honolulu, 2400 miles south immediately after repairs were made, instead of remaining in Alaska for further repairs. Wooley said he had been in close touch with the 17th Coast Guard District Office in Juneau. 'I didn't feel a decision had been made,' he said, 'I felt the district office was waiting for more information from me and that it was up to my discretion when I felt the ship was ready to go to sea. And I didn't think I should depart without an okay from Captain (Donby) Mathieu (district chief of operations, 17th District). My understanding was I had permission to depart when I felt the ship was ready. I had no doubts about my instructions.'"

Commander Floyd Hunter
Legal Counsel for Captain Frederick Wooley

On December 14th, the investigation into the grounding and near loss of the cutter *Jarvis* ended, although completing the final public report took several months. In closing arguments, lawyers for Captain Wooley and the two young junior watch officers made a strong plea that "no negligence was involved in the Aleutian patrol nightmare." Rear Admiral McClelland stated that the report was to go first to Commander Pacific Area in San Francisco, then to the Coast Guard Commandant in Washington D.C.

The *Honolulu Star-Advertiser* reported on the BOI daily. Captain Wooley's attorney, Commander Floyd Dore Hunter, summed up the hearings by declaring that Wooley should be praised for what he did in ensuring that the ship did not sink. As reported on December 15th:

"Hunter said Wooley feels there was no negligence by any watch officers or other crewmen nor was the decision to leave Beaver Inlet for Honolulu a poor or hasty decision. Wooley, Hunter said, felt the ship was seaworthy, that the grounding damage had been patched and the flooding halted sufficiently to allow the ship to return to Sand Island.

"Hunter added that Wooley is a master skipper of unusually solid seagoing experience (he is a former Merchant Marine captain) and that his maneuvering plan to avoid the grounding was sound and proper. Further, He said, Wooley was not critical of the anchor detail which reported that blowing, sleet-filled morning that the anchor was holding.

"Hunter said Wooley was doing what he could to save the situation in the 47 minutes he had in command on the bridge prior to grounding. The moves he made, Hunter said, were the 'hazards of the profession.' Hunter said the skipper—Captain Frederick O. Wooley—could only be found negligent if the absolute standard were applied that he was responsible because he was there and in command when it happened.

"The *Jarvis* grounded, the captain's lawyer suggested, in large part due to the unpredictable Alaskan weather. Attorney Hunter said the captain lacked adequate weather briefing from Coast Guard officials in Alaska. The attorney said efforts should be made to provide ship commanders—especially those without extensive experience in Alaskan waters—with maximum weather and sea information."

Hunter himself had been a commanding officer of two ships, most notably the CGC *Confidence* in Kodiak, Alaska, which had received several commendations. While on active duty, Hunter earned his law degree from the George Washington University Law School in Washington, D.C. He served as a District Legal Officer for two different CG districts.[54]

Board of Investigation

The BOI further discussed an annual Alaska Patrol Conference, which is attended by the commanding officers and other key officers from patrol cutters, to assist with educating them on the Alaska Patrol. Since *Jarvis* was not yet fully operational at the time of the conference, a representative from the ship was not sent.

The remainder of the findings section of approximately eighteen pages, summarized the events leading up to the grounding and listed the ship's damages. As stated in the BOI:

"A recapitulation of damages to the *Jarvis* as a result of this casualty is as follows:

• Sonar dome and transducers sheared off as a result of the grounding.

• Pit log sword arm bent forward and to port.

• Minor flooding in forward magazine above sonar dome cover. No residual damage. The four starboard propeller blades were curled and otherwise moderately damaged. Hull puncture at frame 241, starboard, longitudinal number 9.

• Hull scrapes, gouges, and slight indentations from frame 150 to frame 244, starboard side, requiring no more than one shell plate renewal.

---

[54] Hunter retired in 1976 from the Coast Guard and went into private practice in Boston, Massachusetts. He passed away in December of 2017.

• Flooding of engine room and adjacent pump room to a level of 15 feet above base line with salt water immersion of all machinery to this level.

"Repair costs for the hull repairs, sonar replacement, transducer repairs, turbine overhaul, and propeller repairs are estimated at under $400,000. The costliest item is the turbine overhaul which is necessitated by submergence in salt water. All other damage costs are attributable to the initial grounding."

Opinions of the Board

The latter part of the BOI outlined the opinions of the Board regarding lessons learned of the incident. These included:

1. The basic cause of the initial grounding was high winds experienced in Iliuliuk Bay on 15 November. The anchor commenced dragging rapidly a few minutes before 0215 (2:15 a.m.) when there were frequent gusts to 45 knots. By the time the position was accurately determined at 0225 (2:25 a.m.)[55] and Captain Wooley called, the *Jarvis* was in an extremely precarious position. By 0230 (2:30 am), *Jarvis* had dragged to the edge of the flat 16-18 fathom anchorage area and did not move significantly thereafter until the anchor was aweigh at approximately 0305 (3:05 a.m.). Since it was not recognized that the anchor was aweigh, there was little or no way on and *Jarvis* was driven by the wind into shoal water from which she could not escape unscathed. Captain Wooley's decision to attempt to back clear after he realized that the anchor was aweigh was a proper decision. Under the circumstances, however, the correct course of action would have been to slip anchor at an earlier moment, relying on the weak link at the bitter end of the chain to part.

---

[55] Years later, Robert Loftin would comment: "For the board to say I failed to get accurate radar ranges does not correctly describe what transpired. We were able to check our position with radar for the first hour or so of the watch. Keep in mind when getting a fix even with radar, the ship is moving in the wind. This is why my last good fix formed a triangle. A small triangle is still considered a good and reasonable fix on a large-scale chart we used for Dutch Harbor. We called the captain after the wind speed got to the point the radar was useless. Given the darkness and the weather, we depended on radar to assess whether or not we were dragging anchor."

2. A greater adherence to standard procedures might well have prevent the grounding: Thus:

a. An anchor buoy had not been streamed. Its presence may well have led Captain Wooley to consider slipping anchor or signaled that the anchor was aweigh.

b. The anchor chain was not hosed off as it was brought in. The inability to see chain markings because of mud was a material factor in the failure to determine when the anchor was aweigh.

c. The PA system was not utilized nor the full bridge and CIC watch set. As a result, accurate independent navigational data was not available to the Commanding Officer. An experienced officer was not on the wing of the bridge where he may have quickly determined that the anchor was in fact tending to port. The Commanding Officer was not free from immediate navigational, reporting, and conning duties so as to be free to reflect on alternative courses of action such as slipping anchor. [56]

d. Anchorage ranges were not established in CIC for the watchstanders and no routine position reports were required. No fix was obtained by CIC during the critical one-hour period preceding the grounding and no sufficiently accurate information was at hand to determine if dragging had occurred.

e. A definitive system of anchor range and bearing checks was not established. This could have been accomplished by positive markings on the chart to indicate the original position of anchorage with subsequent position checks plotted on an overlay, marking of the shoreline on the radar scope, or establishment of positive visual and

---

[56] On reflection later, Robert Loftin would remark: "It may be the case that Captain Wooley was carrying too much of the load, but look at the time line on the night of Nov. 15th. The time from when we got underway from Dutch Harbor until the time the MAYDAY went out was eight or nine hours. I think the captain was on the bridge all of that time. There was so much tension, I could see why he might not have felt comfortable giving the CONN to another officer. What officer had more sea time than him? Most of the younger officers were only LTjgs or ensigns. Mr. Smith, the navigator and operations officer, was the only LT, but he had come up as a radioman.

When you consider the quantity and quality of experience in the wardroom, to whom could Captain Wooley turn? This is not to say they were bad officers. It's just that the situation was so scary and outside the norm. It's as if we were in a fire fight. If you're in charge of a rifle company, are you going to take yourself off the line if you're stressed out?"

radar targets for check purposes. As it was, each watchstander on the bridge and in CIC made his own decision, erased all previous work, and destroyed any opportunity to quickly establish that dragging had occurred. Particularly disturbing was the concentration of two OODs on a check range to a single radar target which would not reveal movement of the ship to the north and toward the reef.

3. Damage control steps taken after the grounding were proper and to the limit of on- board capabilities. The patch remained tight and the fracture did not enlarge, the increased flooding of the engine room being due to the working of the hull in a seaway.

4. The conditions under which the authorization for *Jarvis* to depart had been granted by Admiral Palmer and Captain Mathieu were proper and were clearly understood by Captain Wooley. As pertinent, this authorization depended on the adequacy of the patch, a matter solely within the province of the *Jarvis*.

5. The decision to leave sheltered waters was erroneous and the responsibility therefore must rest with Captain Wooley. A flooding rate of 150-gallons per minute which required two submersible pumps to control is not indicative of an adequate patch in such a vital space. The correct decision would have been to bring in divers and install a cofferdam patch as was done thereafter. There were many disadvantages to remaining in Dutch Harbor—intense storms, lack of full protection from the weather, lack of repair facilities, necessity of mounting an extensive airlift operation, etc. But the fact remains that a poor position was traded for a worse one.

6. The increase in flooding at 1630 (4:30 p.m.), which necessitated the use of a third submersible pump, coincided with the first contact with the open sea and was a clear indication that the patch was inadequate. It was an error not to recognize the significance of this signal and to immediately return to shelter.

7. The major increase in flooding at 1800 (6:00 p.m.) was due to the working of the hull in the heavy seas encountered. Captain Wooley's decision not to risk capsizing by coming about and to instead seek the relative calm off the continental shelf was a reasonable one under the circumstances.

8. In theory, the flooding at 1800 (6:00 p.m.) was capable of being controlled by available equipment. For a considerable period of time, the situation was in a precarious balance by the loss of the fire pumps at 1848 (6:48 p.m.) meant the loss of three eductors and the condition deteriorated rapidly thereafter. Though dewatering efforts continued, the engine room flooded to the thirteen-foot level in little more time than would be expected under free flooding conditions. This casualty illustrates the extreme vulnerability of the 378' class vessel to a minor hull rupture in the engine room. If the rupture had been but a few feet away, it would have been inaccessible for patching. Flooding in any other compartment will not seriously cripple the ship. The Board recognized that it is not feasible to effect major changes in this respect and the specific recommendations generated are somewhat minor in nature and will serve only to alleviate damage from relatively minor flooding but will not protect against disablement in the event of a major rupture. An increased effective dewatering capability in the engine room may well have averted flooding of the engine room. It is further the opinion of the Board that working of the hull in a seaway on this class of vessel makes reliance on an interior patch to control flooding unwise.

9. The response by the *Koyo Maru No. 3* to the *Jarvis* SOS call was timely, effective, and in the highest tradition of the sea. The tow was accomplished in a very smart and seamanlike manner and her continued presence on the scene at Beaver Inlet, while awaiting the arrival of other Coast Guard vessels was a gracious act. Also commendable is the response of the *Haruna Maru* to assure that the tow had been successfully undertaken.

10. The conduct of the officers and crew of the *Jarvis* during the damage control and rehabilitation efforts showed a high degree of

effort and esprit. The response by all Coast Guard and Navy units involved in both the SAR phase and rehabilitation phase of this incident was outstanding. The repairs to the hull and rejuvenation of the engine room in Dutch Harbor was a major accomplishment.

11. Adequate information as to weather and local conditions was available to the *Jarvis*. It is concluded that the absence of the vessel's representatives from the ALPAT conference and the lack of a detailed individual briefing by CGD17 had no bearing on this casualty. At the same time, ALPAT briefings and conferences are highly desirable if not for any other reason than allowing commanding officers to trade experiences in these difficult waters.

12. The radar antenna drive mechanism for the S-51A radar on the *Jarvis* is inadequate. The antenna must be capable of rotation in winds in excess of 45 knots without constant adjustment by a technician. No other equipment malfunction requiring correction was noted.

Recommendations by the Board

The Board of Investigation report finished with a listing of errors committed by individuals from the command and the crew, noting that the mistakes were mostly errors of judgment and not violations of the UCMJ. The Board's stiffest recommendation came against Captain Wooley: "The opinion that his errors which contributed to the casualty were ones of judgment and do NOT amount to a negligent hazarding of a vessel; dereliction in the performance of duty; a failure to obey Coast Guard Regulations nor any other offense under the UCMJ." Under recommendations, the Board further recommended that he be "awarded a non-punitive letter of censure and that he be relieved of command."

Jarvis ship recommendations were also put forth:

"That utmost consideration be given in design criteria for future Coast Guard vessels to require a double hull in a single engine room space.

"That SPS-51A radar antenna drive system on the 378' class be improved to provide reliable automatic rotation in high winds.

"That a watertight door be installed at Bulkhead 202-½ to protect the forward pump room.

"That the following changes of an engineering/damage control nature be thoroughly reviewed for possible implementation on 378' class vessels: 1) Add 600 pounds of quick-drying cement to damage control allowance lists, and 2) An improved dewatering capability for the engine room be realized."

The report with recommendations was forwarded through the chain of command to Coast Guard Headquarters, where the Commandant would now finalize and approve the findings and recommendations of the BOI.

April 1973
Honolulu, Hawaii

As of April 27th, the official report on the Coast Guard *Jarvis* grounding was still pending release to the public. The *Honolulu Star-Bulletin* publicly asked: "One wonders if and when Coast Guard Headquarters in Washington will make public the recommendations of its board on the inquiry into the grounding of the cutter *Jarvis* at Dutch Harbor Nov. 15." The article further stated that Captain Wooley of Mililani was presently on temporary duty at Coast Guard headquarters and the repaired *Jarvis* itself on Ocean Station November between Honolulu and San Francisco. "Lawyers for both Wooley and Eger made a pitch that the board of inquiry find no one at fault for the grounding. Wooley is close to mandatory retirement," quoted the newspaper.

Official Report
Board of Investigation

The official report from Admiral Whalen of the Convening Authority was released in March of 1973 with minimal changes to the recommendations, except regarding Captain Wooley. While initially the recommendation was for non-punitive action for Captain Wooley, modification to the BOI resulted in a more severe reprimand of the issuance of a punitive letter, a decision upheld later in June of 1973 by the Coast Guard's acting Commandant, Vice Admiral T. R. Sargent.[57] Vice Admiral Mark Whalen, Pacific area commander, was quoted in the *Honolulu Star-Advertiser* on the Board's findings:

Coast Guard boss upholds action against Jarvis skipper

By BRUCE DUNFIN
Advertiser Staff Writer

Article from the *Honolulu Advertiser,* dated January 1973.

"'From an operational viewpoint, it is apparent that the basic causes of grounding were high winds, failure to follow standard procedures and improper maneuvering of the vessel during the process of weighing anchor. It is impossible to ascribe a particular event or procedure as the significant contributing factor but for which the grounding would not have occurred.' He would add, 'These failures do not reflect credit on basic procedures in effect on board the *Jarvis* at least during the day and night preceding the grounding of the vessel.'"

Other non-punitive actions recommended in the original BOI toward other *Jarvis* crewmembers were upheld.

---

[57] The primary difference between punitive and non-punitive actions is that the punitive becomes a permanent record in the member's official record, while non-punitive is kept between the person and his command.

Chapter 12

THE *JARVIS'S* FUTURE

"Without argument, the most significant historical event, which ever took place on the *Jarvis* was in November 1972, when 170 officers and enlisted men united and prevented the most serious loss of life and property in the history of the Coast Guard. People, who were not there don't realize how close the *Jarvis* was to sinking in icy waters off the Aleutian Islands. In the newspaper articles published in Honolulu, when the *Jarvis* returned from Alaska, crew members were quoted regarding the lack of fear. Things were happening too quickly to even think of fear because we all knew what had to be done to save the *Jarvis*."
—*Dan Edwards,* The Wake Behind Us

Change of Command
May 11, 1973

WITH COMMANDER WHITE acting as the Commanding Officer (CO) of the Coast Guard Cutter *Jarvis* during Captain Wooley's absence, the Coast Guard took the step of appointing Captain Bob Hollingsworth as the next CO.

Once notified he was to be the new CO, Commander Hollingsworth asked for a copy of the official Board of Investigation from the District Legal Office. The report was not yet completed; Hollingsworth insisted he would like a copy in advance because, "I gotta know what I am getting into." With his request, the BOI was completed and released shortly before he was officially sworn in as the next CO. His next question was, "Who am I relieving?"— which was met with glazed eyes. "We'll get back to you," was the response. Soon, the answer came back: "You will be relieving Captain Frederick Wooley."

UNITED STATES COAST GUARD CUTTER

JARVIS
WHEC-725

Change of Command

Monday, 11 June 1973
Honolulu, Hawaii

The *Jarvis* "Change of Command" ceremony
program. June 11, 1973.

On May 11, 1973, a large gathering arrived at CG Base Honolulu for the
official change of command.

For those crewmembers from the original crew, there was some sadness
as they were saying good-bye to their captain and friend. As crewmember
Dan Edwards commented, "There wasn't dry eye aboard that day from those
of who were there from day one."

After he was sworn in, Commander Bob Hollingsworth became the second official Commanding Officer of the Coast Guard Cutter *Jarvis*, a title
he would hold for two years until his departure in 1975. On July 1, 1973,

Captain Frederick O. Wooley, the first Commanding Officer of the Coast Guard Cutter *Jarvis*, was officially retired.

Deep selected for captain[58] with this promotion to take place thirteen months after assuming command of *Jarvis*, Commander Hollingsworth hit the road running, not wanting to fall into the same pitfalls as Captain Wooley had unfortunately encountered. He read the official BOI report from cover to cover and became quite familiar with the *Coast Pilot*, which had described the anchorage area where the *Jarvis* had gone aground as "poor holding ground," with an area subject to winds from the southwest. The *Coast Pilot* is updated annually and is the primary document to supplement nautical charts of the waters of the United States.

Hollingsworth's observations of the incident and the personnel were well known within the Coast Guard: the grounding was the result of not a single mistake but of a series of events, from errors by an inexperienced crew on watch to equipment failures, all of which initiated by extreme harsh weather conditions. The ensign on the bridge had just four months of experience, having come straight from the academy. The reasons he delayed in notifying the captain will never be known. Perhaps he did not want to interrupt the captain's much-needed rest or maybe he was overly confident in his abilities. The crew had a reputation as a well-trained group, highly competent, with excellent leadership. The captain was well-loved by the men and believed in "Do what's right, follow your gut."

Honolulu, Hawaii
December 1972

In the early morning of December 14, 1972, a young nineteen-year old straight out of Storekeeper school, reported aboard the CGC *Jarvis*, currently in the dry dock at Dillingham Shipyard in Honolulu. Walking aboard the gangway and saluting the colors, SASK Marvin Pugh was excited for the opportunity to serve on his first ship in the Coast Guard. Once aboard, the

---

[58] Officers who do exceptionally well with their jobs may be selected for "deep selection." These personnel are promoted ahead of their class.

Quarter Master of the Watch (QMOW) greeted the young man and piped the Officer of the Day (OOD), Boatswains Mate First Class (BM1) Charlie Greene, to the quarterdeck.

Dressed in a chambray uniform and "Dixie" cup hat, BM1 Greene walked out of the open hangar bay to greet the young man. Dark haired with a mustache and standing about 6'3'', coupled with broad shoulders and physically fit, thirty-year-old Greene struck an imposing figure to the new crewmember. "Leave your sea bag and follow me" he was ordered. Without much conversation except for a few cautionary words regarding on where to walk, or where not to strike his head, they crossed over the brow, down the scaffolding stairs to the dry-dock floor, and under the fantail, then proceeded to the starboard side aft.

Greene stopped and turned toward Pugh, stating, "If you remember nothing else about today, remember this. Look up; what do you see?" Pugh observed extensive scaffolding engulfing the *Jarvis*, and repair work well underway. Being hesitant and not wanting to sound ignorant, he wasn't quite sure how to answer the OOD. "It looks like a giant scar running down the length of the ship with openings every so often and people working on it," he responded.

"That's right," Greene said, while both men stared at the huge dent running on the underside of the hull. "This damage occurred when we struck a reef in Alaska."

Greene faced the new crewmember, and then solemnly said, "Despite the circumstances, no one died. Remember that. *No one died.* That was because the ship was saved because her crew knew their job and they knew it well." Pausing, he continued, "As a new crewmember, it's your job to learn it and to learn it well. Failure to do so could cost you and your shipmates their lives. It is my job and yours, to make sure that doesn't ever happen."

Over the years since, this conversation was often repeated, not only to new members of the *Jarvis* but to other commands and Coast Guard classrooms as well. The lessons of the *Jarvis* grounding served not only to highlight the extreme dangers of the Alaskan waters, but also to illustrate the leadership, commitment, and heroic actions of a well-trained crew that saved a ship that fateful week in November 1972.

Decommissioning and Sale
October 2012

On October 2, 2012, at 10:00 a.m., the Coast Guard Cutter *Jarvis*, having served over forty years of service, was decommissioned at the Coast Guard Base Honolulu. Captain Richard Mourey, assigned as the Commanding Officer in July of the same year, was the last to command the vessel. The official Coast Guard party was in full dress whites, while the rest of the military attendees wore the tropical blue uniform. Many guests had been invited, including all former crewmembers. Close to thirty-five of the original "plankowner" members, many who were aboard the ship during the grounding, attended as well.

Richard Brunke, the former BM3 who retired as a commander in 2004, was in attendance and was surprised that the ceremony was more emotional than he had expected. There he met his old *Jarvis* shipmates, who reminisced and told stories about the grounding of which he had not been aware. "While we all stood at attention while 'Taps' was being played and the lowering of the U.S. flag, I began to tear up as if I were putting to rest one of my best friends," he would later recall. "It was not until that moment that I realized just how proud I was of my fellow shipmates, as we battled together to not only save *Jarvis* but ourselves as well. This will remain one of my greatest 'sea stories' of my career."

Others in attendance included the future Commandant of the Coast Guard, Admiral Paul Zukunft (affectionally known to the troops as "Admiral Z"), Admiral James Rendon, Admiral Richard Houck (former XO of the *Jarvis*), and Admiral Joseph McClellan.

Captain Richard Mourey presented his final comments as Commanding Officer of the Coast Guard Cutter *Jarvis*:

"Good morning Admiral Zukunft, Admiral Rendon, Admiral Houck, Admiral McClellan, past crewmembers, distinguished guests, friends, and family of *Jarvis*. What a fine morning it is to honor this great ship and all the members who served aboard her during forty years of dedication to the Coast Guard and the Nation. It is true…we are letting go of this honorable vessel that has carried crews through calm seas and through raging storms. She has brought us home safely time and again in defiance of the sea whose character is to find the weakness of all ships and exploit it. Yet, while we are losing a ship, we are retaining the spirit of the crew, the spirit of the Coast Guard.

"We have a proud crew. You can tell by the way they pitch in together to get things done. You can see it when they hustle to man their stations. You can hear it in the positive pitch of their responses to the most technical or the simplest of questions. I could tell within days of reporting aboard that this would be a great tour.

"A ship can accomplish anything with a proud crew. The spirit of all ships resides in the hearts of the crew, no matter where they go. Even knowing the ship is not long for service, the crew continues to demonstrate their pride in *Jarvis* in every way. The condition of the ship is a reflection of how the crew feels about themselves. Admiral Zukunft mentioned during his last visit that it looks like this ship has some life left in her and I give all the credit for this observation to the crew.

"The magic that has kept these ships deploying through four decades of service is that there is no magic at all. Successful deployments can be measured in the sweat pouring forth from hard working crews. *Jarvis* is no exception and the crew worked hard to prepare for her final cruise to work for Coast Guard District Fourteen to protect our home waters, the Hawaiian Islands. They also demonstrated great pride by putting forth a magnificent effort to prepare her for today's ceremony following our return home only seventeen days ago. I present to you, the current crew of Coast Guard Cutter *Jarvis*. Please give them a round of applause.

"In the last few months, I have had a wonderful opportunity to communicate with past crewmembers who over the decades of the ship's service earned Meritorious Unit Commendation Medals in 1976, 1983, 1988, and 2003 and a Unit Commendation Medal in 2005. They have been chomping at the bit to come back to see the ship, to tell their stories, and to demonstrate pride in the ship. It is no wonder today's *Jarvis* crew has such an indomitable spirit. This most important ingredient to success has been passed down from crew to crew over the years. The proof of that spirit is in the audience today. Fifty-five former *Jarvis* crewmembers, including two Commanding

Officers and two Executive Officers, and twenty-one members of the original crew traveled from all over the country to remember the ship and their time aboard! Please give them a round of applause.

"Of the past members of the crew, the one we've had the most contact with is the 11th Master Chief Gunner's Mate of the Coast Guard, Mr. Jack Hunter. Jack has been the rock, the foundation, and our main link to the past crew. Within every crew you have your stars. Jack is that star among the more than 2,000 people who served aboard *Jarvis* since 1972. Jack, please stand up, you deserve recognition.

"As we headed for home during our last cruise, I asked Jack for a bit of the history of *Jarvis*, and he reached out to the crew. I want to thank the following members in the audience today for their submissions: CAPT Peter Knight, USCG (ret); CDR Richard Brunke, USCG (ret); Mr. Dan Edwards, RDC Art Garcia, USCG (ret); and Mr. Ted Turner. Additionally, I want to thank Ms. Heather Bacon-Shone, Mr. Bob Loftin, Mr. Jerry Sandors, Ms. Pam Brown, Mr. Barry Lichtman, and CWO Bob Frank who were unable to be here today. Their personal stories demonstrate the great character of these individuals as members of the Coast Guard and of *Jarvis*. There are so many good stories that I've struggled over the fact that I can't do them justice here today, so we've placed them in a binder along with copies of the unit awards for everyone to read at the reception before we send them on to the Coast Guard Historian.

"Commander Richard Brunke sent the largest collection of pictures, news articles, and mementos from his first tour in the Coast Guard aboard *Jarvis*. The commissioning program he saved touts *Jarvis* as a 'Jet-Powered' High Endurance Cutter due to her twin Gas-Turbine Engines providing 36,000 horsepower. The pictures tell us that Anna *Jarvis*, the daughter of Captain David *Jarvis*, for whom the ship is named, attended the commissioning ceremony which must have been very inspiring.

"For those who are not familiar with the story, Captain Jarvis, as a first lieutenant in the winter of 1897, while assigned to Revenue Cutter *Bear*, led a famous expedition across 1,500 miles of Arctic ice and snow to save 300 starving whalers stranded North of Barrow Point, Alaska. The link between Captain Jarvis and his namesake remains strong. You see, Seaman Brunke was in the presence of Captain Jarvis's daughter at the commissioning and before he retired, he served as the Executive Officer aboard Cutter *Munro* and led a young officer assigned there named Lauren Dufrene. Lieutenant Dufrene stands before you today as the Engineer Officer of Coast Guard Cutter *Jarvis*. Commander Brunke's wonderful collection is also available for everyone to see at the reception.

"[Radarman Chief] RDC Art Garcia sent in a story about *Jarvis's* unexpected deployment from the South Pacific to Alaska after the 1989 grounding of the *Exxon Valdez*. [Commander] CDR Howard, the XO, had command while CAPT Busick remained in Honolulu to testify for a drug seizure by the ship. *Jarvis* received the call in Guam to divert to Alaska which set the crew into emergency mode to send requests home for the one thing they had none of...cold weather clothing! Three weeks later after a slow steam to conserve fuel which led to some thinning food supplies and the consumption of a fair amount of peanut butter by the crew, CAPT Busick met *Jarvis* in Adak and resumed command for a completely different kind of patrol than they started. Demonstrating amazing adaptability, the crew completed an Alaska Patrol and seized a Russian trawler illegally fishing in U.S. waters before heading home to Honolulu.

"I've saved the biggest story for last. In comments provided by Mr. Dan Edwards and in newspaper stories in CDR Brunke's compilation is the story of the most significant case the *Jarvis* ever experienced, the near loss of the ship itself after grounding in terrible winds and frigid seas on their first Alaskan Patrol near Dutch Harbor in November of 1972. This story hits close to home for me, because I've been aboard a ship of this class in Dutch Harbor in hurricane strength storms before.

"The weather in Alaska is very unforgiving; especially in the month of November as low-pressure systems roll one after the other across the Bering Sea from Siberia. The crew's determination and courage were tested not once, but twice. After the grounding, the crew effected repairs in the harbor and then set sail to return to Honolulu. Only fifty miles into the transit, the bridge again sounded General Emergency, flooding in the engine room! Dan recalls manning a P-250 pump with ST3 Donaldson on the starboard side amidship, watching the ship roll from side to side and seeing how close the waterline was to the main deck. He also remembers taking food below decks to the teams in the Engine Room...in his words, 'You didn't have to ask anyone about how serious it was, it reflected in their faces.'

"The plight of the *Jarvis* made national news. Without the heroic efforts of the damage control teams who saved *Jarvis*, she and her crews would not have gone on to serve for the next forty years and we would not be having this ceremony today. Let's again please recognize the twenty-one members of that first crew here today.

"Before we close, I believe it's important to recognize that *Jarvis* could not have accomplished so much and been of such great service to the Nation without operational and supporting partners and friends, many of whom are represented here today. It goes without saying that our Operational Commander's staff at Pacific Area, based in Alameda, CA, has helped *Jarvis* overcome innumerable obstacles over the years—thank you Admiral Zukunft. Having our home base in Hawaii, we have worked many times for and always maintained an outstanding relationship with Coast Guard District Fourteen represented here today by their Chief of Staff—thank you Captain Merrie Austin, and a former District Commander—thank you Admiral McClelland. I have to believe that nearly all the *Jarvis* helicopter detachments and C-130 flights must have come from Air Station Barbers Point—thank you Captain Tim Gilbride. *Jarvis* has worked with Coast Guard Sector Honolulu countless times over the years – thank you Captain Joanna Nunan[59] for your partnership and friendship. Our crews would not have been capable of accomplishing all their missions without the fine support of Coast Guard Base Honolulu—thank you Captain Jim Koermer. It is very fitting to thank our friends at the Navy League who have helped us so many times over the years and enabled us to have the reception following this ceremony today—thank you Mr. Bob McDermott.

"Finally, an important note about our home, Hawaii. *Jarvis* is one of the rare ships in the Coast Guard that has spent her entire commissioned service based in one place, right here in Honolulu. The

---

[59] Captain Nunan would later preside over this author's retirement ceremony in Honolulu.

people of Hawaii have helped our Coast Guard crews to feel welcome, to be a part of the community. Representing the State of Hawaii, we have with us today Mr. Walter Kaneakua, Senator Inouye's Executive Assistant for Military and Veteran Affairs; Mr. Mike Kitamura, Senator Akaka's State Director; Mr. Kamakana Kaimuloa representing Congresswoman Hanabusa; and Mrs. Lauren Montez representing Congresswoman Hirono. Please accept my humble expression of gratitude on behalf of all our crewmembers over the years, *Mahalo Nui Loa.*

"Because Coast Guard crews have invested so much pride in her, it will be sad to see *Jarvis* go. Yet, the spirit of *Jarvis* will live on, as we will bring our crew back to Hawaii aboard Cutter *Morgentheau* to continue in the great tradition of success set forth by the crews of the Coast Guard Cutter *Jarvis.*"

EPILOGUE

T HE SHIP WOULD, for years, continue to be haunted by "gremlins,"
problems that would pop-up notably with electronic connections that
hadn't been cleaned thoroughly and later deteriorated. "The ship was never
the same, not just the vessel, but the crew too as tour rotations had already
begun," as LTjg Rick Sasse recalled later.

Captain Richard Mourey, the last Commanding Officer of the *Jarvis*, relayed the story of the *Jarvis's* trip to Los Angeles/Long Beach to swap out
the crews with USCGC *Morgenthau*. Just twenty-four hours into the journey, the Engineer Officer called the captain down to the engine room, something she usually wouldn't do unless there was an important issue. Mourey
would further explain:

> "Sure enough, she took me to a quarter-sized hole at the base of the
> hull behind the starboard main diesel engine. Everything was under
> control. They'd used a wooden plug to fill the hole and had already
> sawed it off flush with the deck. Still, I wasn't inclined to cross 2,000
> miles of open water without doing a full assessment and repair, so I
> turned us around and headed back to Honolulu. The engineering
> team did a bang-up job contracting a repair but as I recall this allowed
> us to unexpectedly be at home for Thanksgiving with our families.
> After the repair, we headed out to Los Angeles."

Pretty amazing when you consider the patch had been in place for close
to forty years!

Awards

Despite some push for official recognition of the crewmembers, there were only a few who received official recognition for their efforts; but, as the Executive Officer, Commander White had stated to junior officers, "You don't get an award for almost sinking a ship." A consensus from some of the former crewmembers was that they were "just doing our job," that it was their responsibility as a crew to save the ship. One crewmember summed up his feelings:

> "Stan, Mike, Joel, and the others well deserved the recognition they received because they were fighting this battle on the front lines… they were doing things the rest of us had no idea about until it was all over. But the rest of us, who were part of the support staff, on the second line of defense were all forgotten."

Still, there was some resentment from those who did not receive anything. One crewmember remembers working twelve-hour shifts in the "elephant snot," with very little sleep and extremely cold conditions, and yet was not recognized—an experience shared by others as well. As their careers extended over the years, many would observe lesser achievements receiving recognition, while theirs on *Jarvis* never did. As one crewmember stated: "Heck, we saved a ship. We should have received something." There was no long-term bitterness, just a reluctance to accept things as they were.

Despite the heroism and dangerous rescue efforts of the C-130 pilots and flight crews, no known awards were issued to this group. As pilot Chuck Hughes later stated: "No rewards—that was back in the day that awards were hardly ever handed out. The rationale was that we were just doing our job."

Those known to have received awards included Chief Warrant Officer Third Class (ENG) William Strickland, Damage Control Chief Lowell Montgomery, Chief Boatswains Mate Chief "Stan" Stanczyk, Seaman Joel Cortez, Seaman Travis Deleon, Sonar Technician Third Class Mike Large, and Boatswain's Mate Third Class Mike Campbell. Considering the awards issued, it is most likely Strickland, Montgomery, Cortez, and Deleon received awards for their work in the engine room, while Chief Stanczyk received an award for his deck leadership. Sonar Technician Third Class Mike Large received a Commendation Medal for his work as a diver in the engine

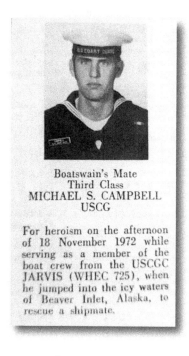

Boatswain's Mate
Third Class
MICHAEL S. CAMPBELL
USCG

For heroism on the afternoon
of 18 November 1972 while
serving as a member of the
boat crew from the USCGC
JARVIS (WHEC 725), when
he jumped into the icy waters
of Beaver Inlet, Alaska, to
rescue a shipmate.

Notice of Boatswain's Mate Third Class Michael Campbell's commendation and the Coast Guard medal he received for his actions aboard the Jarvis.

room. Large's participation as a diver was noteworthy; the Navy divers later stated in Commander White's award recommendation that "they would only do the same in an extreme emergency situation."

Additionally, BW3 Campbell received the Coast Guard Medal for rescuing a fellow crewmember who had fallen into the freezing water while at dockside in Dutch Harbor.

One award letter issued read in part:

"Letter of Commendation Dated Sept 20, 1973
"On 15 November 1972, while on Alaska Fisheries Law Enforcement Patrol, *Jarvis* ran aground in Unalaska, Alaska, and flooded her engine room. After effecting a temporary patch where the hull was penetrated, *Jarvis* attempted to return to her home port in Honolulu, Hawaii.

"However, working of the ship in heavy seas caused a reflooding of the engine room. This caused *Jarvis* to drift helplessly toward a rock shore without power in complete darkness, heavy seas, strong, gusty winds, freezing temperatures, and snow squalls. following a perilous period of twelve hours, *Jarvis* was rescued by the Japanese vessel *Koyo Maru* and towed to safe anchorage at Dutch Harbor, Alaska. There, the monumental task of cleaning and restoring all machinery and life support systems to an operable condition was accomplished in an orderly and expeditious manner.

"During this critical period, you displayed a high degree of professionalism, leadership, proficiency, and versatility in supervising and receiving operations of urgently needed voluminous salvage material and equipment received by sea or dropped by air aboard *Jarvis*; thus *Jarvis* recovered from her ordeal and was eventually restored to full operational status."

—*Signed: W. L. Morrison, Rear Admiral, U.S. Coast Guard*
Commander, Fourteenth Coast Guard District

The last known awards were presented to LT John Huddleston and LT Wolfe, the two helo pilots aboard HH-52A 1383, for their efforts to save the helicopter and for shuttling supplies to *Jarvis*.

Coast Guard Cutter *Jarvis*

The ship was transferred from the United States to the Bangladesh navy under the Excess Defense Articles program; a two-year-long process by which foreign allies of the United States receive notification of the ship's availability. Those countries submitting bids must have national defense objectives that align with the United States; they must also have the ability to support the vessel itself, not only with logistics but a trained crew as well. The *Jarvis* transfer was one of twelve high-endurance cutters the Coast Guard replaced with new vessels. Previously the Coast Guard had transferred two of the high-endurance ships to the Philippines and another to Nigeria.

In December 2012, Coast Guard crews were swapped out between the CGC *Jarvis* and the CGC *Morgenthau* while moored in San Pedro, Califor-

Program from the official transfer ceremony of the *Jarvis* to the Bangladesh navy. May 23, 2013.

nia. The status of *Jarvis* was changed to "in-commission special," while, beginning in March 2013, the new crew from the Bangladesh navy, trained on the ship. Petty Officer 3rd Class Perry Summers relayed how the training was divided into departments: "The engineers would learn the mechanics, damage controlmen would learn the systems, and the electricians would learn the ship electronics."

The cooperation and expertise of the *Jarvis* crewmembers were appreciated by the Bangladesh personnel. First Class Petty Officer Nura Alam of the respective service, praised the Coast Guard as "the best organization in the world." He would further summarize his feelings, reflected by others as well:

"There is a bond the *Jarvis* crew has, from command level to the junior level. The bond they have for each other is absolutely brilliant and friendly. There are high and low levels of bonding. *Jarvis* crew has the maximum. Everyone works together to get the job done."

The Coast Guard Cutter *Jarvis* was formally transferred to the Bangladesh navy on May 23, 2013, at a formal ceremony at Coast Guard Island, Alameda, California. Renamed the *Somudra Joy*, which translates as "Victory at Sea," the vessel is the now the largest ship in the Bangladesh navy. This handover marked the first transfer of a large warship from the United States to Bangladesh.

Captain Gregory Burg, commanding officer of the *Jarvis* during the "in-commission special" period, would hand the ship's hour glass to the Bangladeshi captain. At the formal ceremony at the Coast Guard base in Alameda, several dozen members of the crew stood at attention along the rails of the ship with American and Coast Guard flags and pennants flying. It would be the last time a U.S. crew would man the vessel. In attendance at the ceremony was the future Commandant of the Coast Guard, Vice Admiral Paul Zukunft[60] who stated in reference to the ship: "I can't count the number of lives saved, the thousands of metric tons of contraband confiscated." This does not take into account the invaluable service *Jarvis* contributed to the Alaska fishery patrols.

It was a poignant moment for Captain Burg. After passing the hour glass to the new captain, Burg dismissed the *Jarvis* crewmembers and was suddenly caught up in emotion. As he described:

"I was unexpectedly caught with emotion and really fought to maintain composure. Just the whole sight, no Coast Guardsmen aboard, no flags, it was just more than I expected. Though I had only been the *Jarvis* CO for a few months, I'm a huge fan of the 378s in general I guess I should have expected it, but it just was the moment in time…*Jarvis* wasn't ours anymore."

---

[60] The 25th Commandant of the U.S. Coast Guard, 2014-2018.

BNS *Somudra Joy*. Photo courtesy Jack Hunter.

The BNS *Somudra Joy* departed Alameda for its home port of Chittagong, a city of over 2.5 million, in October 2013 and arrived December 12th. Captain Mohammad Nazmul Karim Kislu would now serve as the ship's commanding officer. Captain Kislu said his country intended to continue using the ship for search and rescue along with law enforcement.

It was a bittersweet moment for those present, but as former crewmember Robert Stranathan stated: "But for its future, I'm glad it remains in service somewhere." Captain Burg reinforced that view: "Whatever ship you command, you grow very fond it. I know Captain Kislu and his crew will take great care of it, it's very hard for me. It's kind of like part of me was transferred today."

Vice Admiral Paul Zukunft, the Commander for the Pacific Area, summarized it best: "We've won the super bowl, but now it's time to take us out of the game."

Thus, on May 23, 2013, the Coast Guard Cutter *Jarvis* (WHEC 725) ended her historic journey in the U.S. Coast Guard. As Commander Kenneth White would most likely would have said, "The Queen of the Fleet has retired."

Coast Guard helo HH-52A 1383

Coast Guard helo HH-52A 1383, instrumental in the grounding incident by transferring vital supplies back to the ship, was later assigned to the Coast Guard Cutter *Polar Star* as icebreaker support. The aircraft has been retired for some time and is currently at the American Helicopter Museum & Education Center in West Chester, Pennsylvania.

Coast Guard helo HH-52A 1383. Photo courtesy the American Helicopter Museum & Education Center.

Captain Frederick Wooley

Now retired Coast Guard Captain Frederick Wooley would begin another phase of his life. Up to 1973, the sea was his calling; now it was time for something new.

With the summer now free to find his dream property, Wooley spent the time looking for the right place at the right price. Starting in New Jersey where his brother and sister lived, he and his wife scoured various farms, moving further west after each search. Finally, they found the perfect farm near Burnt Cabins, Pennsylvania, close to the center of the state.

With over 100 acres of land, Wooley was free to grow crops and raise cattle and horses. He also loved challenges, and the idea of being self-sustaining appealed to him, especially when compared to his sea-going background. While hardly profitable, Fred had a great time trying. All his life he was a people person, whether with his shipmates in the Coast Guard or with his neighbors in the countryside of Pennsylvania. Whereas he knew next to nothing about farming, that did not stop him from pursuing the endeavor and asking anyone who could offer advice; he had no shortage of self-confidence. He believed in a two-way street of neighborly help and would be there to assist others when needed. When a young family was down on their luck, he deeded an acre of land to them so they could get back on their feet. Later when Fred and his wife became elderly, this family was there to look out for their welfare.

He and his wife Margaret lived in a three-bedroom, salt-box style brick home on acreage that was half wooded and had a stream running through the property. He grew wheat, corn, hay, and, with any vacant property left, he would plant trees to provide wildlife cover, and more importantly, because he loved trees. "He was a tree hugger before it was cool," his daughter Sue would affectionately recall.

He loved animals, particularly his horses. A horse rider most of his life, he rode well enough to be on the polo team in Garden Grove, California, when he was thirty-five years of age. When he and his family lived in Louisiana, he converted a three-car garage into a three-stall horse barn. His love of horses continues with his adult children today.

At various times during his farming career, he owned a couple of beef cattle, a goat, an orphaned fawn and a series of dogs and cats. A conflict between the goat and the goat's love of eating his freshly planted trees resulted in the goat's transfer to another owner. Regarding the beef cattle, his daughter Sue relayed one of her favorite stories:

> "My favorite is when my dad had enlisted the assistance of a neighbor farmer and his son to 'dispatch' one of the beef cattle prior to taking the beef to the butcher. So, it's early morning and dad goes out to select the unlucky candidate. I think animals have some sense of knowing what's up, because somewhere in the process of singling out the young beef, it got alarmed and got out of the barnyard gate, with my dad hanging on to the rope he had secured around its neck. The beef ends up dragging my poor dad up the lane past the house, he all the while yelling for help to my mom and I inside, blithely drinking our morning coffee—we didn't hear a peep. The rodeo continued

Captain Wooley pursuing his favorite passtime. Photo provided by Jack Hunter.

until my dad was about to give up from exhaustion—at which time the neighbors arrive to help. They told my dad that the father says to the son as they drive down our lane, 'Oh my, Fred's got the beef out already!' When they finally got the animal corralled and ready to shoot, the neighbor, knowing my dad's tender heart when it comes to animals, takes the gun they were going to use and prepares to shoot. My dad says, 'Give me that. I'll do it.' Which he did with some satisfaction. That one always cracked us up."

Throughout most of his life, Wooley struggled with his smoking habit until he purchased the farm, and continued to drink his coffee heavily laced with sugar. One of his biggest pleasures was visiting his friend and former shipmate Ernie Smith in Montana, where the two would spend much time fishing. Other former *Jarvis* crewmembers would occasionally come to the farm to visit their friend and mentor; golfing was often involved. Two reunions of former *Jarvis* crewmembers were held at his farm as well, a further testament to the men's admiration for their former leader.

Shortly after purchasing the ranch, Frederick Wooley received the following letter from his former shipmates:

"To Captain F. O. Wooley: Commanding Officer, USCGC *Jarvis*:

"We the crew of the Coast Guard Cutter *Jarvis* would like to thank you from the bottom of our hearts. During the time of our grounding and the weeks after, you were a shining inspiration to all. You seemed to be everywhere at once. You always had a few words of hope and courage for all, no matter what our rank or station.

"For many of us this was our first experience with any such adversity, and for a few the first voyage. Your frequent talks and appearances, even in the flooding engine room, fired every one of us to seemingly fantastic feats. But yet in retrospect we see they were not enough to equal your outstanding leadership and never-failing courage. You have won the hearts and souls of the entire crew, our only gift to you is our never-ending admiration and trust, for anything more would seem dowdy and redundant. We think this can best be summed up in once sentence: We will follow you whatever, wherever, whenever, even to the gates of hell!

—*Signed: The crew* (*USCGC* Jarvis)

His daughter Sue once asked her dad on what makes a good leader. He responded in so many words: "Humility. Always keep in the forefront of your mind the welfare of those you lead."

Former crewmember David Landis would remember him as "…a true professional mariner and yes, loved and respected! His leadership style was ahead of the times. There was a lot of talent on the *Jarvis*, and he made use of them."

Landis's friend and former shipmate David Martin, a lifetime mariner himself, also admired Wooley's leadership style. "Captain Wooley did not get stressed. He kept everyone on an even keel. I really liked him. He was a kind man and served as a model for me of how a captain should carry himself."

As Commanding Officer of the *Jarvis*, Captain Wooley took responsibility for what occurred, never exhibiting any bitterness about the grounding or the findings. You do your best; then you move on.

He continued working on the farm until his health prohibited it. Even after twenty years of this lifestyle, Fred and his wife remained on the farm with the assistance of neighbors who helped plow and till the fields, not to mention checking in on their welfare. With deteriorating health, the two sold their farm and relocated to a smaller home in 1998, where they remained until Fred's passing in 2000.

Toward the end, Fred suffered from a variety of illnesses that had grown worse over the years. For the last year of his life, Fred received hospice care while residing at home. During his final days at home, as he lay dying, Sue assisted her dad with phone conversations with her siblings; the last call was with his daughter Anne. Completing this last call, Sue hung up the phone, and her father smiled, then with his final words, said, "All present and accounted for."

Jarvis reunion at Captain Wooley's home in 1999. *Standing* (left to right): Dan Edwards, John Moran, J.D. Miltier, Tim Baum, Tom Baum. *Kneeling* (left to right): Charlie Greene, Harry Lape, and Neal Metzbower. *Sitting*: Captain Frederick Wooley. Photo provided by Dan Edwards.

FINAL COMMENT

THIS BOOK IS not about second-guessing the findings of the Board of Investigation; Monday-morning quarterbacks can be found in any classroom in America. As often stated in maritime circles, an accident at sea is most likely from a series of mistakes, not just one. In this case, the errors and circumstances are numerous: an inexperienced ensign on the bridge, the failure to notify the captain promptly of the ship's movement, radar issues that obscured the position, and illegible markings on the anchor chain from the mud. Other factors included the ship's selected location for safe-harbor from the weather, navigational decisions, and critical personnel missing. When you take into account the severe weather, including the notorious severe williwaws and the extremely cold, windy, icy, and wet conditions and high sea waves—you have the makings of a disastrous situation.

But the ship was saved. When you examine the overall team effort of the ship's crew, and their heroic actions through unimaginable work conditions, these members prevented *Jarvis* from sinking. The individual efforts, however small, contributed to the overall rescue of the vessel.

When the situation was the bleakest, they did not panic; they did not despair. When the ship rolled to a sixty-degree angle, they crawled their way on the bulkheads to their duty stations. When, at the darkest hour, the vessel was dead-in-the-water without power, they continued in their duty to save *Jarvis*. When the engine room flooded, crew members heroically dived into the freezing and polluted waters to plug the hole and unclog the hoses. Later, when anchored and in a repair status, they worked in the ungodly goop of "elephant snot" to clean the engines so they could head home. The reputation of the *Jarvis* crew was that it was one of the best-trained crews in the Coast Guard. She had the enlisted and officer leadership necessary to persevere in dire situations. When the men were tested to their limits, they did not disappoint.

Crewmen queried on who stood out on the basis of their performance, the most common answer was that no one did, that it was a total team effort. Asked about their opinions of Captain Wooley, the unanimous reply was that everyone loved him. He was their captain, their leader, and their mentor. While many disagreed with the findings of the Board, many also noted that he was in charge and, as such, the blame follows the Captain, right or wrong.

Concerning the moment of greatest peril, when *Jarvis* was just thirty minutes away from the shore of Akutan Island, the Board of Investigation noted that the ship was drifting "helplessly toward a rocky shore without power in complete darkness, heavy seas, strong, gusty winds, freezing temperatures, and snow squalls." If not for the timely arrival of the Japanese fishing vessel *Koyo Maru No. 3*, this story ending would have been about the worst Coast Guard ship disaster in their service's history. Happily, it's not.

No one died. The Coast Guard Cutter *Jarvis* was saved.

APPENDIXES

Appendix A

PLANKOWNERS[61] AND CREWMEMBERS
OF CGC *JARVIS* (WHEC 725)

Below are listed the names of the original crewmembers at time of commissioning and those present during the grounding of the CGC *Jarvis*. Some of the members were not present at the time of the incident due to authorized leave or early transfer. Every effort was made to verify the names with rosters that were available, but mistakes and omissions may have occurred.

Officers

Captain Frederick O. Wooley (CO)*
Cdr Ken Ephron White (XO)*
LCDR George F. Buffleben *
LT Ernie R. Smith, Jr *
LT Phil Stager *
LTjg Al J. Sabol *
LTjg Myron F. Tethal *
LTjg Steve M. Bergeron *
LTjg R. (Doug) D. Phillips, III
LTjg Rick C. Sasse *
LTjg Carl R. Schramm, Jr *
LTjg Paul D. Barlow
Ens Jim R. Nagle, II *

Ens Jim H. Richardson
Ens James F. McCarthy, III
Ens Marty C Eger
CWO4 (F&S) Harry E. Lape *
CWO3(ENG) Bill A. Strickland *
CWO2 (BOSN) Michael T. Monroe
CWO2(ELC) Page John Keoni Shaw*
CWO2 J. T. Blackmon *

Enlisted

ETCM Don A. Eckler *
ENCS Charles C. Bateman *

Denotes Plankowner

---

[61] A Plankowner is an original crewmember at commissioning of ship.

ENCS Harold (William) E. Cox *

CSCS Ruben S. Manlangit *

RDC Victor R. Fisher, Jr *

QMC Gerald (Jim) Herman *

YNC Hal K. Hess *

ENC Dale C. Hoosier *

GMC Jack A. Hunter *

SKC Pete J. McCue *

RMC Jim D. Miltier *

DCC Lowell E. Montgomery *

SDC Febrilium Ponce *

EMC Melvin P. Roberts

SKC B.D. Sanderlin

BMC Walter (Stan) M. Stanczyk *

ETC Ted H. Turner

STC John D. Valerga *

HMC Gerald (Jerry) H. Walker *

EN1 Lawrence N. Baker

SD1 Melvin D. Bausa *

QM1 David. D. Berry *

FT1 James Caudill *

FT1 Lee T. Cearley

BM1 Jack Crowley

RM1 Richard (Dick) L. Dupre *

BM1 'Charlie' Greene Sr *

SS1 Ken Laws

EM1 Lewis (Lou) E. Maher *

GM1 Edward McKnight *

EM1 Edward (Neil) Metzbower *

BM1 S. R. Mitchell *

EN1 Marion D. Moon *

SK1 M. (Sam) Siulua *

BT1 Larry W. Stoppelmoor *

CS1 Oscar T. Salang *

ETN1 W. L. Townsed, Jr *

ET1 T. H. Turner *

EN1 Eugene F. Wnorowski

EN1 Donald A. Zupko *

MST2 Michael F. Alles *

BM2 Norm Black

FT2 L. T. Cearly *

ST2 S. P. Curl *

CS2 Roverto D. Demetrio

RM2 George M. Fewell *

RM2 Tom Franke

DC2 Thomas J. Frankhouser

YN2 R. A. Green *

CS2 Lorenzo A. Javier

EN2 Andrew J. Kacsanek, III *

FT2 Gordon J. Kroemer

TT2 Thomas J. Jordan *

RD2 Charles 'Brother Luke' Lucas *

FT2 Thomas A. Murphy

QM2 David L. Landis *

RM2 Roy C. Montgomery

ST2 H. V. Rees *

YN2 Brian Miller

GM2 John O. Nylen

YN2 Schmedding

ST2 John (Zack) Noble

RM2 Robert F. Salmon *

ST2 Robert J. Stranathan *

SD2 Arsenio C. Robles *

RM2 Jim D. Spears *

EM2 Ken J. Wenner

QM2 W. C Sharpe

BM2 Wolff A. Wald

EN2 J. R. Wilson *

EN2 Bruce Tamulion

EN2 James C. Wimbley

SD3 Ernie S. Abad *

BM3 C. Alexander Jr *

SK3 Rodrigo "Rod" Amparo *
RM3 Raymond J. Beaver *
EN3 David D. Blakely *
ST3 John (Joe) T. Borosh *
GM3 Gary L. Boyd
ETN3 S. M. Bristol *
BM3 Lester Bruch III *
BM3 I. L. Coffin *
BM3 Richard G. Brunke
YN3 Mark Carter
EN3 B. W. Crawford Jr *
RM3 David H. Cost
RM3 G. Robert Craig III *
YN3 R. Angelo Cleffi
HM3 Robert A Cupples
EN3 A. S. Del Campo *
CS3 Robert (Bob) A. Devens
CS3 R. D. Demetrio *
YN3 John Dery
RD3 T. (NOLA) B. Eaton *
ST3 Ed Donaldson, Jr *
SD3 D. F. Drig
DC3 T. J. Frankhouser *
EN3 G. Erice
YN3 H. S. Fenn III
SK3 R.G. Hasley
QM3 Tom M. Hall
QM3 William (Bill) Hart
BM3 James (Red) M. Henson
ET3 Herbert Hauck
EN3 R. C. Hirshberger *
EN3 Robert Kraus
MST3 D. A. Holt *
RD3 M. R. Jones
BM3 Tim L. Larson
FT3 G. J. Kroemer *

ST3 Mike C. Large
ETN3 Tom R. Looney
EN3 Henry Lipian *
QM3 Robert L. Loftin *
SK3 D. B. Mattson
CS3 L. Llorente
DC3 Dan J. Marston *
RD3 John D. Moran *
ST3 Ron E. Matuska *
EM3 "Larry" S. Meneses *
SS3 Donny Neuman
ETN3 C. S. Moses
GM3 S. A. Murphy
ST3 Larry Niggle
RD3 Ted W. Noring
EN3 Jack N. Otteren, II *
SK3 T. L. Page *
GM3 J. F. Pardee
FT3 Joey J. Parker
ET3 Don E. Piccone *
RD3 Bill A. Pigman/ Sandstrom
GM3 J. G. Rauk
BM3 Byron (Dick) R. Rice
SD3 A. V. Robillos *
SD3 'Demi' B. Saguiped
ET3 Jerrold (Jerry) B. Sandors *
CS3 Anthony 'Pat' Shea
MST3 J. F. Simmon
EM3 George W. Steier, Jr *
ST3 Denny D. Strutton *
ST3 Robert L. Van Elsberg
RD3 Steve L. Wager *
BM3 W. A. Wald *
BM3 E. Williams
EN3 J. C. Wimbley *
TN Roman A. Abinsay *

SN T. H. Baum *

SN T. S. Baum *

FA Patrick C. Bejarno

SAGM J. W. Bilich *

SA Jack E. Boyd

FA M. Breda *

FA Doug C. Brewer *

SN Ray L. Christianson *

SN Richard N. Bryan *

SN Mike S. Campbell *

FA W. G. Cox *

FNEN Dan E. Cornell

SN Joel H. Cortez *

SN Mike E. Davis *

SNCS N. Cromer Jr *

TN R. D. Dacanay *

SNCS R. A. Devons *

SA Howard W. Debord, Jr *

SA Steve 'Travis' C. Deleon *

SNQM George (Keith) Fawcett, Jr *

TN D. F. Drig *

SA Daniel (Dan) L. Edwards *

SA C. E. Gibbs, III *

TN Guillerrmo R. Eusantos, Jr. *

SNRD3 D. (Joe) Joseph Fasce

FA Paul D. Gregerson *

TN Vergilio M. Febrero *

SNYN H. S. Fenn, III *

SA T. M. Hall *

SA Ken D. Gray

SA Jim G. Green, Jr *

FNEM Howard P. Jensen, Jr.

FN Leo Griffin, Jr *

SN F. (Larry) Halagiere *

SN M. T. Jones *

SNQM W. S. Hart *

FA Willie H. Horton, Jr *

SN Tim. R. Lawler *

FA Eugene L. Johnson, Jr *

FA D. A. Jones *

FA J. J. Meaney, Jr *

SNGM Randy W. Kerr *

SN T. L. Larson *

SNQM Dave Martin *

SN Robert (Bobby) Maclees *

SN Leo L. Manipon

SN Robert Rawlinson *

FA Willis M. Mason

SN Michael D. Mathis *

FA Jim Rodriguez *

SN W. (Sam) G. Mitchell *

SNGM J. F. Pardee *

SN Mike D. Schueler

SN Anthony E. Reed *

SA Richard (Dick) R. Rice*

SNCS A. P. Shea *

SN E. (Cappy) W. Sanders *

SA L. G. Sarver *

FN Gary W. Tyler *

SA P. K. Selvey *

FA William (Bill) Sewell *

SA Greg A. Waggy *

FA G. J. Silva *

SN Farun (Suli) Sulejman *

SN Phillip H. Wittenbert *

SN Ron D. Vergeer *

TN Fernando F. Villaluz

FA J. G. Warren *

SN E. Williams *

SN W. (Bill) L. Webster *

FN R. D. Willis Jr

Crewmembers of HH-52A – 1383

LT John (Ron) Huddleston

LT William (Bill) P. Wolfe

AD1 Erv M. Hawes

AT1 Richard (Tiny) C. Lawson Sr

AD2 Robert A. Page

AM2 Charley E. Hicks

AE2 D. B. Robertson

Appendix B

COMMANDING OFFICERS OF THE
COAST GUARD CUTTER *JARVIS*

Twenty-two men served as Commanding Officer of the Coast Guard *Jarvis* from commissioning in 1971 to decommissioning in 2012. During this period, over 2,000 men and women streamed through tours of duty on the ship. The commanding officers came from a variety of notable backgrounds, including service in Vietnam, and many continued to contribute to society in significant ways after retiring from the Coast Guard. Included in this group would be the first father and son to graduate from the Coast Guard Academy and attain the rank of Rear Admiral.

Of the two men who had served in Vietnam, Ross Bell was seriously injured on the CGC *Point Welcome* when the eighty-two-foot cutter was shot and bombed by friendly forces. This mistake resulted in the commanding officer's death, the first Coast Guardsman to die in the Vietnam conflict. "Axel Jack" Hagstrom had also previously served in Vietnam before his *Jarvis* command. He served as well on many other ships, and he holds the distinction as the very first Golden Ancient Mariner of the Coast Guard. He held that honor until his retirement in 1984. A Facebook post in 2019 described him as "the saltiest Coast Guardsman they had ever met."

Captain Bobby Hollingsworth (1973-75) graduated from the U.S. Coast Guard Academy in 1955, after which he served as Deck Officer aboard the CGC *Ingham*. His tours in the CG included commanding officer of a 95' patrol boat out of Norfolk, Virginia, and Loran Station Eniwetok. He worked primarily in the communications field with an assignment as Executive Officer aboard the CGC *McCulloch*, another high endurance cutter.

Hollingsworth's first thirteen months as commanding officer of *Jarvis* was at the rank of commander, and he was probably the youngest officer to command a 378-foot high-endurance cutter. It was during his assignment on *Jarvis* that he was deep-selected and later promoted to captain.

As the commanding officer of the *Jarvis*, his first patrol in Alaska resulted in the seizure of the *Mitsu Maru Nr. 30* for territorial sea violation off of Unalaska Island in the fall of 1973. This seizure was the first of a foreign vessel in eighteen months and generated a lot of high-level interest due to the refusal of the trawler to cooperate. A Coast Guard C-130 took the accompanying photo as the ship as it was trying to avoid seizure.

Capture of the *Mitsu Maru Nr. 30* concluded after a thirteen-hour chase that stretched over 140 miles. The ship's master later pleaded guilty in U.S. District Court in Anchorage and was fined $30,000. A civil suit against the vessel resulted in payment of an additional $200,000.

Seizure of the *Mitsu Maru Nr. 30*. Photo provided by Admiral Hollingsworth.

On April 18, 1975, at 1:20 am, a Korean owned ore carrier struck the Coast Guard Cutter *Jarvis* while it was docked at Coast Guard Sand Island base. The pilot of the vessel was attempting to turn the ship in the channel between Sand Island and the commercial pier on the opposite side.

Hollingsworth recalled the incident:

"The pilot gave a 'slow ahead' bell and the engine responded with turns for 'back slow.' The pilot observed the ship was being 'set down' and increased the order to 'half ahead' then to 'full ahead' just before the ramming.

"The *Jarvis's* OOD, CWO Monroe, called me at home at the Red Hill housing area with the news and LCDR Walsh and I hurried to the scene and arrived just as the other ship was moving to the nearest anchorage. Fortunately, there was no damage below the waterline, and the only flooding was from some broken overhead pipes in one of the berthing areas."

Immediately the Coast Guard Marine Safety Office and the Legal branch filed a legal action against the owners to ensure payment for the damages. In the end, the company paid for all compensations, including the hotel expenses for the crew during the two- month drydock period.

Hollingsworth concluded the story:

"Change of command was a couple of weeks later, and I turned over the ship with the best looking, best functioning engine room in the fleet! Nothing like two extra months of Charlie Status for the engineers and deck force to get things in great shape. We maintained our operational level by lots of time in the training facilities at Pearl Harbor during the repairs. The crew enjoyed living in hotels and catered meals for a couple of months."

During his two years as CO, *Jarvis* completed three deployments to Alaska. Additionally, the ship represented the Coast Guard in joint Naval operations including the Rim of the Pacific Exercises (RIMPAC), a four-week exercise with thirty-one maritime vessels from U.S., Canada, New Zealand, and Australia.

Rear Admiral Hollingsworth continued his career after *Jarvis*, working various jobs including assignments to Governors Island, New York; Coast Guard Headquarters in Washington, D.C.; and later as Commander, Second Coast Guard District in St. Louis, Missouri. Notable during this time was his one-year assignment by the Commandant to prepare a report for the Study of Coast Guard Roles and Missions.

After the Coast Guard, Rear Admiral Hollingsworth pursued various work opportunities in the information technology field. He retired in 2004 and now spends time with his wife Pat living the "Good Life" in Virginia watching the sunrises over the Potomac.

Captain James (Jim) C. Knight (1975-77) spent thirty-two years in the U.S. Navy and the U.S. Coast Guard, retiring with the CGC *Jarvis* as his last assignment. After his retirement, he completed law school at Western

State School of Law and practiced law until his final retirement at the age of seventy-nine. Captain Knight crossed the bar at the age of ninety on June 9, 2017, in Yorba Linda, California.

An article that ran in the *Pacific Shield in* 1976, highlighted some of *Jarvis's* accomplishments during Captain Knight's tenure:

> "The *Jarvis* could teach a few of her counterparts how to catch foreign vessels in violation of fisheries treaties. She was recently awarded the Coast Guard Meritorious Unit Commendation for single handedly locating seven foreign fishing vessels engaged in unauthorized fishing activities off the coast of Alaska earlier this year.
>
> "Total fines levied were $2,805,000 against four Japanese and one South Korean fishing vessel. Diplomatic protests were filed against one Taiwanese and a fifth Japanese vessel.
>
> "Also, the *Jarvis* recently received the highest numeric grade of any cutter to date for Anti-Submarine Warfare (ASW) exercises conducted 27-30 September at Fleet Training, Pearl Harbor."

Captain John Wilkinson (1977-78) graduated from the Coast Guard Academy in 1954 and served on active duty spanning over twenty-six years including commands of the CGC *Resolute* and his final tour onboard the CGC *Jarvis*. After retirement, Wilkinson returned to college and received a B.S. in Accounting, eventually settling in Norwalk, Connecticut. He passed away on June 1, 2014.

Captain Axel John Hagstrom (1978-79) commonly known throughout the Coast Guard as "Axel Jack," also commanded other Coast Guard vessels including the USCGC *Campbell* and the USCGC *Balsam*.

Axel Jack Hagstrom was born in Iron Mountain, Michigan, and enlisted in the Coast Guard in October of 1946. He served as an enlisted man during the Korean War, entered the Coast Guard Officer Candidate School (OCS) in 1956. Once completed, he was commissioned as a LTjg (O-2), then shortly thereafter he saw extensive duty in Vietnam. As a result of service in Vietnam, he was awarded the Legion of Merit with combat "V" device for his actions during Operation Market Time, an effort to stop the influx of Viet Cong supplies into South Vietnam.

The Legion of Merit that he received read in part:

"From the Secretary of the Navy: The President of the United States takes pleasure in presenting the LEGION OF MERIT to: Lieutenant Commander Alex J. Hagstrom, United States Coast Guard.

CITATION: For exceptionally meritorious service from 30 June 1965 to 31 March 1966 while serving with U.S. Coast Guard Squadron ONE during its development and, later, while engaged in armed conflict against communist insurgent forces in the Republic of Vietnam. As Squadron Operations Officer, Lieutenant Commander Hagstrom developed combat operating procedures which formed the basis for tactical operation of Squadron Cutters in the Coastal Surveillance Force. The thoroughness of the training program instituted by him enabled the cutters to undertake their operational mission immediately upon arrival in Vietnam. As Commander, Coast Guard Division ELEVEN, he achieved an outstanding operational record of endurance and accomplishment with the units under his command. While acting as Commander Task Unit ONE HUNDRED FIFTEEEN POINT ONE POINT NINE, Lieutenant Commander Hagstrom successfully directed his forces and coordinated those of other commands in preventing the capture of two U.S. Navy survivors, weapons and classified material of a mined PCF. As Commander Coast Guard Division THIRTEEN and Task Group ONE HUNDRED FIFTEEN POINT SIX, he deployed Coast Guard cutters and Navy PCFs in the rivers of the Rung Sat Special Zone, south of Saigon. Within two weeks, these forces sank or captured six Viet Cong junks, killed twenty-seven enemy personnel and captured seven others along with arms, ammunition and other contraband. Lieutenant Commander Hagstrom's exemplary leadership, devotion to duty and professionalism during this period were in keeping with the highest traditions of the United States Naval Service. The Combat

"Distinguishing Device is authorized.

"For the President. Paul Nitze. Secretary of the Navy."

In the years leading to his retirement, he received three Coast Guard Commendation Medals with the Operational "O" device along with the Republic of Vietnam Armed Forces Meritorious Unit Citation.

Further accolades came his way toward the end of his career. The Ancient Mariner award was established in 1978, the same year Hagstrom assumed command of the CGC *Jarvis*, as a way to honor those officer and enlisted Coast Guard Cuttermen who possess the dedication and professionalism of the profession and hold the distinction of Cuttermen longer than others. The Cutterman designation is awarded after five years of sea-service, but to qualify as Ancient Mariner, a person must have had ten years of sea-duty.

Captain Axel John Hagstrom became the very first Golden Ancient Mariner of the Coast Guard and held that distinction until his retirement in 1984, having completed thirty-seven years of active duty.

Of note during his tenure as commanding officer of *Jarvis*, was the collision of the M/V *Taiwan Phoenix* and the MV *Star K* in July 1978. The *Star K* suffered severe flooding damage that threatened the safety of the ship. Damage control personnel from *Jarvis* went aboard to assess the extent of damage and carried out dewatering efforts. For their efforts, the team was awarded Letters of Appreciation from the command.

In October, just a few months after that event, *Jarvis* had just moored in Adak, Alaska, when flash orders arrived to proceed immediately 800 miles west toward Russia to the last known coordinates of a U.S. Navy P3 Orion plane that had been forced to ditch into the freezing waters. Air assets were dispatched; however, the *Jarvis* was the closest U.S. surface asset that possibly could rescue any survivors.

Former Coast Guard member Eric E. Mills recalls the trip:

"Upon completion of fueling, we got underway into one of those storms you take every effort to avoid. It took us nearly three days to arrive on scene. Seas exceeded fifty feet, and sustained winds were more than 110 mph, with frequent gusts to 130. The surface of the sea was being picked up and carried away by the winds. By the time we arrived, the survivors had been rescued by a Soviet trawler and whisked to Kamchatka for medical treatment. Our orders had changed: Locate and recover any remains of the crewmen lost and locate and recover or destroy any piece or part of the Orion that was left floating. We completed our mission by sinking the only piece of wreckage we could find."

Ten of the fifteen survived the crash and were miraculously rescued by a nearby Soviet trawler and later returned to the United States. A comprehensive book on this event was written by Captain Andrew Jampoler (USN, Retired), titled *Adak, The Rescue of Alfa Foxtrot 586*. Later it was reprinted for *Readers Digest*.

Several prior *Jarvis* crewmembers who worked for Captain Hagstrom-'mentioned that he "was the saltiest sailor' they had ever met. But what does that mean? Eric Mills adds another story about Axel Jack:

"Axel Jack Hagstrom was well respected by the *Jarvis* crew. We respected his ability, leadership, accomplishments, wry humor, and the fact that he started out enlisted, just like us. He proudly wore his Good Conduct ribbon, and we all knew that decoration was only awarded to enlisted personnel. There were few if any Captain's Masts under Capt. Hagstrom. He had other ways of enforcing discipline, but that's another story...

"Capt. Hagstrom wasn't afraid to render a salute whenever it was deserved. We had a crewmember, a Machinery Technician (MK), who had been in the Navy during the Vietnam war, who had been decorated for heroism. When the ship's crew was mustered for inspection, the Captain made a point of stopping and saluting this crewman each time.

"He had an odd affinity for his 'at sea' cover. His hat, which only came out when we were underway, had taken so much salt spray over the years, that all the gold thread had corroded to a sticky green. His cap wasn't dirty—it was salty, and so was he.

"As a radioman, I could read Morse code, whether sent by radio or sent by flashing light. Captain Hagstrom wanted a radioman on the signal bridge to translate Morse messages from the naval control towers. So, whenever *Jarvis* went to special sea detail, I was on the signal bridge.

"I recall one occasion about 1979, entering Pearl Harbor. Much of the crew had changed into dress uniform because we would be passing

USS *Arizona* on our way to the Pearl fuel docks, and we would be manning the rail and rendering honors.

"As we entered the waterway, a big U.S. Navy vessel was departing. It was one of those enormous amphibious warfare vessels, nearly twice our length and surely four times our tonnage. Hundreds of sailors and marines on her decks, attending to their duties, paying no attention to that 'little' Coast Guard cutter.

"We were closing fast and would soon pass port to port. Now you know that tradition dictates the junior commanding officer initiates rendering honors to the senior,[62] and I'm sure the egos on the bridge of the Navy vessel led them to believe they were senior, but as we approached each other the Navy could see our crew on deck making no effort nor preparation to man the rails.

"Suddenly, the sailors aboard the massive Navy warship were urgently, and rather tardily, ordered to man the rails and render honors on the double! Hundreds of them ran to their lifelines, looking down upon our little boat. Our orders to man the rails came over the 1MC, but about the time we got lined up, our vessels had passed, honors were secured, and we resumed our duties.

"It was a matter of great pride for the crew of the *Jarvis* to know that our Old Man was that salty and that he would not bow to the Navy ego, even though we were entering their turf.

"As a footnote, I learned there is a publication that resides on the bridge of American warships containing the date of rank for the CO. I don't know if our Quartermaster referred to that pub on this occasion, but you can bet your seabag that Captain Hagstrom knew exactly where he was on that list and knew by name which few U.S. warships he would initiate rendering honors to."

Axel Jack Hagstrom passed away on January 1998 and is buried in Tacoma, Washington.

Notable of the officers who served under Captain Hagstrom, Ensign Rich

---

[62] Rendering honors is a time-honored tradition between vessels of the U.S. Navy and the Coast Guard. Ships typically are prepared by listing in advance which vessels will be in the vicinity and creating a seniority list for use on the bridge. The junior ship will render honors to the senior ship based on the captain's rank. Not too many captains were senior to Captain Hagstrom.

One of two seized Korean fishing vessels.
Photo courtesy of Tommy Tuliano.

Habid would serve seven years in the Coast Guard before moving onto salvage work with the company Titan Salvage. His notable accomplishment with this company included leading the salvage of the cruise ship *Costa Concordia* off the coast of Italy, a job many experts thought was impossible. Captain Habid proved the skeptics wrong in the successful salvage operation of the ship. Habid passed away in March 2016.

Captain John Ikens (1979-81) was described by one of his former crewmembers, Robert Desh, as a "Great CO! We accomplished much during his tour." Marty Hagans remarked, "I would have sailed through the gates of hell for Capt. Ikens."

Noteworthy during his tenure was the Alaska patrol in October of 1979. There they boarded three large Korean stern trawlers and soon discovered numerous fishing permit violations. After approval from the State Department, the ship seized two of the vessels and escorted the violators to Kodiak. The seizure resulted in the largest fishing violation case in the history of the Alaskan Fisheries Conservation.

Earlier, *Jarvis* responded to a distress call from a crab boat that was in danger of sinking. A helicopter was soon dispatched and dropped a dewatering pump for the crabber to assist until *Jarvis* arrived on scene. Once the cutter arrived on scene, a damage control team was sent aboard the crab boat to pump the remainder of the water out.

Captain David A. Worth (1983-85) graduated from the CG Academy in 1961 and previously served as the Commanding Officer of the Loran Station on Kure Island for one year in 1964. After the *Jarvis* command, Worth was selected as the chief of staff for the Seventeenth CG District in 1987.

Captain Harry E. Choate Budd (1985-87) was a 1964 graduate of the U.S. Coast Guard Academy. During his twenty-three-plus years of service he served on five Coast Guard cutters: (*Redwood* - XO, *Mariposa* - XO, *Acushnet* - XO, *Storis* -CO), retiring as commanding officer of *Jarvis* in 1987. He received his BCE from the University of Illinois and a Master of Engineering Administration from The George Washington University. Ashore, he served two tours in civil engineering in Boston and in Headquarters and as Public Works Officer at the Coast Guard Yard. He served as Chief, Intelligence and Law Enforcement Branch, Juneau.

In retirement he worked in public works and plant and facilities operations in the Seattle area. He was able to realize his life-long dream of flying; obtained his commercial pilots license in 2003. He passed away in March 2018.

Captain Peter Busick (1987-89) Notable during his tenure as commanding officer, was the ship's response in Alaska after the 1989 grounding of the *Exxon Valdez*.

On September 12, 1988, *Jarvis* received the prestigious Coast Guard Meritorious Unit Commendation from the Commandant of the Coast Guard. The letter attached to the medal reads:

"For meritorious service from 20 June 1988 to 19 August 1988. While undergoing maintenance in Charlie status, *Jarvis* put to sea to evacuate an injured crewman from the F/V JAPAN TUNA NO. 2. A helicopter was launched from *Jarvis* at a distance of 150 miles from the fishing vessel to execute the medical evacuation. A subsequent launch using C-130 aircraft coverage for the helicopter in transporting the crewman to shoreside medical facilities, a distance of 250 miles, was expertly coordinated by *Jarvis*. Upon return to homeport, *Jarvis* entered RIMPAC '88, the largest multinational naval exercise conducted by the allies in the Pacific Ocean. As the only Coast Guard participant among fifty vessels from four nations, *Jarvis* distinguished itself by fully integrating into the areas of anti-submarine warfare, surface gunnery, operational deception, anti-surface barrier patrols and surface attack group missions. *Jarvis* displayed tenacious skill and tactical knowledge as well as superior ship handling and seamanship during five separate refuelings at sea, helicopter operations with aircraft from three nations and repeated close-order formation steaming. On law enforcement patrol one week after completing RIMPAC, *Jarvis* conducted daily flights with an embarked HH-65 helicopter and coordinated eight Coast Guard and United States Navy fixed wing surveillance patrols along the Hawaiian Island chain. Diverted twice in five days for the evacuations of injured crewmembers from the Korean F/V's *Heling Yng No. 1313* and *Tomision No. 2*, *Jarvis* provided critical medical care and coordinated the successful recovery and transfer of both patients at long range, again using fixed wing aircraft to extend the mission radius of the helicopter. An eight-hour law enforcement boarding of the sailing vessel *W. N. Ragland* resulted in the *Jarvis* crew discovering a hidden compartment in a hydraulic oil tank. Three United States military rifles, two .45 caliber pistols and more than 1500 rounds of ammunition were seized.

"The exceptional performance and devotion to duty displayed by personnel serving on board Coast Guard *Jarvis* are exemplary and are in keeping with the highest traditions of the United State Coast Guard."

"The Operational Distinguishing Device is authorized.

"Signed: Vice Admiral Clyde E. Robbins, Commander Coast Guard Pacific Area."

Captain Ross Bell (1989-92) Perhaps the most interesting background of any who served on board CGC *Jarvis* belonged to Ross Bell, who served during the Vietnam War. Over 8,000 Coast Guardsmen served in Vietnam from 1965 to 1975, in a variety of maritime roles, but most notably in patrolling the dangerous harbors and rivers.

During the Vietnam conflict, then-LTjg Bell served onboard the CGC *Point Welcome*, a ship that was patrolling near the 17th Parallel, the top of the patrol boundary, when, on August 11, 1966, she came under attack by U.S. forces! Author Paul Scotti in his book *Coast Guard Action in Vietnam* vividly describes the scene as the cutter is strafed and bombed with 20-mm projectiles by a U.S. Air Force B-57 airplane who had mistakenly taken it for a North Vietnamese trawler. On the watch in the mid-morning hour was the Executive Officer, LT Bell, accompanied by Gunner's Mate Third Class (GM3) Mark McKenney. Bell himself is struck, but not before he sounds "General Quarters." As Scotti writes of Bell:

"Lying on the deck, his vision beginning to cloud over, he saw that some of his toes were gone, but felt no pain. A chunk of flesh was missing from his broken right arm, and he bled in numerous places where metal fragments had raked him."

The ship is hit three times with strafing by bullets and bombs. Two Coast-guardsmen are killed, including the Commanding Officer, LTjg David Brostrom, and Engineman Second Class Jerry Phillips, while numerous others suffer severe injuries. A few years earlier, David Brostrom had entered the Coast Guard Academy with his friend and *Jarvis* crew member George Buffleben.

Author Scotti wrote of the incident:

"Blood was everywhere. It pulsed from wounds. It was underfoot, causing the men to slip as they worked. It slickened the handrails and steps of the steel ladder entryway. McKenney slumped at the bottom of the ladder, where, refusing to let his wounds keep him from lending a hand, he had aided in getting Phillips into the mess deck. Seeing the engineman's dreadful condition in the light, the young gunner's mate became engulfed in despair. The cries of pain, the helplessness of not being able to strike back and the mental anguish of being shot by your own side gripped him all at once. Reaching out for the source of life, he folded his hands and prayed, 'Dear God, help us.'"

The attack continued for an hour before the Air Force received word that the ship was friendly. The crew, unsure if more attacks were soon to arrive, took to abandoning the vessel and found safety on shore, only to wade ashore and be greeted by gunfire, determined later to be by unfriendly forces. Retreating to the *Point Welcome*, the men found the Coast Guard Cutter *Point Caution* had arrived to provide protection and relief. Gunners Mate Mark McKenney [63] received the Purple Heart for injuries suffered as a result

---

[63] Mark McKenny would go on to retire as a master chief petty officer having served twenty-seven years of duty. In 2006, he would donate eight acres, along with a house and two apartment build-ings, to the Coast Guard for future morale and recreation purposes.

Captain Ross Bell. Photo provided by
Jack Hunter

of the attack while Chief Boatswain's Mate Richard H. Patterson was ultimately awarded the Bronze Star with Combat "V," an award that many felt
should have been the Medal of Honor.

The Board of Investigation later determined that the attack on the *Point
Welcome* was caused by a series of mistakes, including the lack of common
communication capabilities between the different services. As Scotti wrote,
"Put another way, one hand did not know what the other hand was doing."
Lieutenant Junior Grade Brostrom, the son of a Navy commander, became
the first Coast Guardsman to perish in the Vietnam War. Because of this incident, concrete steps were made to improve the policies and communication between the various services.

As for LT Bell, he spent weeks recovering in a Marine Corps tent hospital,
and then later at a Navy hospital ship before being transferred to a hospital in
San Francisco. There he spent five months receiving medical attention. While
in the hospital, a local newspaper interviewed him and wrote the following:

"LOVE AMONG THE SERVICES: Remember when the U.S. Air Force planes bombed and strafed the Coast Guard cutter *Point Welcome*, off the So. Vietnam coast, killing two Americans and injuring seven? Well, one of the latter was Lieutenant (jg) Ross Bell, now a patient at the Marine hospital here. While he was being flown back, his ambulance plane landed at Clark Field in the Philippines, where LT Bell ate breakfast. He now has a fascinating souvenir of that stopover—a bill from the Air Force for 27 cents! 'Sure, I'm going to pay it,' grinned the Lieutenant yesterday. 'I'm sure the Air Force needs the money.'"

It could go into a fund for a course on "How to Recognize Coast Guard Cutters," the author of the article quips.

Captain Ross Bell took command of the CGC *Jarvis* in 1989 and served three years. During this period, the ship was temporarily decommissioned in 1990 to begin a $55 million Fleet Renovation and Modernization program (FRAM) that updated the engineering plant, combat systems, and electronics. Living spaces were given upgrades. Later, he also served as Commanding Officer of the CGC *Rush*. When Bell retired, he had accumulated thirty-six years of active duty.

Captain, and later Rear Admiral, Dennis Sirois (1992-93) took command of the *Jarvis* in 1992. Before he took command, in July of 1990, *Jarvis* was decommissioned and began the FRAM. The $55 million complete overhaul included engineering, habitability, electronics, and combat systems upgrades. The pre-commissioning was completed in November of 1991 and she was placed "In Commission Active" status on December 11, 1992. Captain Sirois would serve as the *Jarvis's* first commanding officer in this status. He had previous ship commands of the USCGC *Cape Henlopen*, USCGC *Bittersweet*, and USCGC *Confidence*. Ashore assignments included Associate Professor of Physics at the Coast Guard Academy, Afloat Assignment Officer at CG Headquarters, and the Coast Guard Liaison to the Chief of Naval Operations at the Pentagon.

Later, as Director of Reserve, Rear Admiral Sirois noted the value of Coast Guard Reservists immediately following the 9/11 attacks:

"When the nation was confronted by the immediate need for securing our domestic port infrastructure, the Coast Guard was there. Exercising existing plans and the unique authorities granted the Secretary of Transportation, the Coast Guard Reserve surged immediately on 11 September, with up to 1,100 members on duty by 14 September."

In 2006, his title became Assistant Commandant for Response at Coast Guard Headquarters in Washington D.C; he retired the same year. A graduate of the Coast Guard Academy in 1970, he is the recipient of the Legion of Merit, awarded for actions during the Global War on Terror.

After retirement in 2007, Admiral Sirois was hired by EG&G (URS) to be the Vice President of Counterterrorism and Law Enforcement Programs. RADM Sirois has a Master of Arts in National Security and Strategic Studies from the U.S. Naval War College, a Master of Science in Management from Rensselaer Polytechnic Institute and a Bachelor of Science in Marine Science from the U.S. Coast Guard Academy.

Captain J. Scott Merrill (1993-95) After retirement from the Coast Guard, Captain J. Scott Merrill earned an Unlimited Tonnage Ocean Masters Merchant Marine license in 1996 and worked nineteen years for the Alaska Marine Highway System. He sailed on many of the Alaska ferries, but primarily as a deck officer on the M/V *Tustumena* in the same waters of Alaska where he sailed on the *Jarvis* and the CGC *Firebush*. He retired as Master of *Tustumena* in May 2016. He now spends time building a new home on a lake near Mt. St. Helens in Washington State.

Captain Robert Rzemieniewski (1995-97) graduated from the Coast Guard Academy in 1973 and retired from the Coast Guard January 1, 2003.

Captain Jim Sabo (1997-99). Shortly after he left the command of the *Jarvis*, Captain Sabo led an investigation in 2000 into the near-sinking of the CGC *Dallas* while attempting to moor at the dock.

Captain Robert Stevens (1999-2001). Under his command, *Jarvis* completed a mission of migrant interdiction in the Pacific between Guam and

Hawaii in 1999. On one return trip from Guam, the ship came upon more than 100 Chinese migrants. They were returned to a temporary camp on Tinian of the Mariana Islands until arrangements could be made to repatriate them to the People's Republic of China. After departure from Tinian, the *Jarvis* encountered another migrant boat that was disabled, requiring the ship to tow the vessel. As *Jarvis* was near the ninety-day window for the mission, the Coast Guard cutter *Kukui* relieved *Jarvis* of the tow.

At last report, Captain Stevens serves on the Port of Astoria Board as a commissioner. The port's website outlines his background:

> "Robert, who is known as Steve, was raised in the Midwest, and has lived and served in the Pacific Northwest since 1974.
>
> "Steve began his Coast Guard career as an enlisted man; became a commissioned officer and achieved the rank and position of captain. He commanded two ships and patrolled the waters of Oregon, Washington, and Alaska. Of particular note, he spent four years with the Cutter *Resolute*, homeported in Astoria, where he became familiar with the waterfront, the Port of Astoria, and the local maritime community.
>
> 'I never forgot what it was like starting out at the lowest rank on a ship,' he said, and he is proud of his blue-collar background. After retiring from the Coast Guard service of thirty-four years, he began volunteering in the community and was appointed a Port Commissioner. 'It was time to give back to the maritime community which gave me my start.' Steve and his wife Teresa live in their home in Warrenton, which they bought in 1991, retiring in the community where he commanded his first ship. They are happy to call the Astoria area and the Lower Columbia River Estuary their home."

Rear Admiral Steven Ratti (2001-03) retired July 1, 2014. He is the son of retired U.S. Coast Guard Rear Admiral Ricardo Ratti, thus the two have the distinction as the only Coast Guard Academy graduate father and son to have reached the rank of Rear Admiral in the Coast Guard.

Ratti served as commanding officer of four CG vessels: USCGC *Point Hope*, USCGC *Sapelo*, USCGC *Thetis*, and finally USCGC *Jarvis*. His final assignment was as the Commander of the Fifth Coast Guard District in Portsmouth, Virginia. It was during this period that superstorm Sandy occurred, in which the Fifth District was actively involved with maritime recovery, and search and rescue including the search for the ship HMS *Bounty* during the storm. This ship was built for the 1962 film starring Marlon Brando, *Mutiny on the Bounty*. Fourteen crew members were rescued; however, two perished including the captain. An official investigation report later blamed the captain who had made a "reckless decision" to sail into the storm.

Previously Ratti had also served as Director of Operations, J-3 for the United States Southern Command and as director of the Joint Interagency Task Force West at the United States Pacific Command in Hawaii. He holds a degree with a Bachelor of Science in economics and management from the United States Coast Guard Academy and later received a Master of Science degree in human resources management from Rensselaer Polytechnic Institute and a Master of Science in instructional technology from Florida State University.

Captain Michael Jett (2003-05) retired from the Coast Guard in August of 2007. His last assignment was serving two years as Chief of Resources, Seventh Coast Guard District in Miami, FL. His responsibilities in this position included maritime enforcement operations in the Seventh District as well as the sizeable Caribbean basin. The area spans 1.8 million square miles and includes Central America, northern South America, and the entire Caribbean Sea. These duties included drug interdiction, coastal security, anti-terrorist operations, fishery enforcement laws, and vessel safety laws—to name just a few of the vast responsibilities.

Captain Michael Inman (2005-07) retired July 1, 2010 after thirty years of active service. His extensive experience included ship operations, search and rescue, law enforcement and command and control. When the Coast Guard started expanding operations in the Arctic in 2007, he was the leading architect, operations planner, and implementer of the new program. His experience also included the design and implementation of enhanced use of force techniques for dealing with drug interdiction.

Noteworthy during his tenure was the accomplishment of the first ever joint security exercise for the North Pacific Heads of Coast Guard Agencies, with the Russian Northeast Border Directorate vessel *Vorovsky*.

Captain John Prince (2007-09). During his tenure as Commanding Officer of *Jarvis*, Captain Prince completed three Alaska patrol crews. After this assignment, he was assigned the same position on the Coast Guard Cutter *Bertholf*. In recognition of his leadership, he was presented the Meritorious Service Medal by Vice Admiral Manson Brown during the ship's change-of-command ceremony in July of 2011. Previous to the *Bertholf*, Prince had accumulated over twenty-six years of active service with sixteen of those years afloat on seven different classes of CG cutters. His last known assignment was serving as the 11th Coast Guard District's chief of staff in July 2012.

Captain Aaron Davenport (2009-10). Upon completion of a *Jarvis* drydocking period in San Francisco, Captain Davenport relieved Captain Prince and sailed the ship back to Honolulu. During his tenure as Commanding Officer, *Jarvis* accomplished a historic EASTPAC patrol, seizing over six tons of cocaine. She also completed a successful South Pacific International Fisheries Patrol near Tahiti and Samoa. Previously, Davenport had served as Commanding Officer of the CGC *Valiant* and as Deputy Chief of the Office of Counterterrorism and Special Missions at CG Headquarters. Captain Davenport was also detailed to the White House Staff as a Special Advisor for Homeland Security and Counterterrorism to Vice President's Cheney and Biden. His final assignment was Chief of the Office of Cutter Forces and Professional Officer for a fleet of over 250 ships and 8,400 sea going personnel, while also providing oversight to a multi-billion/multi-year surface fleet recapitalization program.

Captain Davenport retired after thirty years of active service in 2014. Today Captain Davenport owns and operates a disabled veteran's company, Valiant Partners, LLC. He also serves as senior policy researcher with the Rand corporation. He holds a BS in Marine Sciences from the Coast Guard Academy; an MS in Environmental Sciences, with a concentration in Industrial Hygiene; and a Minor in Hazardous Materials from UCLA Fielding School of Public Health.

Captain Webster D. Balding (2010-12) retired in July of 2013, having served various missions as the Commanding Officer of the *Jarvis*. These missions included joint maritime law enforcement, search and rescue fishery enforcement, and enforcing maritime sovereignty. During his command, several law enforcement cases resulted in fines of over $750,000 per case. He also represented the Coast Guard in international functions, including the 2010 Maritime Multi Mission Exercise in Vladivostok, Russia, and the 2011 Pacific Partnership Civil Support with Pacific Command and international forces in Va'vao, Tonga. He later served as the Atlantic Area chief of Preparedness Division, in Portsmouth, Virginia.

Captain Richard Mourey (2012 - Decommissioning) is a 1989 graduate of the Coast Guard Academy with more than fifteen years of sea time aboard six cutters, serving various positions including as Commanding Officer of the CGC *Thetis*. In addition to his sea time, Mourey served as the U.S. Military Deputy for the United States Northern Command Future Operations division and as the Director of Interagency Coordination for the North American Aerospace Defense Command and United States Northern Command. He retired in 2019 with thirty years of service.

List of Commanding Officers for the Coast Guard Cutter *Jarvis*

Captain Frederick O. Wooley	1971-1973
Captain Bobby Hollingsworth	1973-1975
Captain James Knight	1975-1977
Captain John Wilkinson	1977-1978
Captain Axel John Hagstrom	1978-1979
Captain John Ikens	1979-1981
Captain Terry L. Lucas	1981-1983
Captain David A. Worth	1983-1985
Captain Harry E. Choate Budd	1985-1987
Captain Peter Busick	1987-1989
Captain Ross Bell	1989-1992
Captain R. Dennis Sirois	1992-1993
Captain J. Scott Merrill	1993-1995
Captain Robert F. Rzemieniewski	1995-1997
Captain Jim Sabo	1997-1999
Captain Robert Stevens	1999-2001
Captain Steven H. Ratti	2001-2003
Captain Michael Jett	2003-2005

Captain Michael D. Inman	2005-2007
Captain John Prince	2007-2009
Captain Aaron Davenport	2009-2010
Captain Webster D. Balding	2010-2012
Captain Richard Mourey	2012 - Decommissioning

Appendix C

REFLECTIONS

Interviews were conducted with as many of the crewmembers that could be found. The following are some of the comments and recollections regarding the incident and of the command.

Jarvis Grounding

"I stepped out and checked the fantail. The water is flowing on the main deck. The *Jarvis* is like a speed boat on high speed except it was not running. The bow was pointing up and aft was down and in addition to that, icebergs were floating all around. Looks like she was going to sink. I thought of the danger that the ship will sink. We might survive swimming, but hypothermia would kill us if not rescued right away." —*Leo Manipon*

"What I do know is that night was one of the worst nights of my life. I knew I would die from exposure if I had to go overboard and ride out the storm in an open raft. I thought for some hours that it was the last night of my life. I had a sweetheart I intended to marry back in Honolulu. What really depressed me was the thought I would never live to see our children opening their presents under the tree. After we got towed back to Dutch Harbor and I had a chance to get ashore I called her to let her know I was all right. She told me her mother had awakened her early in the morning saying the news had reported the *Jarvis* having sunk with all hands. You can imagine how that hit her." —*Robert Van Elsberg*

"…All the while wallowing in a mess of sea water, oil and asbestos insulation from the turbines. We called it "elephant snot". We blew it, wiped it, wore it and scrubbed it. It followed us back to our bunks after eighteen-hour days in the engine room where we slept in it. For weeks there were no showers, no clean coveralls." —*Ken Wenner*

Jarvis Crew Performance

"Reputation of the *Jarvis* was a well-trained crew."
—*Admiral Bobby Hollingsworth (2nd CO for the* Jarvis)

"What I will always remember about the *Jarvis* was the excellent crew that I got to serve with. Many of the crew were handpicked, and others like myself, happened to be in the right place and the right time to serve on her." —*Richard Sasse*

"It was a very busy night- excellent crew. If it had been a different crew, you would have had deaths." —John Moran

"I remember there was no panic. We were concerned about sinking, but everyone was so busy doing whatever was assigned to them, that there was not much time for thinking about anything else. To me, the whole crew were heroes." —George Fewell

"We were scared, but there was no panic. Everyone was working too hard. And morale was sky high. Everyone felt we had to save the ship."
—*Crewman ET3 Jerrold Sandors*
(*From the* Honolulu Advertiser, *December 9, 1972*)

"I have had lots of adventures in my life and I have met lots of wonderful people, but it is my time on the *Jarvis* that holds the fondest place in my memories." —*Carl Schramm*

"He (Joe) always had a special place in his heart for *Jarvis*. It sometimes felt that the *Jarvis* was his firstborn. He really felt that those 170 men created this massive mythical thing and breathed life into it. There was always great pride in his stories during that time with the feel-good stories as well as some dark stories. My dad as a young man just twenty-one years of age being thrown into an unimaginable life-threatening situation in one of the most brutal, terrifying and isolated parts of the world is something he always tried to explain but could never fully convey those days and the events that unfolded. The fortitude, youthfulness, naivety and bravery that all 170 men on the *Jarvis* had was a testament to each one of their characters. The ability to stare a life-threatening crisis in the face not once, but twice and do it with precision and a calmness is beyond admirable."

—*Nick Borosh, son of Joe Borosh*

"The ship's crew fought valiantly, risking life, limb and their health in the freezing Alaska floodwater [while] trying to save the ship."

—*Helo pilot John Huddleston*

"Those timely repairs kept *Jarvis* afloat and allowed the vessel enough time to receive more air-dropped P-250 pumps and for dive personnel to arrive. (Lowell) Montgomery's actions were key to our vessel's survival." —*Mark Carter*

"Outstanding crew…without a doubt, finest crew I ever served with. Travis Deleon was invaluable during incident along with Joel Cortez."

—*Stan Stanczyk*

"I truly do not remember any particular crewmember standing out. We all did what we were trained to do, improvised when necessary, and came home." —*Richard Brunke*

"We did everything right- professionalism and pride." —*Tim Lawler*

"The men I worked with throughout the grounding and flooding of the ship, the rest of ship's crew all acted professionally responsive, and I never saw any emotional breakdowns. As a matter of fact, it seemed like they went about business as usual, almost like they had rehearsed this situation all their lives." —*James "Tiger' McCarthy*

"Anyone stood out: The engine room personnel, diving into the freezing water. Bucket brigade- worked for long hours." —*John Moran*

"The crew of the *Jarvis* was by far the tightest and friendliest crew I ever served on. It was one of the best 'team' events I have ever seen and been a part of in my sixty-eight years here. Tight crew that stays in touch today. A whole bunch of us grew up in a hurry there."

—*Denny Strutton*

"I have had occasion to go to Dutch Harbor many times since 1972, and each and every time that I was there my thoughts inevitably drifted back to my time on the *Jarvis*. And I don't mean just the events surrounding the grounding, but rather my entire time on the ship. Frankly, my tour of duty on the *Jarvis* was one of the happiest periods of my adult working life. It would be difficult to overstate the degree of camaraderie that existed among the junior officers on the ship— particularly those of us who came aboard on the pre-commissioning detail. It was a 'Band of Brothers' thing that, for me at least, would never be duplicated." —*Carl Schramm*

"Chief Stanczyk was an inspiration as well as the CO/XO and OPS and entire crew of *Jarvis*. Master Chief Hunter also kept me in line as gun boss and inspired me to greater heights. Throughout, the crew I worked with was determined, resolute and professional. I am proud to have served with them all." —*Paul Barlow*

"Memories of that event still bring tears to my eyes at the heroism demonstrated by the 150 men aboard the *Jarvis* and what we did to save the *Jarvis* and the lives of the crew, which had the potential of being the worse disaster of life and property in Coast Guard history. None of us gave up during the two phases of the disaster, the initial grounding in Dutch Harbor and the taking-on of water and almost sinking when we were sailing back to Honolulu." —*Dan Edwards*

"To look back, I am proud. I am part of the crew who saved the *Jarvis*." —*Leo Manipon*

Leadership Learned and Other Lessons

"I will never forget seeing him [Captain Wooley] walk down the ladder into the engine room dressed in overalls with a rag in his hand to help the rest of us clean up and ultimately get at least one of our diesels running to bring us home." —*Robert Van Elsberg*

"The incident helped me in my later career as a ship's captain—I learned: don't panic, keep your head about you. Stay relaxed, be an example of calm in the middle of a crisis. That way the crew will keep their wits about them and together we will resolve the crisis as a team. Captain Wooley did not get stressed. He kept everyone on an even keel. I really liked him. He was a kind man and served as a model for me of how a captain should carry himself. This was the most influential event of my career [career sailor and ship's master]."

—*Dave Martin*

"I was at the *Jarvis* decommissioning and got to tour the ship. I went down to the 3rd deck and got to take a look at the new location for the radio spaces. So completely different. If the radio spaces were down on the 3rd deck when we had our Alaska problems, the flooding might have affected the radio spaces and we might not have had comms. Scary thought." —*George Fewell*

"My mother heard a news brief [WTIC TV Connecticut]—*Jarvis* had run aground with no other details 'fate of the crew unknown.' For three days she thought I was dead." —*John Moran*

"In Anchorage a Coastie couldn't buy a drink in a bar as someone would set them up because their relative or friend was saved by the Coast Guard." —*Ken Wenner*

"I was able to call home once in port, it seems the news was reporting the ship and all hands lost at sea." —*Wayne Debord*

"The Coast Guard's mission doesn't wait for a war to happen—it's 365 days a year. There is something noble and special in that. My girlfriend told me that her mother woke her up early in the morning to tell her the *Jarvis* had gone down with all hands. I think that was probably a news broadcast." —*Robert Van Elsberg*

The Weather

"I was able to review some of the events of the grounding with my brother-in-law, Steve Herbert, who I wrote was on the *Ironwood* the night of the 15th and 16th. His opinion was that when the weather gets bad in Alaska, you will find yourself in trouble. Even if we had been able to successfully get underway, we still may have been blown onto a shoal. The williwaw was *the* issue. Quartermaster Petty Officer 2nd Class (QM2) David Landis stated that we were no doubt caught in a williwaw. I would say that describes the wind condition the night of the grounding. It could also explain why the radar antennae was intermittently stopped—not constantly stopped so that we would have noticed the problem immediately." —*Robert Loftin*

"A williwaw was definitely what caused the grounding. That was on design negative of the 378' cutters. The bow super structure caught the wind like an umbrella, and at times could affect the maneuverability of the vessel. The first SAR case I was on was when I was on the USCGC *Chautauqua* (a 255' WHEC). A freighter had sunk a several hundred miles west of Midway Island, and us and the USCGC *Mellon* (the other 378' homeported at Base Sand Island, Honolulu) were dispatched. We were both on scene and only found debris of the freighter. The winds were so strong that *Mellon* could not turn to pick up debris."
——*Richard Brunke*

"It was windy, wet and cold. Winds came from between the mountains." —*John Moran*

"The weather was terrible. Huge seas and rain. The ship rolled like a cork in a tub." —*Roy "Monty" Montgomery*

"The *Jarvis* was on the rocks and listing to the starboard side. I could not tell much about the height of the waves as the wind was blowing pretty hard. When you are dropping stuff in the dark around the mountains, most of your time your eyes are in and out of the cockpit. To make it simple, I was sure glad I was in the airplane and not on the *Jarvis*." —*Tom Scoggins, C-130 crewmember*

"After flying as a Marine helo door gunner in Vietnam, I figured flying with the Coast Guard in Kodiak would be a piece of cake—*major* miscalculation. Ended up loving every minute! Turbulent winds and snow [on scene] with *Jarvis* looking like a toy boat in a dishwasher."
—*Dave Watkins, C-130 crewmember*

The Command

"You know how I feel about Captain Wooley. The captain always goes down with the ship, even if it is figuratively." —*Robert Van Elsberg*

"He [Commander White] was dedicated and supportive of the CO and ship's policy. He was previously enlisted and was the most decorated person in the CG at that time. He had more than five rows of ribbons." —*Tom Blackmon*

"I think ninety percent of the crew felt that Captain Wooley, Commander White, and all of the chiefs really cared about us and tried to make us the best crew ever." —*Denny Strutton*

"The adventures that we experienced during the first year will always be remembered reminding us in part of the trials and tribulations that Capt. David Jarvis experienced in his Alaska crossing to save the marooned whalers. The moments of boredom, the times of excitement, the absolute sense of accomplishment surrounded us all during 'The First Year.' It is with this book that we hope to relive those memories." —*Page "Keoni" Shaw, editor of* The Wake Behind Us

General Comments

"Without argument, the most significant historical event, which ever took place on the *Jarvis* was in November 1972, when 170 officers and enlisted men united and prevented the most serious loss of life and property in the history of the Coast Guard. People who were not there don't realize how close the *Jarvis* was to sinking in icy waters off the Aleutian Islands. In the newspaper articles published in Honolulu when the *Jarvis* returned from Alaska, crew members were quoted regarding the lack of fear. Things were happening too quickly to even think of fear because we all knew what had to be done to save the *Jarvis*." —*Dan Edwards*

"My opinion here is that the dangers of a williwaw wind wasn't truly understood by the watch standers; Alaska is known for them and Dutch Harbor is susceptible to these winds on a fairly regular basis. Yes, the winds played a major part of why the anchor started to drag, however, there were other events that lead to the actual grounding, Also, the night orders were not administered as written and the least experienced personnel were also on watch. Just my opinion here as I remember who was on watch. In my experience, marine accidents are a series of events that lead to negative and dangerous conclusions. Such conclusions can take years to develop.

"Most radars antennas of that era were good up to 80 knot winds before they started to what I call chatter, and somewhere around 100 knots they stopped in their tracks, as I found out one SAR night in 1978." —*David Landis*

"I was part of the group to leave early. I remember being flown to Base Kodiak on a Coast Guard C-130 on Thanksgiving Day, 1972. After arriving at the base, we stored our gear and went to the dining hall where all—it seemed like all—the people on base had gathered for Thanksgiving dinner. We joined in and to this day, it's my most memorable Thanksgiving. It took several days for us to be transported back to Base Honolulu and there really wasn't much for us to do while waiting. It was a bittersweet period with us having nothing to do in

Kodiak and the *Jarvis* in Dutch Harbor needing help that we couldn't provide." —*Jerry Sandors*

"Whatever ship you command, you grow very fond of it. I know Captain Kislu and his crew will take great care of it, but it's very hard for me. It's kind of like part of me was transferred today."

—*Captain Gregory Berg on the transfer of* Jarvis *to Bangladesh*

"The Elbow Room Bar on Dutch Harbor created the drink 'Jarvis on the Rocks' after the *Jarvis* ran aground in 1972." —*George Fewell*

Appendix D

LIFE AFTER *JARVIS*

Commander Kenneth White. White's first enlistment in the Navy was in 1941 was when he was underage (and subsequently discharged when discovered); two years later, with his dad's written permission, he again enlisted in the U.S. Navy. He would later enlist in the Coast Guard in 1950 without a break in military service.

White's final assignment was in Seattle at the Thirteenth Coast Guard District where he was in charge of the CG Auxiliary program. Nelson Hunt, a former Coast Guard officer and a retired judge in Lewis County, Washington, worked for the commander in Seattle. He describes Commander White as a strict enforcer of Coast Guard regulations as they pertained to the Auxiliary. Known as "The Bear" due to his size and personality, White may have been severe toward those who he viewed as poor performers, but he was also generous toward those who he felt deserved it. As Hunt relayed, "He gave me the best fitness reports ever."

In his autobiography, White outlined the rest of his career:

> "My officer promotions came regularly, and I was in the line for promotion to captain (O-6), when I retired. My assignments as an officer were both challenging and rewarding. They served to help develop me into a better officer, leader, and manager.
>
> "In 1975, I was faced with transfer back to Washington, D.C., which I would not have enjoyed, even though it would have involved a promotion. I decided that had done enough, earned a good pension, and would like to see my grandchildren grow, which I missed with my own children due to sea-duty, and I applied for retirement on July 1, 1975.
>
> "Changing my status to civilian life did not still satisfy my hunger for learning and education, and after a few months rest, I started back

to school, which I am continuing now. I call myself a self-employed consultant and have been hired as such during the past two years, but I will eventually have to get back in the saddle again to keep busy with work and pressures which I enjoy.

"Working with people has been my whole life. I am people oriented and successful in that area. As an underage enlisted man, I started with supervising older men, and ended my career supervising many military personnel, some civilian employees, and over 3,000 volunteer Coast Guard Auxiliarists.

"Some things worthy of note in my career which I am proud of are: I was a rated petty officer at the tender age of fifteen, I received an enlisted appointment to Annapolis at seventeen, I was the first Fire Control Technician in the Coast Guard, I was the first person accepted for OCS (Officer Candidate School) training in the Coast Guard in peacetime with less than two years formal education, and I was the first Coast Guard Officer assigned to postgraduate training at the Armed Forces Staff College."

Upon his retirement, White enrolled and graduated from City University in Everett, Washington. He would spend his spare time umpiring baseball and volunteering as a scout leader with the Evergreen Council of Boy Scouts of America. At the age of fifty-five, White developed ulcers and was admitted to the hospital where he passed away in 1981. He left behind a wife, Ann, daughters Barbara and Patty, and son K.C. White.

Lieutenant Commander George Buffleben. George Buffleben spent twenty years in the Coast Guard before he retired as a commander in the Bay area. He graduated from the Academy in 1963, and his class was the first to serve in Vietnam. After the Coast Guard, he worked as a consulting engineer, then later as a civilian government employee with the Coast Guard at the Coast Guard Island in Alameda, working as head of the licensing department. His final retirement was in 2014, now residing just outside the San Francisco Bay area.

Lieutenant John (Ron) Huddleston (Pilot). Ron Huddleston retired as a commander with the Coast Guard and presently lives in southern California.

Lieutenant Chuck Hughes (Pilot). Chuck Hughes rose to the rank of Commander and retired in 1988 having flown over 8000 hours. After retirement, he and his wife built a new home in Coeur D Alene, Idaho where he continues to work selling real estate.

Lieutenant Ernest R. Smith. Lieutenant Smith served as operations officer on the bridge at the time of grounding and at the time of disablement. After retirement, Captain Wooley would visit Ernie in Montana and the two of them would go fishing. At last report, he still lives in Montana, most likely with a fishing pole in his hands.

Lieutenant Phil Stager. Phil Stager was transferred from the *Jarvis* just before the Alaska patrol. He continued to serve in the Coast Guard as a naval engineer, completing twenty years of service and retiring as a LCDR. After retirement, he authored a book: *Mine to Mill: History of the Great Lakes Iron Trade: From the Iron Ranges to Sault Ste. Marie.* He is a nationally accredited philatelic judge and continues to enjoy the sunny retirement life in Florida.

Lieutenant Junior Grade Carl Schramm. Carl Schramm's last assignment was as the executive officer of COMSTA Kodiak. At the end of that assignment, he left the Coast Guard in 1983 as a LCDR. While in Kodiak, Schramm joined the flight club at the air station and learned to fly.

After the Coast Guard, he became a state trooper in Alaska, flying in and out of remote villages throughout the state. Carl's last role as a trooper was in King Salmon with the responsibility of law enforcement for the Aleutian Islands. This duty included numerous trips to Dutch Harbor, a community with which he was now quite familiar. He is now retired and spends a significant amount of time traveling America in his RV while devoting as little time as possible in front of a computer.

Lieutenant Junior Grade Rick Sasse. Richard Sasse retired as commander in 1993, having worked in various facilities management positions throughout the country including one detail in London. One notable assignment was at Coast Guard Headquarters, working on the 1993 presidential inauguration. After the Coast Guard, Sasse worked as project manager for a few companies, including his current company VFA (Vanderweil Facility Advisors), which was acquired by Accruent in 2014. His ultimate goal is to retire to Cape May, New Jersey. Rick's wife is the sister of George Buffleben's wife.

Lieutenant Junior Grade Myron F. Tethal. Myron F. Tethal went on to have a successful career in the Coast Guard, retiring as captain with over twenty-seven years of active service. A 1970 graduate of the Coast Guard Academy, Tethal was widely loved by enlisted and officer alike. Commander White noted that Myron was his son's hero, and further stated, "If I were a boy, Myron would be my hero, too." Rick Sasse commented that Myron was a unique personality who we all admired. Myron passed away in 2013.

Lieutenant Junior Grade Paul Barlow. Paul Barlow's initial tour after graduating from the Coast Guard Academy in 1971 was aboard the CGC *Winnebago* until her decommissioning in February 1972. At that time, he was transferred to the CGC *Jarvis* where he served as deck watch officer until his next transfer in April 1973. After *Jarvis*, Barlow continued going to sea, with a final assignment as commanding officer of the newly commissioned CGC *Thetis* in Key West, Florida. One of his notable missions was serving as commander of the Maritime Interdiction Force in Bahrain in 1992. After retiring as captain in 1997, he became Assistant Director of Auxiliary for the Ninth CG District. He served forty-two years of combined military and civilian duty in the Coast Guard. He now lives happily with his wife Renae in Juno Beach, Florida.

Lieutenant Junior Grade Al Sabol. Lieutenant Al Sabol went on to become a captain with the Coast Guard, serving twenty-seven years and retiring in 1997. He was a 1966 graduate of Bethlehem-Center High School in Fredericktown, Pennsylvania, and voted the "Most Athletic," excelling in football, baseball, basketball, golf, and track. He graduated from the CG Academy in 1970 with a BS in Oceanography. During his tenure with the Coast Guard, he was awarded numerous medals and commendations, including the Coast Guard Special Operations Medal with Bronze Star and the National Defense Service Medal with Bronze Star. After retirement from the Coast Guard, he could most often be found on the golf course or with his grandchildren. Al Sabol, commonly, called by his friends as "The Captain," passed away at the age of sixty-four in Leesburg, VA on March 25, 2013.

Ensign James "Tiger" McCarthy III. James "Tiger" McCarthy III went on to complete twenty-one years of active service with the Coast Guard, retiring at the rank of commander. As he relates, McCarthy earned his nickname due to a somewhat aggressive "Type A" personality. Jim earned two master's degrees ((Naval Architecture/Marine Engineering and Mechanical Engineering) and passed the New Jersey Professional Engineering (Mechanical) state licensure exam. After the Coast Guard, he finished his civilian career as a GS-14 with the Coast Guard in Washington, D.C., retiring with over fourteen years of civil service.

Ensign James Nagle. Jim Nagle would serve twenty-three years of active service with the Coast Guard, retiring as a commander in 1989. After the Coast Guard, he worked at Inmarsat in London for ten years, later working at various consulting jobs. Jim holds a master's degree in Systems Management from the University of Southern California and a Bachelor's degree in Electronics Engineering from DeVry Institute. He co-authored a book on Global Navigation Satellite System (GNSS) principles and applications and has written numerous articles in technical journals and conference papers related to GPS/GNSS. Additionally, he holds a British and French patent for a Satellite Radio-determination System.

Ensign Martin Eger. Martin Eger retired from the Coast Guard as a commander with twenty years of active service. One of his later assignments was serving as the Assistant Operations Officer for the CGC *Bramble*, where he worked for then-LT Scott Merrill, who would later become commanding officer of *Jarvis*.

Chief Warrant Officer Keoni Page John Shaw. "Keoni" Page John Shaw retired as a LCDR in 1993 having served thirty-three years. He was the original editor of the *The Wake Behind Us*, the short history of the first year of the CGC *Jarvis*. Upon his Coast Guard retirement, Shaw lived on the Big Island near Hilo in an old sugar plantation house on a couple of acres. There he ran a successful Asian handicraft business in Hilo until 2017. He passed away December 2018 in Bremerton, Washington.

Gunners Mate (GMC) Jack Hunter. Jack Hunter joined the Coast Guard in 1962 and completed Gunners Mate School after boot camp. Before the *Jarvis* duty, he was assigned to the USCGC *Minnetonka*. This ship was soon deployed to Vietnam for ten months, arriving in January 1968, just a few days before the infamous *Tet* offensive by the North Vietnamese. Later assigned to *Jarvis*, Jack spent four years on the ship, departing as an E-8 (Senior Chief). Upon advancement to E-9 (Master Chief), he was transferred to Coast Guard Governors Island, New York, assigned as the Master Chief at Gunners Mate School. Jack was the 15th Master Chief Gunner's Mate of the Coast Guard. After retirement in 1982, Jack procured a job as a mail carrier with the U.S. Postal Service until he retired from that position. Today he and his life-long wife Claudia reside in Colorado, with Jack collecting "all-things *Jarvis*" in his spare time.

Damage Controlman (DCC) Lowell Montgomery. Lowell retired as chief warrant officer (MAT3) in 1973. After retirement, he moved to Florida and had a woodworking shop. He was affectionately known by the locals as "Polar Bear," until he passed away in 2006. Like Captain Wooley, he served in the Merchant Marine during WWII.

Boatswain's Mate (BMC) Walter "Stan" Stanczyk. Walter "Stan" Stanczyk retired as a CWO4(BOSN) in 1988, having served twenty-eight years in the Coast Guard. One of the more beloved men aboard the *Jarvis*, Stan initially worked at a cement plant after his Coast Guard career. Now at age seventy-nine, he continues to work in Florida and has no plans to fully retire. He served two tours on the *Jarvis*: 1971-75 and again later as a warrant officer from 1981-1983.

Electrician's Mate (EM1) Edward (Neil) Metzbower. Neil Metzbower originally enlisted in 1958 and retired after just shy of thirty years in the Coast Guard, with his last rank as master chief. He grew up between Baltimore and the Eastern Shore where he resides today.

Quartermaster (QM1) David Berry. David Berry stayed in the Coast Guard until he retired from the CG station in Cleveland. He became a mining safety inspector and started his own business. He died in 2018 from an automobile accident in South Carolina.

Radioman (RM2) George Fewell. George initially signed up for the Navy in 1965 and was discharged in 1969. Soon after, George saw the light and enlisted into the Coast Guard, where he remained until his retirement in August of 1995 as a CWO4. After this retirement, he worked at an engineering firm in Seattle for five years, then went into consulting work until 2007. He continues to work for a company conducting quality assurance for the U.S. Army, managing people in the field who install telecom cabling.

Radioman (RM2) Thomas Franke. Franke works as a CPA with the Cleveland Clinic. He completed four years of active duty and twenty-six years in the reserve, that included duty in Operation Desert Storm.

Radioman (RM2) Roy Montgomery. Petty Officer Second Class Montgomery retired in 1990 with Kodiak, Alaska, as his last duty station. After he left the Coast Guard, he moved to Las Vegas to begin a career as a 21 dealer at a local casino. He subsequently moved up in the organization to dice boxman, floorman, surveillance agent, and finally as a shift manager in smaller casinos. He permanently retired in 2015.

Sonar Technician (ST3) John (Joe) Borosh. Joe completed four years in the Coast Guard and went on to a career with AT&T as Chief Information Officer (CIO) and later as Executive Director for McKesson. Joe passed away in May of 2015.

Electronics Technician (ET3) Jerry Sandors. Jerry chose the Coast Guard because his father had been a Coast Guardsman and had been present on the CGC *Taney* as a radioman during the Pearl Harbor attack. At the *Taney* floating museum in Baltimore, you will see his father's uniform and diary in a display case as examples of someone serving on the ship during that era. Sandors completed one tour in the Coast Guard and later became an electronics technician with the Federal Aviation Administration, working throughout the eastern region. He retired in 2013 having completed over forty years of federal service, the last ten as division manager of the frequency engineering group. He resides in Springfield, Virginia, with his wife and two cats. He can often be found cruising the Chesapeake Bay and the Potomac River in their thirty-seven-foot cruiser.

Boatswain's Mate (BM3) Richard Brunke. Richard Brunke remained in the Coast Guard for over thirty-three years, retiring as a commander in 2004. His last assignment was as XO of the USCGC *Munro*. Along with his duty aboard *Jarvis*, Brunke served five years in Hawaii on three ships and three shore assignments. He became a Coast Guard Special Agent, achieving the rank of E-7 (BMC). In 1983 he was selected to Officer Candidate School. As an officer, Brunke worked various assignments in the field of Intelligence and Law Enforcement.

After retiring from the Coast Guard, Brunke worked for a short period as the shipping and receiving manager for Home Depot, then as an HR manager for a construction company for a few years. With grandchildren now in his life, permanent retirement came calling.

As often the case with Coasties, Brunke quipped: "I swore when I enlisted, I would never serve a day over four years, and thirty-three-and-a-half years later, I realized the Coast Guard was one of the best organizations anyone could be a member of."

Yeoman Petty Officer (YN3) Mark Carter. Mark Carter retired with twenty-one years of service as a CWO3 in 1992 having served numerous assignments aboard Coast Guard cutters. After the Coast Guard retirement, he earned two Master of Arts degrees and a Ph.D. After attaining his degrees, he worked for the Department of Veterans Affairs and other governmental agencies. In 2010, Mark retired from all activities to pursue a career in the recording industry as a contract musician with various labels including Capitol Records and Sony Studios. He later worked as Chairman of the Millennium Group. Today Mark is "somewhat" retired, working occasional music contracts, most often with Sony.

Radioman (RM3) Robert Craig. Robert retired as a chief radioman with twenty-two years of active service. After the Coast Guard, he worked in a machine-making firm, then ten years as a payroll manager for another company until his final retirement in 2014.

Quartermaster (QM3) Keith Fawcett. Keith spent almost nine years in the Coast Guard leaving as a chief quartermaster. After the Coast Guard, he worked for twenty years in the maritime field unloading supertankers. Later he returned to the Coast Guard as a civilian with ten years in vessel traffic work and the last nine years working as a marine casualty investigator in predominately high-profile cases.

Quartermaster (QM3) Tom Hall. Tom Hall retired from the Coast Guard, with distinction as the Command Master Chief of the First Coast Guard District after thirty-one years of service. After his retirement, he worked part-time at a small engine repair shop. Since then, Tom has been enjoying the retired life with family and friends.

Quartermaster (QM3) David Landis. Landis retired in 1982 as a QMC after which he became a captain in the U.S.-flagged cruiseship industry for the next twenty-six years. In that role, he made annual trips to Akutan Bay. He also started Latitude 46 Marine Consultants in 2006, and became a founding member of Water2Wine cruises in the Tri-Cities area (Washington state) in 2015.

Sonar Technician (ST3) Mike Large. Large spent four years in the Coast Guard, afterward becoming a commercial diver for Taylor Diving and Salvage. During this period, he completed some work in Columbia, where he met his wife. He has worked in a variety of countries, including in Nigeria as a diving supervisor. Currently, he works for Chevron, with his retirement slated within the year.

Quartermaster (QM3) Robert Loftin. Robert spent four years in the Coast Guard after which time he left the service and attended graduate school in Urban Design and Architecture at Virginia Tech in Blacksburg, Virginia. Coincidently, former *Jarvis* crewmember Jerry Sandors was his roommate at VPI. After graduation, Loftin became a licensed architect in Virginia and continues to practice in Lancaster, Pennsylvania. "All in all, I would say, life has been good," he would comment years later.

Damage Controlman (DC3) Daniel Marston. Dan retired as a CWO3 in the Coast Guard and now serves as a pastor in Florida.

Quartermaster (QM3) Dave Martin. Dave spent four years in the Coast Guard, then continued to work on ships in the marine industry. He worked his way up to the rank of captain, and his first assignment in that position sailed to Dutch Harbor. He is currently captain of the University of Hawaii's scientific research vessel *Kilo Moana* based out of Honolulu. Dave continues to live a dream life, working three months on, three months off, residing a mile above sea level in the beautiful country of Costa Rica, with his wife and son.

Radioman (RD3) John Moran. Retired at age sixty-two, John now spends a lot of time on boats while also an active member of his local yacht club.

Seaman/Storekeeper (SN/SK3) Marvin Pugh. Soon-to-be SK3, Pugh was not on *Jarvis* during the grounding, but he provided such a great story that he could not be ignored. Pugh retired from the Coast Guard with twenty-two years of service, having attained the rank of senior chief (SKCS). Before his retirement, his last duty station was serving as an instructor at the Chief Petty Officers (CPO) Academy. He graduated with a BS in Sociology and later attained a Human Resource Management certification. Upon retirement, he worked for the City/County of San Francisco as a training officer with the human resources department. He has since retired and resides in Oregon.

Sonar Technician (ST3) Denny Stratton. Denny retired in 1990 as a master chief sonar technician. During his twenty-two years in the Coast Guard, he served on four of the 378-foot High Endurance Cutters. After the Coast Guard, he worked with the Bentonville (Arkansas) Police, retiring in 2007.

Yeoman Petty Officer (YN3) Angelo Cleffi. After serving on *Jarvis*, Cleffi later worked at the Office of Commander, Atlantic Area, rising to the rank of chief yeoman (YNC). He passed away in 2014.

Sonar Technician (ST3) Robert Van Elsberg. Robert completed an initial tour in the Coast Guard, then worked for the Army Reserve and later the Air Force Reserve as a journalist. He has over thirty-four years as a military newspaper writer and editor, working on four Air Force magazines and three Army magazines. He quipped that he left the Coast Guard, "…because I never again wanted to experience being aboard a sinking ship." He is now fully retired.

Seaman Mike Campbell. Mike stayed on the *Jarvis* for two years, then was transferred to the presidential security detail on the *Point Hobart* out of Oceanside, California. Later he was on temporary assignment for the Coast Guard to evaluate hydrofoils for Coast Guard use. His final assignment was working at the small boat unit in Cape Disappointment, Ilwaco, Washington. Campbell departed the Coast Guard in 1978. He retired from the Astoria, Oregon, fire department after twenty- five years of service and still resides in the area.

Seaman Ray Christianson. Ray spent four years in the Coast Guard, then went to college and became an accountant. He presently resides in Minnesota.

Seaman Joel Cortez. Cortez spent four years with the Coast Guard, after which he left the service and returned to Texas.

Seaman Apprentice Wayne Debord. Wayne spent two tours in the Coast Guard, then made a career change. Working with the National Oceanic and Atmospheric Administration (NOAA), he performed as the chief quartermaster. Later he made another career shift toward computer programming. He fully retired a couple of years ago.

Seaman Frank "Larry" Halagiere. Larry served four years with the Coast Guard before moving on and graduating from Western Illinois University with a degree in sociology. He retired from the City of Ottawa as a building and zoning official. He passed away in 2014, recognized in his life for "humor and charismatic presence."

Seaman Howard Jensen. Spent four years in the Coast Guard; later worked as a photo lab technician. After this career, he worked in the advertising field. He presently lives in Florida.

Seaman Tim Lawler. Lawler completed four years of service, including two months at Kauai Coast Guard Loran Station in 1974, where he originally met this author. After the Coast Guard, he sold real estate for thirteen years and now works as a chef.

Seaman Leo Manipon. Leo retired as CWO4(F&S) after thirty years and presently works as the housing program analyst for the Coast Guard in Alameda; a job he has held since 2001.

Fireman Leo Griffin. Leo retired as an AD2 (Aviation Mechanist Mate, Second Class) after sixteen years of service; his last duty station was at ATC (Aviation Training Center) Mobile, Alabama. After the Coast Guard, Leo worked for the U.S. Postal Service and later for the VA as a mechanic. He is fully retired now and living in Dallas, Texas.

Fireman/Electrican's Mate (FNEM) Ken Wenner. Ken spent four years in the Coast Guard, after which he worked thirty-two years with the Pennsylvania Department of Environmental Protection. He now owns an electrical business. He spends his spare time playing the trombone, working as a river guide, Scout leader, and "babysitting four of the loveliest little girls a grandfather can have."

Fireman Apprentice Doug Brewer. Doug spent four years in the Coast Guard and later opened up his own business, where he worked thirty-four years building and modifying equipment for the handicapped. He retired in 2006 and spends his time as a snowbird and visiting as many NASCAR events as possible.

Fireman Apprentice Bill Sewell. Bill spent twenty-two years in the Coast Guard before retiring as an MK1 and moving to Omaha, Nebraska. After the Coast Guard he continued working as a mechanic on over-the-road trucks. He is now retired, but works part-time in his own business building bunk beds. His Facebook page is Bills Bunk Beds Omaha.

Seaman Bill Webster. Bill spent four years in the Coast Guard, after which he attended air conditioner school. He spent forty-six years in this field of work, with twenty years as a state contractor.

The following personnel were not interviewed but continued to serve in the Coast Guard until their retirements. Information courtesy of Jack Hunter.

Name	Last Rank
QMC Gerald Herman	CWO
RMC Jim Miltier	RMCS
SKC Pete J. McCue	CWO
ETC Ted H. Turner	CWO
HMC Gerald (Jerry) Walker	CWO
FT1 James Caudill	CWO
FT1 Lee Cearley	CWO
GM1 Ed McKnight	GMC
RM2 George Fewell	CWO
QM2 David Landis	QMC
YN2 Brian Miller	YNC
FT2 Thomas Murphy	CDR
GM2 John Nylen	CWO
RM2 Robert Salmon	LCDR
RM2 Jim Spears	RMC
ST2 Robert Stranathan	CWO
GM3 Gary Boyd	GMC
YN3 R. Angelo Cleffi	YNC
QM3 Tom Hall	QMCM
BM3 James (Red) Henson	CWO
EN3 Henry Lipian	LT
ST3 Ron Matuska	STCS
CS3 Anthony Shea	CWO
FN Leo Griffin	AD2
SN Michael Mathis	CWO

Appendix E

RATING DESCRIPTIONS

The following job descriptions for the various Coast Guard ratings were taken directly from the 1967 *The Coast Guardsman's Manual*, often called the *Blue Jacket Manual*. The 1967 edition would have been the applicable manual for those serving on the CGC *Jarvis* in 1972.

Note that in the following job descriptions, computers and satellites did not exist. This manual was published by the United States Naval Institute, Annapolis, Maryland.

Seaman – SN (E-3): Training for a rating in deck, ordnance, electronics, precision equipment, administrative and clerical, or miscellaneous groups: Perform general deck and other detail duties; maintain equipment, compartments, lines, rigging, and decks; act as lookouts, members of gun crews, and security and fire sentries.

Fireman – FN (E-3): Training for engineering groups: Lighting-off boilers, operating pumps, motors, and turbines; record readings of gauges; maintain and clean engineering machinery and compartments; stand security and fire watches.

Stewardsman – TN (E-3): Training for steward rating: Assist in preparing and serving meals; clean officers' galley, the wardroom, and officers' living quarters. Stand security and fire watches; serve as members of gun crews: participate in working parties.

Petty Officers (Pay grades 4 through 9)

Deck Group

Boatswain's Mate (BM): The boatswain's mate serves aboard all types of ships and at most shore stations; in battle, acts as gun captain, member of damage control party, or is stationed on bridge; requires thorough knowledge of seamanship, and understanding of all deck work connected with boatswain's mate and anchor watches, as well as familiarity with rigging, hawsers, winches, hoists, tackle, lines, and cargo nets; may take a turn at the wheel, sew canvas, or double as gun captain; must know signal flags, lights, and navigation instruments; directs handling and stowage of cargo; maintains and operates hoisting and landing gear; must know how to handle small boats; directs boat crews in landing or rescue operations.

Quartermaster (QM): Quartermasters are assigned to all types of ships and serve in the pilothouse on the bridge or signal bridge, or in the charthouse. A quartermaster takes care of the ship's navigation publications, charts, and tables; must know how to use and care for navigational instruments; trains and supervises helmsmen; checks bearings and soundings, and plots courses; must know whistle, bell, and light signals, Rules of the Road, visual communications, blinker signaling, semaphore, and signal flags.

Sonarman (SO): The sonarman serves on ships fitted with sonar equipment, at Training Stations, and at certain district offices; he [64] interprets sonic and magnetic information received by electronic and magnetic defense equipment; may use international Morse code in transmitting and receiving messages on sonar equipment; operates sonar countermeasures equipment where installed; performs routine tests and adjustments on equipment, and makes minor repairs.

Radarman (RD): Radarmen are stationed on all types of ships and small craft and at some shore stations. The radarman must know the function and operating principles of all radar equipment on board, and be able to use such equipment in tracking and searching, in intercepting aircraft and surface vessels, and where indicated, in tracking weather balloons; he interprets and plots all information received; makes routine tests and adjustments, and performs minor repairs.

Ordnance Group

Gunner's Mate (GM): Gunner's mates are assigned to all fighting ships; in battle, they may be at guns or in magazines to supervise ammunition handling. The gunner's mate is responsible for operating and maintenance of guns,

---

[64] In 1972, the active duty component of the Coast Guard was composed of all men; women would be allowed into the Coast Guard two years later.

rocket launchers, and turrets; he maintains and stows ammunition, projectiles, powder bags, fuzes, rockets, bombs, and pyrotechnics; repairs and maintains recoil mechanisms, bearings, breech mechanisms, firing attachments, loading mechanisms, and hoists; inspects magazines for proper temperature, and tests powder; acts as demolition expert in placing and firing explosives.

Fire Control Technician (FT): Fire control technicians operate, repair, and perform maintenance on fire control equipment including computers, fire control radars, directors, switchboards, control components of ordnance power drives, and associated units aboard Coast Guard vessels. Conduct operational tests and alignment checks. Possess general knowledge of ordnance equipment, ammunition, and magazines.

Engineering

Engineman (EN): The engineman serves in almost all types of ships, at naval shipyards, and at repair facilities afloat and ashore. He maintains, operates, and repairs internal combustion engines; usually operates and repairs engines in diesel-driven craft, but may work on high- powered gasoline engines, such as those used in patrol boats; operates and maintains auxiliary engines and the refrigeration and air-conditioning equipment on diesel-driven vessels; uses all ordinary hand, shop and machine tools, and all precision measuring instruments employed in engine overhaul; supervises engine watches and takes full charge of engine-room on diesel-driven craft; keeps necessary records and prepares reports; supervises the work and training of engineman strikers.

Electrician's Mate (EM): The electrician's mate serves on all types of ships and at bases. He installs, maintains, and repairs generators, electric motors, searchlights, yardarm blinkers, and the general lighting and power distribution system employed aboard ship; locates and repairs defects in wiring; uses electrician's hand tools and electrical measuring instruments; performs soldering and brazing operations. In addition to maintenance and repair duties, he may stand an engine-room watch, being at such time responsible for the proper operation of all electrical equipment and control panels.

Telephone Technician (TT): Maintains telephone equipment, including switchboards, electronic repeaters, instruments, teletypewriters, etc. Also maintains telephone lines and cables, including poles and underground lines. Usually serves ashore. This rating is being phased out.

Damage Controlman (DC): Damage controlmen are assigned to all but the smallest ships, and are specialists in the theory, techniques, skills, and equipment of fire-fighting, chemical warfare, carpentry, painting, and general damage-control. In this rating a man instructs and coordinates the activities of damage-control parties; has responsibility for maintaining and repairing damage- control equipment; performs all types of carpentry work; repairs and maintains woodwork aboard ship, including small boats; prepares shoring, braces, and other jury rigs used in damage control; has charge of the paint shop and paint locker, and can mix paint and rig scaffolding, as well as perform required painting.

Electronics Technician (ET): The electronics technician serves on all types of ships and at shore stations having electronic equipment. At general quarters, he stands by to perform instant electronics repair. He is responsible for maintenance and repair of all shipboard electronic equipment, and other types of communication, detection, and ranging equipment employing electronic circuits; he uses many types of precision test equipment, such as cathode-ray oscilloscopes, frequency meters, and vacuum-tube tests; needs a knowledge of circuits and circuit theory, direct and alternating current, various types of vacuum tubes, and electronic and wave theory; understands construction and function of all electronic equipment aboard.

Administrative and Clerical Group

Radioman (RM): Radiomen serve aboard all ships and at all radio stations ashore, operating radios, radio-direction finders, teletypewriters, and facsimile equipment, transmitting and receiving messages in international Morse code. The radioman makes adjustments and performs upkeep in equipment; obtains bearings with radio direction finders; stands watches on teletypewriters, voice radio, and telegraph circuits; copies broadcasts and keeps required logs; lubricates, cleans, and detects mechanical difficulties in radios and typewriters; rigs emergency antennas; supervises and trains strikers.

Yeoman (YN): Most Coast Guard activities ashore and afloat require the services of yeomen. A yeoman must be familiar with official letter and report forms, routing and correspondence, and with the Coast Guard filing system. He performs typing and clerical duties, prepares reports, maintains office records and files, and operates office machines; is an expert on Coast Guard regulations, manuals, circular letters, and directives; is in charge of personnel records and furnishes information on ratings, insurance, transportation, and promotions.

Storekeeper (SK): All shore activities require storekeepers, as do all ships except the smallest types. A storekeeper procures, stows, preserves, packages, and issues clothing, spare parts, provisions, technical items, and all other supplies needed; keeps inventories, prepares requisitions, and checks incoming supplies and stocks for quantity; he may perform some disbursing duties; operates a typewriter and other office machines. In the higher pay grades, he processes all matters pertaining to Coast Guard payrolls and the disbursing of funds for various payments; prepares and types financial accounts and reports; has knowledge of basic principles of Coast Guard accounting system, is familiar with allowances for subsistence, uniforms, re- enlistment pay, family allowances, longevity, etc.

Commissaryman (CS): Commissarymen serve at shore stations and onboard ships. They ordinarily serve as cooks and bakers, but at large shore stations and in large ships they may also serve as butchers. They prepare menus, keep cost accounts, assist in ordering provisions, and check deliveries for quantity and quality; are responsible for proper storage of all food products and for the care of galleys, bake shops, refrigerator spaces, and provision-issue rooms.

Steward (SD): Stewards serve in wardrooms and officers' quarters, afloat and ashore. While the Commissaryman is concerned with food in the general mess, the steward serves as cook and baker for the officers' mess; he also assigns, directs, and supervises stewardsmen in making officers' beds, clean officers' living quarters, and serving meals in officers' messes; prepares menus and assists in ordering provisions; has responsibility for proper stowage of food; estimates quantities and plans for varieties of foodstuffs in preparing for cruises; supervises cutting and preparation of meat, baking of bread, pies, cakes, and pastries, and cooking of soups, vegetables, and meats; maintains high standards of service, cleanliness, and discipline in his area.

Medical Group

Hospital Corpsman (HM): Hospital corpsman and hospital apprentices serve in sick bays, dental offices, or dispensaries of any ship or shore station, and may be assigned to a Public Health Service Hospital for duty as liaison officer. The corpsman performs medical, dental, and clerical duties; gives first aid and performs ward and operating room duties; may be technician in such fields as X-ray, pharmacy, or epidemiology; may serve independently on small ships, performing all but major surgical duties; serves as assistant to medical officer in preventing and treating warfare injuries and in giving physical examinations.

ACKNOWLEDGMENTS

T HIS STORY COULD not have been possible twenty years ago before the Internet. At the beginning of the research phase of this project, I relied heavily on social media and other Internet sources to reach out and find former crewmembers. The research was challenging because these events happened in 1972; several of the crew have passed away, while others are now in their sixties or older. Of those I found, it was somewhat surprising that so many not only wanted to tell their stories but also to hear other stories from their fellow crewmates as well. As mentioned earlier in this book, the timing was such that many of the members transferred when *Jarvis* returned to Honolulu; therefore, they only knew a small portion of the whole story.

I was impressed with the compassion the former crewmembers felt toward the ship and Captain Frederick Wooley. I repeatedly heard about how proud they were of *Jarvis* and how well trained they were as a crew, how they loved the Captain. Many—notably the junior officers—felt that Captain Wooley was ahead of his time in his leadership qualities. He knew the names of every crewmember and would stop them in the passageways to visit and ask how their families were. He cared about his men, and he loved the *Jarvis*. Those attributes led to a loyal crew who were willing to go the extra mile to accomplish the mission; those attributes to exceed may have saved the *Jarvis*.

Over 1,000 pages of research were acquired from phone interviews, e-mails, and personal visits. Notable from the crewmembers were Richard Brunke, Stan Stanczyk, Robert Van Elsberg, Keoni Page Shaw, Dan Edwards, Carl Schramm, Charlie Greene, Leo Manipon, Richard Sasse, and Paul Barlow. These are just a few who have contributed; many others are listed in the chapter on sources. Their input, not to mention their encouragement and enthusiasm toward this story, was priceless. Admiral Hollingsworth, the second commanding officer of *Jarvis*, also contributed a steady stream of information to me.

Unfortunately, Keoni Page Shaw passed away before the book was completed, a regret on my part as we had some great discussions about the *Jarvis*. Fellow crewmember Randy Kerr also crossed the bar while this book was in the final stages of editing. A couple of other sources have also gone silent, and I can only hope for the best.

A special thanks to David Martin and David Landis who frequently explained naval terminology and equipment to this landlubber.

The families of those who have passed have also been fantastic in their contributions, notably Sue Wooley, daughter of Captain Wooley, and K.C. White, Commander White's son. Their insights into their respective father's background and life history were invaluable to this story. A special thanks to the other Wooley children as well: Rick, Sally, and Anne.

The National Personnel Records Center Military Personnel Records in St. Louis provided Commander White's extensive Navy personnel record, with over 100 pages forwarded. The Commander's Navy background was impressive and added to his portion of this story.

In San Bruno, California, I visited the National Archives Center at San Francisco to retrieve the original *Jarvis* logs. I wish to thank Aaron Seltzer from the Center, who went the extra mile to find the records and who ensured they were there waiting for me when I arrived.

Tony Freeman from the American Helicopter Museum & Education Center in West Chester, Pennsylvania, and I exchanged numerous e-mails on the HH-52A 1383 helicopter that now resides at their museum, awaiting a new paint job next year. Helicopter pilot LT John (Ron) Huddleston was gracious enough to provide some gripping detail on the nail-biting take-off from the crippled *Jarvis*.

I would be remiss if I didn't mention retired Master Chief Gunner's Mate Jack Hunter, whom I call "Mr. Jarvis." Over the years, he has personally captured everything *Jarvis*. Pictures, maps, interviews, emails—you name it, he saved it. We met in Coeur d'Alene, Idaho, for a Coast Guard reunion of the CGC *Winona*, where he passed over 1,000 electronic files (estimation) to me. While I reviewed them all, quite frankly I probably missed something important. As I told him later, "Thank you for the files…I think." The complete telling of this story could not have happened without him.

I wish to convey thanks also to Bob Carmack, my good friend, and fellow

"Deep Water Horizon" Coast Guard captain, for his extensive editing inputs and suggestions. Not to be outdone, Terry Grant[65] spent countless hours reviewing my manuscript, often making suggestions and recommendations that were crucial to the success of this book.

I am sure I am missing those folks who were invaluable during this writing phase, from those who provided stories, to those who assisted me with suggestions or proof-reading. You have my gratitude. To those who I could not locate and are now reading this book, send me an email at Scraig7002@gmail.com. I'll reply, I promise.

Finally, a big "thank you" to my wife Rachel for her editing skills. I couldn't have done this without her.

---

[65] Terry Grant had an illustrious career in the Coast Guard, retiring as captain in 1984. Terry graduated from the Coast Guard Academy in 1958 and later received his bachelor's degree in Physics at the U.S. Naval Postgraduate School; ultimately, he received his MBA. He had over 8-1/2 years of sea duty, including icebreaking in the eastern Arctic along with fisheries patrols and search-and-rescue ops in the Bering Sea.

SOURCES

THIS BOOK IS a work of non-fiction with information derived from historical documents and memories of the Jarvis crew members. There were no changes or edits made to names or events. The quotes identified in each chapter are actual conversations or e-mails obtained from the crewmembers or from related news articles as noted below. The research phase itself took close to a year, with much of the effort devoted to searching for the crew members involved. The official Board of Investigation and the actual Jarvis logs provided the times and dates throughout the book. The crew members interviewed provided their memories of what happened from their perspective. Every effort was made to contact those primary individuals involved, despite the forty-seven years since the incident occurred. Even with the challenges, thanks to the Internet, I found and interviewed many crew members or the next of kin.

Preface

Most of this section is relatively generic material relating to the 1970s. Much of the Coast Guard information is derived from my memories as a junior "Coastie," having just enlisted in August of 1972. From that time until early 1975, I served in Alameda, California, and Governors Island, New York, for training purposes; then I transferred to Hawaii and served on the CGC *Planetree*, CG Base Honolulu, CG Air Station Barbers Point, and finally in the Group Office/Loran Station Kauai.

Chapter 1

Information retrieved from the following book: *The Impossible Rescue*. Martin W. Sandler Candlewick Press 2012.

Extensive information retrieved from the following book: *Report of the Cruise of the U.S. Revenue Cutter Bear and the Overland Expedition*. United States Revenue-Cutter Service, U.S. Government Printing Office, 1899.

Additional information from: *The Wake Behind Us: Coast Guard* Jarvis. Editor CWO Page Shaw, 1972; and website "Badass of the Week—David Jarvis": http://www.badassoftheweek.com/Jarvis.html. Retrieved December 13, 2018.

Dr. Albert N. Kittilsen (Kittleson). *Reindeer, Gold, and Scandal.* Kenneth O. Bjork (Volume 30: Page 130). https://www.naha.stolaf.edu/pubs/nas/volume30/vol30_05.htm. Accessed July 10, 2019.

Chapter 2

Liberty ship and merchant marine information obtained from the following websites:

1. "Vessel Type EC2: The Liberty Ship." http://www.skylighters.org/troopships/libertyships.html. Retrieved December 13, 2018.

2. "Liberty Ships and Victory Ships, America's Lifeline in War." https://www.nps.gov/nr/twhp/wwwlps/lessons/116liberty_victory_ships/116liberty_victory_ships.htm. Retrieved December 13, 2018.

3. "Merchant Marines Unsung Heroes of World War II." https://turnstiletours.com/merchant- marines-unsung-heroes-of-world-war-ii/. Retrieved December 13, 2018.

4. "Ten Minutes to Abandon Ship." http://www.usmm.org/washington.html Accessed January 9, 2019.

5. *The New York Times.* September 14, 1942. Electronic files, accessed January 9, 2019.

Frederick Wooley's information received from daughter Sue Wooley: Record of Service, United States Lines letter dated September 13, 1949 to Commandant, New York City. CWO Shaw's handbook *The Wake Behind Us. Coast Guard* Jarvis (1972). Consulate General of the United States letter to Admiral Chester Bender, July 28, 1970.

Chapter 3

Information was retrieved from the following websites:

1. https://www.military.com/coast-guard-birthday/coast-guard-history.html 1

2. https://www.patriotwood.com/blogs/news/16490661-a-brief-history-of-the-revenue-cutter-service

3. https://media.defense.gov/2017/Jun/25/2001768438/-1/- 1/0/USCGPOLARICEOPSCHRON.pdf

4. https://www.todaysmilitary.com/joining/coast-guard

5. https://www.statista.com/statistics/232330/us-military-force-numbers-by-service-branch- and-reserve-component/

6. Discover Hawaii Tours.com. https://www.discoverhawaiitours.com/ford-island/. Accessed February 8, 2019.

7. "Ford Island, Pearl Harbor."https://www.pearlharboraviationmuseum.org/pearl-harbor-blog/ford-island-pearl-harbor-hawaii-december-7-1941-article-i/. Accessed February 8, 2019

8. Census Viewer http://censusviewer.com/county/HI/Honolulu. Retrieved December 14, 2018.

Newspaper articles were obtained from the *Honolulu Star-Bulletin* and the *Honolulu Advertiser*.

Katrina book information from *Chronicles of Katrina*, Steven Craig (2007).

Coast Guard Special Edition 2005 Magazine. "KATRINA. The Gulf Response." PAC Elizabeth Brannan, editor.

Jarvis information for the first year: CWO Shaw's *The Wake Behind Us: Coast Guard Jarvis* (1972). Personal interviews and emails provided from the following crew members to Steven Craig: Ken Wenner, Dan Edwards, George Fewell, Jack Hunter, Denny Strutton, Robert Loftin, Tim Lawler, Roy Montgomery, Carl Schramm, Richard Brunke, and Walter "Stan" Stanczyk.

Coast Guard helicopter HH-52A 1383 information obtained from LT Huddleston's *Coast Guard Aviators' Oral Histories & First-Person Accounts*, along with personal e-mails.

K.C. White provided his father's short autobiography. The *Jarvis* logs were obtained from the National Archives Center at San Bruno, California, by Steven Craig.

Boot Camp experiences were from the author's memories. And no, he never did learn how to swim.

Chapter 4

The following websites were utilized:

1. "Alaska Weather. The Wreck of the Kulluk."https://www.nytimes.com/2015/01/04/magazine/the-wreck-of-the-kulluk.html. Accessed October 2018.

2. "History.com." https://www.history.com/topics/world-war-ii/battle-of-the-aleutian- islands. Accessed January 10, 2019.

3. "The Economist. A Cold Coming We Had of It. January 18, 2007" https://www.economist.com/united-states/2007/01/18/a-cold-coming-we-had-of-it. Accessed February 4, 2019.

4. "Coast Guard Aviation History." https://cgaviationhistory.org/aircraft_/sikorsky-hh-52a-seaguard/. Accessed February 4, 2019.

5. "Dutch Harbor." https://www.ci.unalaska.ak.us/community/page/history.

6. https://www.travelalaska.com/Destinations/Communities/UnalaskaPort-of-Dutch-Harbor.aspx.

7. "Merriam-Webster." https://www.merriam-webster.com/dictionary/williwaw

8. Williwaws. Professional Mariner. March 28, 2007. "Williwaws and other extreme conditions challenger Alaska pilots." http://www.professionalmariner.com/March-2007/Williwaws-and-other-extreme-conditions-challenge-Alaska-pilots/. Accessed July 27, 2019.

Other information retrieved from:

1. United States Search and Rescue Task Force.

2. U. S. COAST GUARD, OFFICE OF INVESTIGATIONS AND ANALYSIS. "A Review of Lost Fishing Vessels & Crew Fatalities, 1992–2007."

3. Decommissioning Ceremony. CGC *Jarvis*. October 2, 2012.

4. *On the Edge of Survival A Shipwreck, a Raging Storm, and the Harrowing Alaskan Rescue That Became a Legend.* Spike Walker. St. Martin Griffin, New York. October 2, 2012.

5. *Kodiak Mirror,* Kodiak, Alaska, newspaper. October 6, 1972.

6. *The Wake Behind Us.* CWO Page Shaw, 1972.

Personal interviews or emails from Richard Brunke, Robert Loftin ("My Favorite *Jarvis* Memory," with Jerry Sandors), Nick Borosh, David Landis, Keith Fawcett, Ron Huddleston (recollections), Jack Hunter, Paul Barlow, and Admiral Bobby Hollingsworth.

Chapter 5

Personal emails or interviews were received from the following crew members: Paul Barlow, James "Tiger" McCarthy, Ron Huddleston, David Landis, Leo Manipon, Robert Loftin, Mike Large, and Carl Schramm.

Information retrieved from the *Honolulu Advertiser* newspaper, December 14, 1972. Coast Guard Board of Investigation, dated February 13, 1973.

Chapter 6

Information received via e-mails or phone calls: Dave Martin, Roy Montgomery, Robert Van Elsberg, Leo Manipon, Ron (John) Huddleston (recollections), Richard Brunke, Denny Strutton, James McCarthy, Jack Hunter, Ray Christianson, Mike Large, Bill Sewell, Mark Carter, Ken Wenner, Joel Cortez, Randy Kerr, Andrew Kacsanek, Nick Borosh, George Fewell, Tim Lawler, Lawrence Baker, Mike Large, and Wayne Debord. Notable from the crewmember comments were the extensive recollections submitted by Robert Loftin.

Newspapers *Honolulu Star-Bulletin* and *Honolulu Advertiser* were utilized, along with the CG Aviation website: https://cgaviationhistory.org/1959-first-of-the-hc-130-aircraft-were-obtained/.

K.C. White provided a letter typed by his father Commander Ken White.

Chapter 7

Information received from the following crew members: Dave Martin, Leo Manipon, Roy Montgomery, Richard Brunke, Ken Wenner, Bill Sewell, Paul Barlow, Robert Craig, George Fewell, Ron (John) Huddleston (recollections), Wayne Debord, and Howard Jensen.

Chuck Hughes provided extensive notes regarding the C-130 support to the *Jarvis.* Additional aviation support information received from the following members: Tom Scroggins, Kirk Colvin, Dave Watkins, Andy Anderson, and Ken Monty. Other pilots and crewmembers involved in the support include Rick Gallien, Bill Jacobs, Denny Morrissey, Bob Miller, Melvin Williams, Jack Schidlmeier, Jim Keller, John Denninger, and Tom Nickols. Many others were involved as well.

The local newspapers *Honolulu Star-Advertiser* and *Honolulu Star-Bulletin* provided *Jarvis* articles.

Akutan Island map courtesy of the U.S. Geological Survey. Akutan Island picture courtesy of Bob Webster.

The following websites were utilized:

1. "Akutan—Official Website of Aleutians East Borough, Alaska." https://www.aleutianseast.org/index.asp?SEC=8500EDE0-9F88-43B2-AEE0-E3919CE04345&Type=B_BASIC. Accessed January 17, 2019.

2. "Trident." https://www.tridentseafoods.com/Our-Story/Our-Plants. Accessed January 19, 2019.

3. "*Coast Pilot Number 9.*" https://nauticalcharts.noaa.gov/publications/coast-pilot/files/cp9/CPB9_C07_WEB.xml. Accessed January 20, 2019.

Writer and traveler Myra Scholze provided information on Akutan Island. The story of the Volkswagen being flown inside a C-130 actually occurred with the author and his transfer to Kauai from Oahu.

Chapter 8

The following crew members provided information: Thomas Franke, Roy Montgomery, Ron (John) Huddleston (recollections), Dan Edwards, Lawrence Baker, Bill Webster, Walt "Stan" Stanczyk, Richard Brunke, George Fewell, David Martin, Leo Manipon, Ken Wenner, Charlie Greene, Robert Van Elsberg, Denny Strutton, Jim Richardson, David Martin, Paul Barlow, Tim Lawler, Ray Christianson, George Buffleben, and Jim Nagle.

Information retrieved from books *On the Edge of Survival* by Spike Walker and *Winona Memories Handbook* (Coeur D'Alene CG reunion 2018), and website for the CGC *Citrus*, "An everlasting Citrus with very long roots": https://laststandonzombieisland.com/tag/uscgc-citrus/. Accessed February 14, 2019.

Additional information from Facebook comments by Jim McDonough and Steve Wiezorek, Mr. Tolentino email to Jack Hunter, and Coast Guard SAR message file 0247-73/NP Dutch Harbor, Alaska.

"Towing procedures." Captain Terry Grant, USCG, retired. E-mail dated July 27, 2019.

Articles from newspapers were retrieved from the *Honolulu Advertiser* (December 9, 1972), *Billings Gazette* (November 18, 1972), *The Daily Journal*, (Nov 17, Fergus Falls, MN), *Honolulu Star-Bulletin* (Nov 18), *The Bee* (Danville, VA), and two CG media releases (CCGD17 November 16, 1972. M. Joseph Leahy, Journalist, and PIO office, San Francisco, CA. 17 November 1972).

Captain Wooley's daughter Sue Wooley and this author also provided some input to this chapter.

Chapter 9

Jarvis crew members providing information include: Denny Strutton, Ron (John) Huddleston (recollections), Dave Martin, George Buffleben, "Stan" Stanczyk, Roy Montgomery, Dale Hoosier, Ken Wenner, Richard Brunke, Leo Manipon, Paul Barlow, Tim Lawler, Jim McCarthy, Howard Jensen, Dan Edwards, Jim Richardson. and Rick Sasse.

Newspaper articles retrieved from the *Honolulu Star-Bulletin* and the *Honolulu Advertiser*. Coast Guard media release: "Coast Guard Daily Operations Summary, Flag Plot," USCG HQ, Washington, D.C., 20 November 1972.

Chapter 10

The following crew members provided information: Richard Brunke, Robert Van Elsberg, Carl Schramm, Ron (John) Huddleston (recollections), Bill Sewell, "Stan" Stanczyk, Charlie Greene, Joel Cortez, George Buffleben, Rick Sasse, Andrew Kacsanek, George Fewell, Dave Martin, Dan Edwards, Denny Strutton, Ken Wenner, Ray Christianson, George Buffleben, Howard Jensen, and Admiral Bobby Hollingsworth.

Research articles retrieved from the *Honolulu Star-Bulletin, Honolulu Advertiser, The Wake Behind Us,* CWO Shaw (editor), and CG HQ message dated 292028Z from Captain Durfee, Rm 8315, Ext 62267 to Secretary of State, Washington, D.C.

Website information obtained: "Coast Guard Compass. Official Blog of the USCG." February 7, 2013. LT Galen Varon, posted LT Stephanie Young. http://coastguard.dodlive.mil/2013/02/americas-queen-coast-guard-cutter-storis/. Accessed January 28, 2019; Speech at CGC *Storis* decommissioning, 2007. RADM Brooks. Accessed February 10, 2019.

Chapter 11

Most of the chapter retrieved from the official Coast Guard Board of Investigation, 5830, dated 13 FEB 1973. Commander (d), Thirteenth Coast Guard District, Seattle, WA. "Report of Formal Board of Investigation into the circumstances surrounding the grounding of USCGC *Jarvis* (WHEC 725) at Dutch Harbor, Alaska, 15 November 1972, and the subsequent flooding and loss of power."

"Report of Formal Board of Investigation into the circumstances surrounding the grounding of the USCGC *Jarvis* (WHEC 725) at Dutch Harbor, Alaska, 15 November 1972, and the subsequent flooding and loss of power." Report 5830 dated 15 MAR 1973. Action of the Convening Board. Commander (dl), Twelfth Coast Guard District, San Francisco, CA.

"Investigation into the circumstances connected with the grounding of USCGC *Jarvis* (WHEC 725) at Dutch Harbor, Alaska and the subsequent flooding and loss of power on 15 November 1972." Report 5830 dated 5 JUN 1973. Action by Final Reviewing Authority. USCG Headquarters, Washington, D.C.

Coast Pilot website: https://nauticalcharts.noaa.gov/publications/coastpilot/files/cp9/CPB9_C07_WEB.xml. Accessed May 6, 2019.

Additional information retrieved from the individual crewmen as noted plus the *Jarvis* logs.

The following newspaper articles were utilized:
Honolulu Advertiser, Dec 9, 1972
Honolulu Advertiser, [date unk] 1973
Honolulu Star-Bulletin, Dec 14, [year unk]
Honolulu Star-Bulletin, Dec 15, [year unk]
Honolulu Advertiser Dec 15, [year unk]
F. Dore Hunter obituary, *Boxborough Beacon*

Chapter 12

Admiral Hollingsworth provided input into the chapter. Captain Mourey, Richard Brunke, Charlie Greene, Dan Edwards, and Marvin Pugh also provided information.

Epilogue

Former *Jarvis* crewmember input came from Rick Sasse, "Stan" Stanczyk, Dan Edwards, Leo Manipon, James McCarthy, and Mike Large. C-130 pilot Chuck Hughes, and former *Jarvis* COs Captain Richard Mourey and Captain Gregory Burg also provided input.

Website research included:

1. https://coastguardnews.com/coast-guard-cutter-Jarvis-transferred-to-bangladesh-navy/2013/05/23/

2. https://www.globalsecurity.org/military/world/bangladesh/bns-somudra-joy.htm

3. "Ex-Coast Guard cutter to serve Bangladesh." The *San Francisco Chronicle* website. https://www.sfgate.com/bayarea/article/Ex-Coast-Guard-cutter-to-serve-Bangladesh-4544562.php Vivian Ho. May 23, 2013.

Thanks to Tony Freeman of the American Helicopter Museum & Education Center in West Chester, Pennsylvania, for his pictures and information regarding the *Jarvis's* helicopter.

Appendix A

CGC *Jarvis* and HH-52A crewmembers lists were provided by Jack Hunter.

Appendix B

Numerous websites were researched, including: Linkedin, Facebook, Coast Guard Register of Officers, U.S. Coast Guard Academy Alumni Association, and Ancestry.com.

Newspaper articles: *Jacks Joint, Military Times, CG Retiree News,* and *Naval Proceedings.* Specific weblinks can be obtained from the author via e-mail.

Personal input through emails or phone calls from Captain Richard Mourey, Captain Aaron Davenport, Captain Bobby Hollingsworth, Jack Hunter, and George Buffleben. Captain Richard Mourey also provided some information on other commanding officers.

Coast Guard information on Vietnam obtained from *Coast Guard Action in Vietnam* by author Paul C. Scotti, Hellgate Press. 2000.

Mark McKenney information from Coast Guard Retire Council newsletter, October 2006, website. "Viet Nam Vet Gives His Land to Coast Guard." https://www.cgretirenw.org/nwsltroct06.pdf. Accessed March 2019.

Captain Ikens CGC *Jarvis* information including the photo provided by Tony Tuliano. Brian J O'Keefe input on Captain Sabo.

Daniel Bowers provided mission information about Captain Stevens's tenure as commanding officer.

Captain Robert Stevens: Commissioner Robert Stevens. https://www.portofastoria.com/Commissioner_Robert_Stevens.aspx

Thanks to Eric Mills for the information regarding the U.S. Navy P3 Orion that was forced to ditch near Adak, Alaska. *ADAK: The Rescue of Alfa Foxtrot 586* was written about the event by author Captain Andrew C.A. Jampoler; Naval Institute Press.

Appendix C

Comments provided by the crew members themselves through phone calls or e-mails.

Appendix D

Most of the information was provided by the members themselves or by the next of kin. Nelson Hunt and Commander White's son, K. C. White, provided insight on Commander White.

Al Sabol obituary. https://www.legion.org/memoriam/215768/capt-albert-j-sabol-us-coast-guard.

Final Note: Nationally, when including U.S. Coast Guard maritime, aviation, administrative and leadership, not to mention other governmental and Department of Defense support, it was literally thousands of people who participated in the rescue and recovery of the USCGC *Jarvis*. BZ![66]

---

[66] Naval term meaning "Well Done!"

ABOUT THE AUTHOR

S TEVEN CRAIG IS a retired Coast Guard Reserve captain with over thirty-eight years of both active and reserve service. He is also a retired Postmaster with the U.S. Postal Service. During his period of Coast Guard service, he actively participated with Hurricanes Katrina and Ike, the 2010 Haiti earthquake port recovery planning, the 9/11 response in Seattle, APEC maritime security planning in Honolulu, the 1984 Olympics in Los Angeles, and the Deepwater Horizon oil spill response—to name a few. Prior to his commissioning, Craig held the rank of senior chief petty officer in the Coast Guard. He holds a Master's degree in Emergency Management and has held associated jobs with federal, state, college, county, and local agencies.

Steven Craig previously taught as a professor at a university in Italy and has spoken at several disaster conferences. He and his wife Rachel, along with two dachshunds, are frequent travelers between homes in Washington State and Arizona. His contact e-mail address is Scraig7002@gmail.com and his website is www.stevenjcraigbooks.com.

www.hellgatepress.com